BECOMING COLLEAGUES

BECOMING COLLEAGUES

Women and Men Serving Together in Faith

Carol E. Becker

JOSSEY-BASS
A Wiley Company
San Francisco

Jossey-Bass books and products are available through most bookstores. To contact Jossey-Bass directly, call (888) 378-2537, fax to (800) 605-2665, or visit our website at www.josseybass.com.

Substantial discounts on bulk quantities of Jossey-Bass books are available to corporations, professional associations, and other organizations. For details and discount information, contact the special sales department at Jossey-Bass.

Manufactured in the United States of America on Lyons Falls Turin Book. This paper is acid-free and 100 percent totally chlorine-free.

Library of Congress Cataloging-in-Publication Data

Becker, Carol E., date
   Becoming colleagues : women and men serving together in faith / Carol E. Becker.
     p. cm.
   Includes bibliographical references and index.
     ISBN 0-7879-4709-1 (alk. paper)
   1. Group ministry. 2. Man–woman relationships—Religious aspects—Christianity. I. Title
BV675.B38 2000
253'.8—DC21
                                                          00-027383

FIRST EDITION
HB Printing 10 9 8 7 6 5 4 3 2 1

CONTENTS

PART FIVE
Communicating and Working Together

PART SIX
Influencing

PART SEVEN
Modeling

PREFACE

MORE AND MORE men and women are working together in teams. Yet, it seems, few teams are as effective and satisfying as both the men and women in them would wish. Apparently, teams need something more than techniques for working together.

What must happen in order for men and women (working together) to have a more effective and mutually satisfying ministry together? This book answers that question. It presents nine criteria for effective mixed-gender teams. When these criteria are met, teams say they are *effective* in their work. Furthermore, the teams provide a *satisfying* work environment for both men and women.

Who Should Read This Book?

The specific concern of this book—and the primary audience for it—is mixed-gender teams in church-related settings, including congregations, agencies, educational institutions, and other church-affiliated nonprofit organizations. That's why the central question of the book is posed in terms of the team's ability to have a satisfying and effective ministry together. In the context of this book, *ministry* does not refer only to the work of clergy in a parish but to all the mission-focused work of church organizations, including congregations. Furthermore, although the nine criteria are relevant for all mixed-gender teams, this book addresses them in the context of nonprofit work.

Two other team audiences will find this book useful. First, teams in secular nonprofit organizations, because they too have a mission focus for their work, can benefit directly from the wisdom of the teams in this study. Second, even though men and women in corporate teams work to achieve profit rather than mission goals, they too can learn from this book to create more effective teams. In particular, the book's emphasis on a balance between reflection and action is wisdom much needed in the corporate world. Its absence as a value in corporate teams may be the single most unaddressed reason why corporate mixed-gender teams do not succeed more often.

Finally, this book presents individual women and men, discusses how they are alike and different as leaders, and addresses the unique challenges for women in leadership. For these reasons, it is also a book for women and men who are not now in teams but who work with others on a regular basis. The wisdom of the nine criteria for change is applicable to our daily interaction with one another as well as to our teams.

How This Book Is Organized

This book is organized in seven parts. Each part addresses one or more of the nine criteria for effective mixed-gender teams. I present each criterion from the perspective of recent literature and from the perspective of the teams in this study. Thus each section includes chapters on the criteria and chapters on specific teams. In all, nine teams tell their detailed stories. I selected these nine teams from the twenty-three that participated in the study because of the unique way they illustrate the nine criteria.

The specific team "stories" are dialogues taken from interviews with the team members. They are, literally, what the team has to say about the criteria for effective mixed-gender teams. Of course, it is important to know what the recent literature about leadership, teams, management, and church-related organizations has to say about the criteria. But the perspective of this book is that theory has more meaning when it is understood through the real-life experiences of men and women working together.

Part One presents an overview of the nine criteria and explains the first criterion, *reflect*. It explains the unique relationship between reflection and action in effective teams and offers the reader a thorough analysis of exactly what reflecting is. Part Two presents the second criterion, *learn*. It suggests and explains two learning tasks for teams today. Part Three presents the third criterion, *believe*. It presents the theology of major religious traditions relative to the leadership of women and suggests practical ways teams can create gender equity statements. Because they are so closely related to each other, Part Four presents criteria four and five, *name* and *include*. It discusses the relationship between knowing ourselves and our partners and becoming truly inclusive in our teams.

Because they are closely related in practice, Part Five presents criterion six, *communicate,* and criterion seven, *work*. It addresses how teams communicate and work together and concludes with a chapter on the traps men and women encounter as they work together. Part Six presents the eighth criterion, *influence*. It defines power and shows how power helps teams influence others toward constructive action. It also illustrates how power works in effective mixed-gender teams. Part Seven presents the final criterion, *model*. It shows how effective mixed-gender teams model teamwork, thereby assisting other teams as well as the systems in which they exist.

How Teams Can Use This Book

Teams that wish to use this book to examine their own effectiveness can do so in several ways. Some teams may wish to read the book as a group, discussing each section as they go. I suggest this rather than a chapter-by-chapter approach. The sections of the book are set up to assist readers in understanding the nine criteria by grouping the criteria with team stories that illustrate the points made. Furthermore, some criteria are considered together because of their relationship to each other, as the preceding summary of the book's organization explains.

Other teams may wish to assign sections of the book to different persons on the team. In this case, team members assigned to a specific section of the book will want to review for their teammates both the criteria and the team stories in their assigned section of the book.

A list of study questions at the end of the book will be helpful to all teams. These questions are written by section, in keeping with my suggestion to study the book by section rather than by chapter. For each section, I offer two types of questions. First, there are questions for personal reflection. These questions will be useful for each team member to consider individually, before discussion with the team. Second, there are questions for team discussion. Team members should consider these questions as a group after reviewing the relevant section.

I offer one word of caution about the questions for team discussion: the level of trust in a team will determine how well its members are able to discuss these questions together. If trust levels are low, the team will need to select questions that feel "safe" for team discussion at this time. Using this book to evaluate team effectiveness may help to build trust so that at a later time the team will be able to discuss additional questions in the study guide. If trust is an issue, working with an external facilitator may also assist the discussion process and help the team build trust.

Defining and Verifying the Nine Criteria

The nine criteria for effective mixed-gender teams developed from research I began in 1994 to investigate the central question of this book: "What must happen in order for men and women (working together) to have a more effective and mutually satisfying ministry together?" I started with a series of focus groups in my own Protestant tradition. Women and men from many Protestant denominations assisted me by conducting the initial focus groups among their colleagues. In all, sixteen different leaders held nineteen focus groups in fifteen different locations throughout the United States and Canada. Men and women from nine Protestant denominations participated in these focus groups. A nominal group process ensured that each focus group answered the key question in a uniform fashion so that the results were reliable.

Ten criteria emerged from the focus groups held in 1994. They provided a template for the 1998 study, in which I tested the criteria with twenty-three different mixed-gender teams from throughout the Judeo-Christian traditions. In the current study, I set out to determine whether the criteria actually make mixed-gender teams more effective. To reveal the roles played by the criteria, I used a structured interview process, conducting in-depth, confidential interviews with each individual in each team. In all, seventy-two people participated in these interviews. On the basis of the interviews, I was able to verify nine of the original ten criteria, amplify them, and define their roles in actual teams.

The 1998 research confirmed that the nine criteria are critical to effective mixed-gender teams. Often the criteria work in surprising ways. Furthermore, the complex ways the criteria work in real teams are often hard to describe. It is not simply a matter of connecting a criterion with examples in various teams. That approach would assume that the teams are superficial structures around the working lives of the men and women in them. Much to the contrary, *effective* teams are very organic, dynamic entities. One has to get into the life of the team and begin to see how it really works. Having done that, the researcher can begin to discern how the criteria work.

A significant challenge in describing how the nine criteria work is that they are not linear. Although this book of necessity presents them in linear fashion, chapter by chapter, they do not function that way in the life of the team. A team does not, for example, address the first criterion, then go on to the next and the next and the next until all are "done." It is an advantage when teams reflect first and act after reflection has begun. As a practical matter, however, teams work on all the criteria at once, integrating them into their working lives as they are relevant and needed. In consequence, team examples and team stories in this book never illustrate one criterion or another without also illustrating the others in some way as well. To elicit good examples, one can go around and around with these teams, always finding more and more.

The Teams in This Study

The teams in this study are from eight Protestant traditions, the Roman Catholic Church, the Reform Jewish tradition, and some nondenominational church-related settings. They are equally divided between those that serve congregations and those that serve in other organizations of the church. Fifteen of the twenty-three teams consist of one man and one woman working together. The remaining teams include between three and eight members; most of these were teams of three or four people. The teams are diverse in ethnicity as well as gender, as the team stories will show. In addition to white Euro-Americans, these teams include African Americans, Asians, and Hispanics.

Because this book is based on a qualitative research study that provided anecdotal feedback, it is particularly important to understand how these teams came to participate in the research. Had I selected the teams from my own network, I would have built bias into the research. Therefore, my approach was to "put the word out" for teams that were unknown to me before beginning the project. Using a designated Web site as well as Ecunet (an ecumenical network serving primarily Protestant denominations), word of mouth, and letters to a wide range of opinion leaders in the denominations, I sought to study mixed-gender teams that had been together a minimum of two years.

I did not seek *effective* mixed-gender teams. I simply sought mixed-gender teams. The difference here may be only a single word, but it is an important one. At the outset, I was willing to look at all kinds of teams. The teams that came to me *described themselves as effective*. This makes sense when we think about it. What team member, believing that his or her team is *ineffective*, would want to participate in this study? What did become clear as I selected teams for the study is that I had "found" an interesting group of mixed-gender teams *that self-selected as effective* by their own criteria. I also found that they all met two criteria by which *they defined* their success as an effective team. First, each person on each team verified, independent of the others, that the team is effective. Second, team members were able to demonstrate results related to their mission. I did not impose any other definition of *effective* on the teams because I did not want to presuppose what the elements of an effective team are. Thus the teams themselves helped me define what an effective team is.

Ultimately, I defined an effective team as one that performs quality work meeting the standards and expectations of the organization in which the team exists, contributes to the personal well-being and development of the members, and provides a team experience that builds the capacity of the team members to work and learn together in the future. Other key terms necessary to understanding the nine criteria are defined in relevant chapters.

I have limited this study to teams that have been together for a minimum of two years in order to be able to assess their effectiveness and glean insights useful for other teams. I felt it was too difficult to know if the short-term experience of new teams would hold over time and therefore be useful to others. Nevertheless, the learnings presented here are useful for short-term as well as long-duration teams. In fact, many more short-term teams would move through the phases of team development quickly and successfully if they applied the nine criteria to their experience.

The teams are represented in the book in at least three ways. First, nine teams are highlighted in extended stories or dialogues that illustrate the nine criteria. These teams have agreed to tell their stories and have had the opportunity to review the published content. Although I have identified these teams to a point, I have attempted to give them a measure of anonymity by withholding last names and the organizations in which they work. Many other teams are represented in shorter anecdotes in the text of the chapters. Some have agreed to be identified, others have preferred to remain anonymous, and I have changed names accordingly. Finally, I have used many quotes taken from the interviews to illustrate the nine criteria as they are lived by real teams. In most cases, these quotes remain anonymous to protect the privacy of teams and individuals in teams.

In all cases, agreeing to have one's team story told has meant agreeing to some revelations. To be honest, team members had to share both the positives and the negatives of team life. Even effective teams have their troubles. Even the best teams make mistakes. In order to show how effective mixed-gender teams really work, the foibles as well as the fun, the fancy, and the finer side of the teams have to show.

The motivation of teams to participate in this study was twofold. Although team members described themselves as effective, they did not necessarily know why. The chance to investigate the secrets of their own success was, for many of the teams, an incentive to participate. Still, many of these teams are well aware that they have something special. Knowing that they are the exception rather than the rule, they want to share their insights with other teams.

The men and women in these teams were very gracious about telling the truth. This is a gift that the interviewer (and ultimately the reader) should receive with reverence and gratitude. It is not to be taken lightly. As the interviewer and author, I started each interview with a set of questions, a name, a phone number, and an appointment time. Beyond that, one never knows what one will get. Out of seventy-two interviews I can think of only one in which I was not eventually invited "in" to the real material about the individual, his or her life, the team, and the way the team works in the particular church-related organization. As a result, I too am changed. I have new respect and admiration for these individuals and the work they do together. I know that this book tells only a part of their very rich team stories. I hope you, the reader, will also be changed by what these teams have to say.

As we engage the criteria to work with each other, we are changed. We become colleagues in a new way. We learn to reflect as well as to act. We gain a new civility that is largely missing in our time. Ultimately, we work more effectively together. We become leaders together. This, after all, is the nature of the nine criteria. It is what this book is about.

Park Ridge, Illinois   CAROL E. BECKER
February 2000

ACKNOWLEDGMENTS

INEVITABLY as I complete this book, the voices of many people linger in my mind. These are the people who have surrounded me throughout the project and made it complete in the end.

First, I hear the voices of the many men and women who shared their stories with me for the purpose of helping others learn about effective teams. Theirs are stories of pain and triumph, disappointment and success, joy and sadness, and deep learning about each other. I am mindful that their generosity in sharing very personal stories was a gift to me individually as well as a gift to my readers. Many of them prayed for and with me as well. I have been changed by my encounters with each person, and enriched by the two years I have spent talking to them all and learning from them. Most of them came to me unknown. Now they all feel like friends.

Next, I hear the voices of my own clients, with whom I shared sections of this book in its development. During the months of writing they provided me with many opportunities to test my emerging ideas about mixed-gender teams. They also allowed me the privilege of sharing in their lives as teams. I hope for their sakes that they learned something from me as I was learning from them.

I also hear the voices of my own teammates at Growth Design Corporation, where we specialize in working with nonprofit organizations. I am privileged to work with many talented colleagues in many different work teams, in an environment where we are always learning more about each other and about serving the needs of organizations. This environment was in many ways the incubator for my interest in the special concerns of mixed-gender teams. As I struggled and delighted in working with my own colleagues, I began to reflect on what it takes for men and women to work successfully together. I thank my colleagues for making me struggle and ponder deeply.

Individual voices also linger in my heart and mind. Special thanks to Kay Edwards, who designed the research instrument and guided my thinking about what I was learning. Choua Thao, Michelle Schultz, and Jeanne Michaels formed my office support team. Claire Buettner at the Evangelical Lutheran Church in America library was a faithful research assistant.

Ellen McCormick read and critiqued and searched for details that would enrich the final draft. This book would not have been written without the support and encouragement of all these voices behind the scenes.

The most constant voice was my father's. Surely this book would not have been *this book* without his thoughtful and gentle critique. In a real sense, he and I formed our own mixed-gender team to edit this book. He was the model partner—encouraging, challenging, available, and truly interested in my project. I found the process of working with him on this book as rewarding as the product itself. I will never be able to look at this book without thinking of him and thanking God for him. So it is with all effective mixed-gender teams.

There were many other intimate voices of friends and family besides Dad's. My mother always made me feel that it was such an important accomplishment. Barbara Boigegrain asked the best questions about teams and encouraged my answers. Ellen McCormick and Judy Braham were prayer partners, and they know how important that was and is. My daughter Emily and son Ethan provided a special kind of encouragement by periodically asking, "How is it coming?" with the genuine interest of young adult children who are beginning their own intellectual pursuits. My younger children Heather and Eric had one question: "When will your book be done?" They asked it over and over, like a refrain, but they were not a burden. Their question was a reminder that books do need to be completed so that mothers can be mothers. My lifelong friend Lynn devised trips for the two of us and waited patiently until the time was available to take one. My husband Paul's voice was one of constant love and encouragement, as it always is. He fixed my computer's problems and held me in the dark nights too, and all of this at the same time he was writing his own book.

Finally, Mary's voice lingers in my mind even though it has been stilled by death. Mary Behrendt, my friend, colleague, and mentor, died just before I started this book in earnest. How I longed to share it with her, to hear her wisdom again, to have her encouragement! I had to be satisfied with the memory of all that she taught me. I let her voice whisper in my mind too.

THE AUTHOR

FOR NEARLY twenty-five years, Carol E. Becker has helped nonprofit organizations achieve their goals through effective planning and communication. Becker is a senior consultant at Growth Design Corporation, a firm
that specializes in providing resource solutions to nonprofit organizations,
including denominations, church-related agencies, and congregations. She
specializes in strategic thinking and continuous planning, personal presentation skills, team development, and marketing communication planning. In 1992 she created *Communication by Design,* a unique planning
process that assists organizations in more effectively communicating their
mission and purpose.

Before joining Growth Design, Becker headed the communication office
of the fourth largest Protestant denomination in the United States, the
Evangelical Lutheran Church in America (ELCA). She designed the communication office at the time the ELCA was formed, hired a staff of more
than twenty-five professionals, and managed a budget of several million
dollars to provide the church with comprehensive communication services. Becker remained with the ELCA for the first five years of the life of
the new Lutheran church.

For ten years beginning in 1977, Becker operated her own business,
specializing in communication planning, public relations support, pro-
duction services, writing, and fundraising communication for a wide variety of business and nonprofit clients.

Becker has published over a hundred newspaper and magazine articles,
book chapters, and journal articles. Many of her articles were written to
promote the work and vision of her professional clients. Her specific research interests include women's issues, leadership, team development,
and interpersonal communication. Her first book was *Leading Women:
How Church Women Can Avoid Leadership Traps and Negotiate the
Gender Maze* (1996).

Becker is a graduate of Ohio State University, where she received her
master's degree in English with a specialty in English language.

PART ONE

REFLECTING AND TAKING ACTION

BRIAN AND MARTHA

CREATING A SUCCESSFUL MIXED-GENDER TEAM

FOR TWELVE YEARS beginning in 1985, Brian and Martha worked together in a large United Methodist parish in a conservative midwestern city. Brian was the senior pastor and head of a large staff. Martha came to the congregation to work in the nursery school, eventually went to seminary, worked with the youth group, and upon graduation was appointed as an associate pastor in the congregation. Her appointment to the same congregation in which she had worked as a layperson prior to her ordination was unusual, Brian and Martha agree, but this gave them an even greater opportunity to get to know each other over a long period of time. The congregation had the same opportunity to get to know them both. That was part of the formula of their successful shared ministry.

Then quite suddenly, in late 1997, Martha was reassigned to a small solo pastorate just twenty minutes away from the congregation where she had served with Brian. The United Methodist Church has itinerant clergy who agree to move at the will of the denomination. Martha actually moved within weeks of being reassigned. Originally asked by the conference not to reveal her reassignment to Brian until after her interview with the new church, Martha objected and was permitted the time to say goodbye.

○

Martha's Commitment

I see a lot of senior-associate teams doing effective parallel ministry, but they don't know each other. We had a deeper relationship, and it served the congregation well. Our relationship included deep respect for each other, a sense of safety in sharing our theological ideas with each other, deep listening to each other personally as well as professionally, speaking the truth to each other and to others on our team, and a commitment to helping each other see things from our individual perspectives. These things were most important in building our relationship.

Getting to this point definitely required personal preparation. For one thing, I had to be secure in who I am as a woman. I learned that I do not have to be like a man, but I don't have to force feminism on anyone either. I must confront what's wrong but also be able to step back when it's my issue. I must also be very secure in my own calling to ministry but at the same time flexible enough to realize that change takes time. It's not fair, but that's the way it is. I have to be willing to love people into change. Knowing all this was important since I was the first woman pastor in this congregation.

It helped to have clear boundaries. We got to the point that we could be with each other in emotionally intimate ways as work colleagues without breaking boundaries. We also set working boundaries using a process Brian initiated. We looked at my gifts and his gifts and decided who would do what, how to trade assignments if we found the other could do better, what to do together, and so forth. Some activities, like Bible study, we chose to do together because they require both men's and women's perspectives. This kind of careful boundary setting helped us acknowledge each other.

At the same time I had to be willing to speak my truth. It's hard when you disagree with your partner. I had to do this about a youth worker who said he was supportive of my ministry but who was not supportive in his actions. Brian didn't see it, so I had to tell him. We strongly disagreed. I kept at it when I thought Brian was not hearing me. Partners need to do that because trust stops somewhere when the misunderstandings begin to creep in. It hurt a lot of the time—for both of us. Had either of us stopped talking, it would have been a major problem, and both of us are conflict avoiders. So it was hard work to keep at it. But that's part of acknowledging your partner too.

Eventually the dialogue brought us to a deeper trust. If you're not connecting with your partner, you don't just throw up your hands and walk away from it. You've got to keep at it. In our debriefing later I could see where I had not been clear and Brian could not hear what I was saying. I needed to hear that I had some issues on my own to work on, and I needed to trust Brian to tell me. It was a rough time in our partnership, but we did have the advantage of some common ground even in the disagreement. We are in the same place theologically. We enjoy each other's company, and we have a similar philosophy about how to treat people.

A lot of our success had to do with Brian's leadership. He made the vision for the staff team very clear. We helped each other see our gifts. The women (and men) still on staff are all strong because they are affirmed and constantly encouraged to improve. I can think of one especially memorable time when this happened during my ministry with Brian. We were at a conference together. The "old boy network" was very much in evidence. Yet Brian treated me as an equal, assuming I would go everywhere the others went. Because he treated me that way, I was accepted that way. It was extremely affirming.

It was clear that Brian was the senior pastor in our situation, but I never saw him buying into hierarchy. He gave me a lot of power to do what I wanted. There were some differences that came with knowing that we were not copastors, but those were put in place by the system, not by Brian. Equality was in place in the team so effectively that I was able to take over Brian's role managing a building project when he went on leave for six weeks. The congregation perceived my power as equal to Brian's. Throughout our ministry together Brian had done things to make that happen. He always treated me as though I had equal responsibility. He made me visible on Sunday. We did team teaching together. And there were areas where I was definitely the one in charge. In the building project, I was always included in the leadership meetings and always consulted when decisions were made. When the architects ignored me, Brian turned the situation around to make sure I was visible. He set the standard with the committee that I was also in charge of the project. Every team member here gets that same kind of treatment.

I think you have to have a deliberate desire to do ministry in partnership to be a team. Otherwise, it's real easy to go along in parallel tracks. Then you lose the enormous amount of goodness that comes from having a relationship. You lose the mutual trust and the deep caring. To do partnership ministry, at some level you have to stretch the boundaries to become friends. You have to like one another.

I miss being in a team now. I can do effective ministry in my present congregation—I am doing so—but I miss the energy of a team. I also question why our team was split up when we had worked so hard to become effective. The conference says they want good male-female teams. At one point they asked us to do some work mentoring other teams. Then suddenly they split us up.

○

Brian's Leadership

Getting to know one another does not happen in isolation. We did a lot to build our team. We talked constantly. We spent time together, both working and socializing. And we spent structured time building the team. We also used team reflection as a structured activity to consider our decisions together before we announced them. For me, all of this was an outgrowth of my personal reflection, which was—and is—an integral part of how I do ministry. That is precisely why the reflective tasks must come first. I need to balance the activity by getting away from it. I need to know where the Spirit is leading me. I also spend lots of personal time thinking about where we are going as a congregation. I write my reflections, sometimes for me, sometimes for the congregation. So, yes, the criteria ring true in terms of our experience. But they begin with me.

It must come first from the senior pastor, especially if the senior is male. White males particularly are part of the dominant structure. That has to change. We change not only by how we act but also by how we talk about how we act. I try to talk about women's right to be clergy. We intentionally address this both biblically and theologically in this congregation. It's especially important in this community where most churches belong to denominations that do not ordain women. Everything we can do to build the case—to help men understand what women have to offer—is important. And we benefit. I think women provide a whole way of understanding ministry that is so good for men. It's good for women too, of course, but it's very good for men to see women in ministry. The benefits for me personally have been many. I've learned to understand my spouse better. I had a colleague with whom I could share about my kids, something men don't do so easily together. And I had the opportunity to talk theologically with Martha about how women and men perceive things differently. I could also see how effective Martha was as a counselor and role model for the women in this congregation. The things some of them said about her were truly humbling for me. As far as the congregation as a whole is concerned . . . Martha and I presented a more well-rounded understanding of the nature of God than I or any man could do alone.

I was surprised by the ease with which the congregation accepted a woman in ministry. Much of the groundwork was laid here before Martha became a pastor, since she was with us as a lay staff member first. But when she became my clergy colleague, we began right away by stating boundaries. Here again, it was my responsibility to take the lead. Martha has talked about how we set work assignments, but that's not where we started. The first issue we decided was what to do about the intimacy issues that are present in a mixed-gender team. We were explicit in recognizing them, in stating that we would both honor our marriages and respect our spouses. At the same time, we decided not to build in boundaries that were unnatural to the working relationship. Pastors working together have to meet in private sometimes. We had to develop trust in each other and model that. Then the congregation could develop a sense of ease about the appropriateness of our relationship. After that we could go on to two other boundary-setting activities: writing a staff philosophy for working together and making work assignments.

We spent a long time developing trust. It wasn't just between Martha and me, but among all the staff. Whenever anything happened to crash that, it was a pretty tough time.

The disagreement we had over another staff member who was not supportive of Martha's ministry was largely a disagreement about how we would respond to that person. I needed to hear what Martha had to say because I did not have the whole picture. I needed the opportunity to get her response to what I was planning to do. And when the final confrontation came, I needed her to be there. I can't overstate how important the trust between us was in that situation. I felt enormously relieved by the sense that we could have that kind of back-and-forth. You have to reach beyond the conflict to preserve the integrity of the team.

Unfortunately, I know from subsequent experience this does not always happen. Having had one good mixed-gender team, you can't necessarily translate that experience to all situations. My very next mixed-gender team did not work well at all. Many things contributed to a bad situation that the people in it could not resolve. Martha was moved suddenly and quickly. She was placed on her own in a small congregation within twenty minutes of us, even though she was open about her preference to be in a team. We waited seven months before requesting another appointment. We asked for a woman because we felt that's what the congregation needed. But it didn't work out. Asking for a woman again didn't mean she would be a woman like Martha or that we would be a good fit as a team. For me to expect that would be stereotyping of women. But I did hope for another good

2

NINE CRITERIA FOR
MIXED-GENDER TEAMS

MIXED-GENDER TEAMS in which all the members say that their work is effective and mutually satisfying are the exception rather than the norm. Some, like Brian and Martha, work hard at working together effectively, only to be dissolved as a team by circumstances beyond their control. Other men and women work together for many years as colleagues, then suddenly run into a barrier to their shared leadership that neither can explain or remove. Yet other mixed-gender teams succeed as long as the team remains intact. As soon as someone in the team leaves and is replaced by a new member, the "magic formula" is lost and success is up for grabs. No one on the team seems able to articulate or replicate the factors that contributed to the original team's success. Similarly, in another scenario described to me, some men and women participate in a successful team for a time, then go on to another team situation that does not work at all. The team members don't know why and seem unable to replicate the positive elements of one team in the next.

All of these situations and more are represented by the teams described in this book. Few and far between are the teams that, over time, remain successful as they grow and change. Contributing to these real-life team problems are the prevailing gender realities. First, women are still underrepresented as team leaders and they often find that their roles in mixed-gender teams are subservient. Second, men must take big risks to advocate for more women in leadership.

We can readily see that our struggles over the past twenty years and more, using resources and wisdom already available, have yielded limited success for mixed-gender teams. Something is missing. What is it? Both individuals and teams I have interviewed over the last four years demonstrate that there are nine criteria to meet if as men and women we are to have an effective and mutually satisfying ministry together. These criteria immediately reveal what we have overlooked. They show us that we have not recognized the difference between our reflective and our active tasks. This is a simple answer, yet at the same time it is a complex one. It's one thing to enumerate the criteria and *say* that we have to recognize the difference between our reflective and our active tasks. It's another thing to *understand* that difference and put it into practice.

Nine Criteria for Mixed-Gender Teams

The nine criteria form a template for us to follow in our quest for successful mixed-gender teams. They fall roughly into two categories that are useful in helping us understand the dynamic relationship between reflection and action. The first five are *reflective criteria*. The last four are *active criteria*. (See Exhibit 2.1.)

The Reflective Criteria

The reflective criteria include all those things that we do individually to prepare ourselves to be effective team members. They are about our inner work, not about work that we do in the world, among or with other people. The reflective criteria call us to pause and ponder rather than act. They include making the commitment to reflection, learning, believing, greeting, and including each other.

CRITERION ONE: REFLECT. The first step we can take to prepare ourselves for effective teamwork is to reflect. In the course of this book, we shall discover how effective teams continually reflect about themselves, their teammates, the team as a whole, and their work. We shall catch a glimpse of the deeper awareness they gain from reflecting, an awareness

---

Exhibit 2.1. Reflective and Active Criteria for Teams.

Reflective Criteria	Active Criteria
Reflect	Communicate
Learn	Work
Believe	Influence
Name	Model
Include	

that goes beyond knowing each other by what they do to knowing each other for who they are and what they are like. This kind of knowing requires a willingness to know ourselves better. It also requires acceptance of gender differences and individual differences within genders. It is only achieved by careful listening to ourselves and each other, and it takes time.

Why commit to this extra emotional and mental work? The best teams say that reflecting helps them integrate theology and practice. This is particularly important for mixed-gender teams because they are still forging new ground in church-related (and indeed in all) organizations.

Reflecting is the first criterion. Repeatedly, in both focus groups and private interviews, men and women working in successful mixed-gender teams emphasize that reflection comes first and continues throughout the life cycle of the successful mixed-gender team. Action will accomplish little, they say, until reflection has borne fruit. Of course, it is always possible for a team to begin reflecting. The benefits of reflecting can be realized anytime in the life cycle of the team, once team members learn the discipline and practice of reflecting. The purpose of starting with reflection is to emphasize a critical point: mixed-gender teams have the best chance of success when they include individuals who are able and willing to be reflective before they form the team.

In Chapter Three we will look carefully at what the reflective tasks require of us. We shall also discover why it is so difficult for us to sustain our commitment to reflection.

CRITERION TWO: LEARN. Accepting gender and individual differences requires first that we understand them. This requires *learning*, the second criterion.

Five years ago, when I first began to write about this criterion, I said that we needed to learn more about creating a place for women in leadership. I also pointed out the practical educational tasks necessary to help women become leaders. I especially emphasized leadership development skills training (Becker, 1996). Although we still need to pay attention to the demands of creating women leaders, I do not think that is the major focus of our learning challenge now. Women have begun to find a place at the table alongside men, in both business and nonprofit settings. We are present in great enough numbers that men are also beginning to learn from us. Furthermore, we are creating a wide variety of programs that provide major funding to create women leaders for the future.

This does not mean the challenge has been met. Certainly, we should still pay attention to the opportunities we provide for young women and girls to become leaders. But our learning should be broader because we can now begin to pay attention to how we work together. With this shift in mind, I believe we face two challenges when we consider learning as a criterion for our ability to work together. First, we need to know more about the challenges of leadership in our time. Second, we need to know what it takes to build a team. We shall discuss these learning challenges in Chapters Four through Six.

CRITERION THREE: BELIEVE. We all want to *believe* in what we do. It gives our work meaning. This is not just a trite phrase. It is important. When our work has meaning, *what we do* and *how we do it* square with our values (the *why* of our work). The third criterion calls on us to examine what we believe (our values) as a way of enhancing our ability to work in a mixed-gender team. There are two ways we can reflect on our values in relation to our work. First, we can consider our values about *what we do*. Second, we can consider our values about *how we work*.

First let's consider what we do. In nonprofit, church-related organizations, our work is service to others. This work is meaningful, but it is also demanding, endless, and perpetually underfunded. We never get it done, and we often cannot see what we have accomplished. Yet in a unique way, our strong belief in the value of what we do, and the urgency of doing it, can be a catalyst to the success of our team. It can help us weather the stresses of working in a mixed-gender team. We shall see how this works in the teams in this study.

Now let's consider how we work. Since our particular concern is the mixed-gender team, an important aspect is that we work in a mixed-gender team. In order to work effectively in our teams, we need first to consider the value of having both men and women leaders. The third criterion, *believing*, calls on us to examine what we believe about the leadership of men and women and to recognize how our values influence our ability to team with persons of the other gender. Do we believe it is important to have both men and women on the team? Do we believe women can and should be peers with men in leadership? Do we believe women as well as men can be team leaders? Answering these questions will determine the shape and substance of our teams.

In Chapters Seven through Ten we will look more closely at elements of *believing*. First, in Chapters Seven and Eight we will briefly examine the theological barriers to women as leaders. These are a part of our history, and in some denominations, a part of the present that still prevents women from playing a role as leaders alongside men. Where these beliefs prevail, the possibility of effective mixed-gender teams is limited. In Chapters Nine and Ten we will learn how and why some teams have developed theological statements explaining their belief in mixed-gender leadership. We'll examine the difference between a theology and a work plan for a mixed-gender team. Finally, we will see how a shared mission and a sense of urgency sustain mixed-gender teams.

CRITERION FOUR: NAME. Working together effectively requires that we know one another. I am not talking about acquaintanceship here but rather the deeper knowing that is a part of truly acknowledging one another. I like to think of this as naming each other in much the same way that Native Americans name people: they give names that describe some trait of the person who has the name. For this reason I call this fourth criterion *naming*. Naming is the preeminent reflective task. It includes knowing each other deeply, respecting each other as individuals, building trust, understanding our differences as men and women and as leaders with a variety of styles, seeing and acknowledging each other's skills and strengths, and assigning value to each other.

It's surprising how few teams recognize the importance of naming each other. Women and men have been working with each other for a long time without knowing or truly acknowledging each other in this way. It may seem obvious that we should acknowledge each other, but it isn't apparent as part of our daily routines. Because acknowledging each other is a reflective activity, it is largely hidden from us until we have made the commitment to know ourselves better and to see and hear the other person.

CRITERION FIVE: INCLUDE. We can't be a team unless we include each other. That's why *including* is the fifth criterion. Of all the criteria that I classify as reflective, this one requires the deepest inner work.

Including each other is the true challenge of diversity. It goes far beyond accepting the fact of gender or any other kind of diversity, even beyond managing diversity. Including each other requires opening ourselves to each other, allowing ourselves to be changed by each other. We cannot do this unless we get beyond stereotypes and even acknowledge our own individual prejudices about each other. When we have confronted our prejudices we can embrace diversity with the knowledge that everyone is changed by it. The minority persons change as they come into the sphere of the majority, and the majority persons are changed too, by the positive influence of the minority.

Including is closely related to *naming* for one simple reason. We are more able to acknowledge each other fully when we have overcome the personal prejudices that get in the way. Therefore, in Chapters Eleven through Thirteen we shall discuss *naming* and *including*. We will see more clearly the relationship between acknowledging ourselves and acknowledging each other. We will consider the role of prejudice in limiting our ability to acknowledge each other. Finally, we will examine what it means to call someone of the opposite sex a leader and a partner.

The Active Criteria

The active criteria engage us with the world. They call upon us to take specific actions to change our way of working together. They include communicating, working together, influencing, and modeling.

CRITERION SIX: COMMUNICATE. In so many ways, *communicating* is central to mixed-gender team success. In my first writing about this criterion five years ago, I focused on language and the imperative for inclusive language. Today, I think the demands of communication for mixed-gender teams go beyond the need for inclusive language to the need for practical communication skills that help men and women understand one another better. Communicating is no simple task. It requires both speaking and listening to each other.

In many respects, the requirements of communication are practical. Every team I interviewed stressed the importance of constant communication, including a willingness to share personal stories, a commitment to working out the many details (including disagreements and misunderstandings) of daily tasks, and a habit of regularly giving each other feedback. Communication, as we shall see, is also at the heart of a cluster of specific activities that help teams continually learn how to be better as teams.

By stressing the practical, I do not mean to deny that language is important. Without doubt, inclusive language helps the gender awareness that is so important for mixed-gender team success. Language is the embodiment of our thoughts, our ideas, our way of conceptualizing the world. It reflects our attitudes. Women and men in successful mixed-gender teams say we must be sensitive about language if we are serious about shared ministry. Our language about God is a particular aspect of inclusive language that is perhaps most difficult, and therefore merits our most careful analysis. It too influences our language about and attitudes toward each other. Language can help us name the variety of experiences of the divine.

In Chapters Fourteen and Fifteen we will examine how both language and communication influence effective mixed-gender teams.

CRITERION SEVEN: WORK. The verb *work* is good shorthand for the preeminent active criterion: *working together*. Working together should remind us that women and men need to be together in the same work setting. This is nothing more or less than coexistence. Acknowledging each other, listening to each other, building trust—all the reflective tasks we have mentioned as well as the active tasks that we shall discuss next require being together in the same space, working together, day after day.

Working together successfully requires much more than taking political action to ensure that men and women are present in the leadership of the denominations, their agencies, and their congregations. Above all, it requires communication. Working together in the day-to-day also requires clear boundaries within which each member of the team has permission to play his or her role with some measure of independence. At the same time, it demands wisdom from all members of the team about intimacy and how intimacy works appropriately between members of the opposite sex who are not sexual partners.

Taken together, all the small ways in which team members work at the daily tasks of being together add up to one big thing: commitment. The commitment of the team is not a burden when members share both humor and a serious commitment to shared spirituality. In Chapters Sixteen through Eighteen, we shall see how teams manage the hard work of being together in the day-to-day.

CRITERION EIGHT: INFLUENCE. To be effective partners, we need to know how to use our power positively and well so that we will be able to influence others toward constructive action. Effective mixed-gender teams do this. Because the ability to influence is the outcome of using power, I call the eighth criterion *influencing*.

This criterion is particularly important for men, almost always requiring a change in their view of power. The story of many failed mixed-gender teams might be different if the person in the position of power, often a man, viewed his role differently. For women, the task is different but just as difficult. We women must stop fearing power and learn to welcome our own unique power as an ally. To do this, we have to overcome our tendency to rule out the use of power on the assumption that it's always abusive. This is a skill we can learn from men, who are not afraid to use power as a leadership tool. Before either gender can accomplish these tasks, both must understand a great deal more about power. There are many different kinds of power and there is a vast difference between power and the abuse of power.

In Chapters Nineteen through Twenty-One we shall examine how power is held in effective mixed-gender teams and how it is often understood differently inside the team, regardless of what those outside the team observe about the power dynamic.

CRITERION NINE: MODEL. Women and men in successful mixed-gender teams work hard to model new ways of leading. Thus *modeling* effective partnership is the final active criterion.

It's not a matter of women adapting to hierarchical models or men learning to be more relational. It's ultimately a matter of finding new ways of leading together that men and women can both appreciate, understand, and use. Once we do this, gender-inclusive leadership will be easier. Openness and flexibility to change, to take a chance on new ways of leadership, are required for our future. "We can't afford to waste the talent of a single person, male or female. As we look at leadership with a 'new way' in mind, we become more and more gender blind, focusing on the gifts we have at our disposal rather than male, female, black, white, or anything else. Our goal is to create an effective team, not to adopt 'my way' or 'your way'" (Becker, 1996, p. 180). This is what modeling is all about.

When I first wrote about these criteria, I defined a tenth criterion about the need for change in systems. "It is not enough for people to change; systems must change as well," I emphasized (Becker, 1996, p. 180). I have chosen not to write about that tenth criterion in this book for several reasons. First and most important, I now believe that the most effective system change comes from teams exerting pressure on systems from within. People, not systems, allow us to experience partnership and collegiality in our workplace. For this reason, I want to keep the focus on teams and what they are doing (and not doing) to bring about change in systems.

Second, coming at the question of change from the system point of view puts the emphasis on the political and organizational issues that many others are writing about. To be sure, we need models for authority that are not patriarchal. We need salaries for women that equal those of men for comparable work. We need policies and practices that will bring women into leadership and free them to do their best work. These tasks are structural. They cannot be achieved by individuals working alone. They start with individuals but require many people working together on the structure of our denominations to be accomplished. Other people are writing about these changes and I defer to them while I keep the focus of this book on working teams.

Finally, I am a skeptic. I do not think much effective change in systems is yet taking place. To be sure, we are beginning to see some of the first signs. At this writing, one Protestant denomination is structuring for more collaborative leadership at the top. Agencies and congregations are also experimenting with more collaborative teaming in administrative circles. But I have seen many more examples of ways in which systems are *not* nurturing mixed-gender leadership. Martha and Brian's story is but one example of effective teams that are intentionally separated. Others have told me of organizational policies that actually make their teaming more difficult. Furthermore, it is obvious that attitudes and theologies still limit the participation of women in mixed-gender teams in many denominations.

In Chapters Twenty-Two and Twenty-Three, then, the focus will remain on teams, looking at how they model change. We will discover how individuals change their own behavior to be more successful team members. We will see how teams discover new ways of leading together. We will also examine the intense and somewhat surprising external pressures that tend to break down the new ways of working together that are crafted by successful teams.

The way the nine criteria work in individual lives is complex. But our examination of these criteria will show us that creating and sustaining an effective mixed-gender team requires time, commitment, and hard work. It demands a constant mix of the reflective and active tasks. The temptation to see the nine criteria as linear and short-term is compelling. But it's not so. They cannot be conquered in linear fashion, like so many hurdles in a race. They aren't consecutive, like chapters in a book. They are circular, connected, overlapping. Thus as we hear the stories of mixed-gender teams to highlight one or another of the criteria, we shall also see other criteria at work in the lives of the individuals and the team. We know, in fact, that we encounter and address each one over and over again in our journey to shared leadership.

How the Nine Criteria Work in Real Teams

We can see in Brian and Martha's experience many of the criteria at work. Brian and Martha recognized the importance of reflection and were fortunate to have an extended period of time to get to know one another before becoming a clergy team. They put an emphasis on reflection, spending lavishly of their time in building trust and learning about one another. They both understood the barriers to women in ministry. Brian took responsibility for building a mixed-gender professional team and presenting it, as it were, to the local hierarchy of The United Methodist

Church. Both Brian and Martha were ready, willing, and able to be present with one another in the day-to-day, even to the point of resolving a difficult disagreement. They set boundaries to make the daily work possible and understandable to the congregation. Thus they could go on to the more active criteria. Though their story does not include comments on these points, Brian and Martha together helped the congregation develop inclusive rather than exclusive theology and language. In both areas, Brian, as the one with more power in the hierarchy, took responsibility. Brian also asserted his authority as the senior pastor of a large congregation to object to the way Martha was moved. As a result, he and other clergy in his conference expect changes in the itinerant system that will allow for more consultation with a congregation when a pastor is moved. It was a small way of changing systems that sent a big message throughout the denomination.

Brian and Martha were a fairly typical effective mixed-gender team. Yet we cannot assume that all successful teams are like Brian and Martha. There are, in fact, many different ways in which effective teams organize themselves. What is similar about them all is their depth of understanding about what it means to be with each other, and particularly the emphasis they put on communication, the way they use power in the team, and their common commitment to a set of values or a shared purpose. This is just another way of saying that *these teams integrate elements of all nine criteria in order to build an effective mixed-gender team.* Before we begin to address the nine criteria in detail, here's a quick snapshot of how all the teams in this study integrate the criteria in practice.

Being with Each Other

When we are truly present for another person we are with that person in all ways. Being with each other includes both accepting each other (greeting, including) and working together effectively day-to-day (working, communicating). There are a number of ways in which effective mixed-gender teams demonstrate this level of presence with each other, both in how they acknowledge each other and in the many things they do to work effectively. The outcome of their radical presence with each other is that they are very creative in putting the team first. Yet at the same time they do not have any sense that they have sacrificed the work that needs to be accomplished in order to nurture the team. The most frequently mentioned ways that effective teams maintain presence with each other include the following:

- Believing in the strength of every member of the team. They are confident in each other's strengths, and they tell each other so. This does not mean, however, that they are all alike. On the contrary, they cite differences among team members in personal style, ways of thinking, and skills as essential to team success.

- Trusting one another. Although they trust one another, at the same time they know that trust can be broken by misunderstanding, missed signals, behaving in ways that other team members (especially team members from another ethnic background or gender) do not understand.

- Achieving and maintaining parity among all members in the team. Everyone counts for everyone else.

- Knowing the benefits for each team member of being a part of the team.

- Continuing some kind of activity that builds the team.

- Talking to each other a lot.

- Including affirmation as a normal part of their idea-action-feedback cycle.

- Stating and honoring contracts and boundaries that team members (and often outsiders as well) understand and honor.

- Avoiding decisions that one or more members cannot support. Yet at the same time, team members remain relatively free to make individual decisions when necessary because they are trusted by others on the team.

- Maintaining accountability to each other. Even when they disagree with each other in private, team members usually support each other publicly; however, there are exceptions to this rule. Some team members agree to speaking their own minds publicly even when they disagree with each other.

We can observe from this list that there are elements of being and doing involved in the level of radical presence that effective team members achieve with one other. The fourth and fifth criteria (naming and including) are reflective. They involve being with one another in all the ways we can acknowledge one another. In this sense they are about *individuals in the team*. The sixth and seventh criteria (communicating and working) are active. They help team members create their own rules for working together day by day. They have to do with individuals *becoming the team*.

Using Power in the Team

All teams manage power both inside and outside the team. The uniqueness of effective mixed-gender teams is that they do not focus on power.
They focus on the team and manage everything, including power, to the
benefit of the team. Some individuals are so focused in this way that they
find the word *power* itself awkward in describing anything their team
does. Analysis of the interviews, however, verified that even when they did
not think the use or management of power was an element of their team's
functioning, it was. Here's how.

- Effective mixed-gender teams are constituted differently in relation
  to power in the external environment. Some are hierarchically constructed, with a person who is clearly the senior member; others
  are very egalitarian and refuse to buy into hierarchical structures.
  Both types were represented in the sampling of effective teams.
  Regardless of the way these teams manage power in relation to the
  external environment, all members share power within the team.
- Individuals in effective mixed-gender teams do not use power to
  "show who's boss."
- In order to succeed, mixed-gender teams need the commitment and
  leadership of the person in the team who holds the most power in
  the external environment.
- Most teams resist pressure from external sources to break down
  the team structure and find a person who will "take charge."
- How well these teams manage their own power dynamics, both inside and outside the team, is a critical factor in their overall success.
- Shared power within the teams often has a positive influence on
  the systems around the team.

When mixed-gender teams use power in these ways, they are *influencing*. They are attending to the eighth criterion. Furthermore, they are *influencing appropriately*—using power as a positive force for their team's
success.

Common Commitment to Values and Purpose

Members of effective mixed-gender teams often cited compatibility, trust,
strength of teammates, good communication, clear boundaries, written
covenants, and plain old-fashioned hard work as factors contributing to

their success as a team. All these elements are dependent on the participation of the team members in a shared working life. They are typical of the things we know to be factors in the success of any team, diverse or not. In addition to these, I found another quite different element at the heart of the success of the teams in this study. It is based not on hard work but rather on shared values or common purpose. This is one element of *believing*.

These team members talked about a determination to succeed because of the important work they are doing. For them, a successful team is central to achieving their purpose. They are so committed to this purpose that they will resolve or even overlook any number of differences and problems in order to be able to continue that work. One person called it "our passion for the mission of this organization." Accompanying this passion may be a sense of urgency. In such cases, the mission of the organization is so urgent in the minds of the staff that there is no time to waste being ineffective. This perspective does not seem to prevent the team from taking some time to work at making the team effective, however.

Sometimes these team members expressed their commitment in terms of values rather than purpose, saying they "have shared values" to bind them together in their work. In teams that hold values as central, team members demonstrate that their behavior in relation to each other is congruent with the values of the organization. Obviously, these are organizations that encourage in their teams much discussion of the values of the organization and what those values mean for individual employees as well as for constituents.

The binding character of common purpose and values in the organization may be unique to the nonprofit church-related organization. More research is necessary to know. However, it was definitely a unique characteristic that provided motivation for success among most teams in this study.

Verifying the Criteria

In reviewing the common behaviors of effective mixed-gender teams, we can readily see evidence of seven of the criteria at work: *reflect, believe, name, include, communicate, work,* and *influence.* What about the other two, *learn* and *model*? The learning these teams have done in order to become effective is most evident in their structure. The preeminent learning tasks are learning about leadership and learning about teaming. These teams have set themselves up to be teams according to their best understanding of what teams are like and how they function. It's as simple as that. We shall see this in every story. Second, learning is evident in the ways these team members have individually integrated their knowledge about "what leadership requires" into their own style as leaders. Again, we shall see the evidence in their stories. Modeling is a bit easier to verify. By virtue of the fact that these teams are effective teams, they model what an effective team is and does. Again, the evidence will be in the stories.

Overall, the feedback of the successful mixed-gender teams in this study verified the nature and importance of the nine criteria originally suggested by focus group participants in 1994. In consequence, they affirmed the importance of reflection and even gave deeper meaning to what the reflective criteria are and how they should be addressed. They showed that action, when it is in counterpoint to reflection, is very effective.

This is not to say that the criteria are unaffected by this second study. Much has changed in my thinking about the criteria. "What's involved" in each one seems different and more complex five years after first writing about them. These changes are a function of time, to be sure, but that's not all. They are also, and more important, a function of what I learned from listening to teams.

The stories of the mixed-gender teams are especially significant. Much like Brian and Martha, the teams bring to life the meaning of the ideas they share in this book. They give personal, political, and theological meaning to being with each other day by day in the workplace. They demonstrate why we need to know our history and the history of our denominations. They show the dynamic and circular ways in which reflection and action work together. They prove to us over and over that we can never tick off the tasks like chores in a list but must instead commit to going over and over them, constantly integrating. They also demonstrate that the active criteria are as much personal as political in nature. They show what we can each do alone and what we must do together. Each one also comes back to a common theme that is intangible: the great joy that men and women experience when they are working together effectively.

3

REFLECTING

REFLECTING IS INNER WORK that prepares us to understand the world, and our fellow human beings, more deeply. It is the first of the nine criteria and the basis for the four that follow it. Effective mixed-gender teams reflect regularly because doing so helps them integrate their values about the team (we might call this their theology) with the daily practice of being a team. What are their values about the team? They care about one another as well as their work. Reflecting allows them to attend to their relationships as well as their tasks. It's as simple as that.

Our tendency to overlook or minimize the value of reflecting is almost unavoidable given the high value we place on action in our culture. Ned's story illustrates the role of reflection and the many ways in which reflection and action counterpoint each other in one man's life. Using Ned's story as an example, we will then consider in some detail what reflecting involves.

Ned's Story

Ned grew up in the Midwest in the 1950s in a typical white middle-class environment. His father was the breadwinner, while his mother, in the terminology of the day, was a homemaker. In reflecting back on what his life has taught him about the work of women and men in the church, the first thing he recalls is the way congregations worked in the 1950s. "Men in our church served on the council. Women coordinated the potluck suppers and taught Sunday school," he remembers. "The superintendent of the Sunday school was always a man; except in 1963 when Mrs. H., who was easily three inches taller and probably eighty pounds the senior of most men in the congregation, in an act of courage a bit less risky (but not much less) than what Rosa Parks did on the bus, questioned why men always served as Sunday school superintendent. She successfully achieved an election upset and served as superintendent from fall 1963 to the spring of 1964, until the men in the church had recovered and did whatever it was they needed to do to assure her removal. At the time I was a youth and thought not much of it. It wasn't until the late 1970s that a woman served in such a leadership capacity in our church again."

It wasn't until 1968, when Ned was in graduate school, that his own journey toward awareness of gender issues in leadership really began. He reflected with me on the meaning of the nine criteria by recalling several women he worked with over the years and several things he learned that, woven together, brought him to fuller awareness of what it takes to succeed in working together.

"When I began my seminary training, I entered as part of the first class under a new experimental curriculum. My class had the first women students in our denomination, some of them becoming part of that pioneering group that had to excel beyond all reasonable expectations in order to prove their value to the church as serious students of theology, let alone as real candidates for ordained ministry," he recalls. "The seminary in those days taught listening, self-reflection, candor, and collaboration. High levels of accountability were maintained for our words and our behavior. Intent was equally as critical as method. With hindsight, I now realize those learning techniques were, in actuality, leadership attributes on the more feminine end of the continuum. But I could not have articulated this understanding back then."

In 1972 Ned entered parish ministry in the inner city where, he says, "I learned a lot about gender and ethnicity from the African American women who had been leading for a long time. They were leaders because many of the men were absent, for all of the historical, racial, economic, and sociological reasons we have come to understand much better now than we did then.

"I also learned about authenticity," Ned continues, "for it was in the inner city that I met Barbara, one of the first women ordained in my denomination. Barbara lived life from a wheelchair, having achieved her ordination in spite of profound cerebral palsy. Early in her career she was highly sought after because she provided an opportunity for the church to demonstrate its openness to women clergy and people with disabilities. But within a few years Barbara died in a tragic fire, alone and unemployed. In large part, Barbara's fatal career mistake was that she refused to be a complacent symbol for a church desperately wanting to make an image correction in a rapidly changing world; a church erroneously thinking it could concoct such a change quickly through a few exceptional examples. Barbara resisted becoming such an example because she knew it would rob her and her church of authenticity. And so she was forgotten."

As the 1980s began, Ned began working for a comprehensive social service agency. Many of its clients were mentally ill adults who were at that time being moved out of institutions into group homes. "These were tumultuous times," Ned recalls, "years of deinstitutionalization, growing regulation, and community placement. Neighborhoods were scared and angry by the intrusion of the people who were being deinstitutionalized. Families were scared and angry by the forced removal of their loved ones from the safety of the institution. Other families who had never placed their loved ones in the institution were judgmental and angry with those who had. These were complicated times.

"There and then we needed resiliency," Ned says. "There and then we needed approaches other than polarizing confrontation. There and then, I realize now, the capacity to achieve came more effectively from the women administrators who joined our fledgling division than it did from the men. How effective any one person could be proved to be a matter of resiliency and the capacity to craft resolutions through collaboration. Again, to the extent generalizations are true, the male administrators burned out; the females did not. The male administrators could not as effectively as the females bring achievement out of the ambiguity of the times and the setting. Somehow, the women group-home administrators were solving the difficulties differently than the men."

Watching from the sidelines, Ned observed that "it had something to do with operating from a base of listening rather than asserting. Clearly control (that is, utilization of power) was a factor, and it was understood and managed differently. Information was also used differently and managed to different ends. Dominating was less important to the female administrators than it was to the males. Being right at all costs was less important. Demonizing the opponent was less important. In a fundamental way, achievement was perceived differently, though I could not articulate it then. I could only reflect on what I was observing."

Later in his career in social work, Ned had the unhappy experience of mentoring a woman for a job that had once been his, only to find that she achieved it at last by abusive means. "Covertly, she made sure that others preceding her in the position (including me) were perceived as severely flawed," Ned recalls. "This is a technique I have seen many—mostly males—use for their own advancement. It hurt when applied to me. It was nothing more than achieving power through the use of effective distortions, rewriting history to assure a desired conclusion. Far too much of this goes on in the organizational world, where the abuse of power over others is commonplace, and power with others for the sake of building community is less often our experience."

Years later, Ned says, this memory still hurts. "It was not an easy lesson to learn in my own journey. But what is instructive for my own reflection is less what happened to me *one time* than the realization that what has happened just once to me has happened over and over again to many women attempting to enter the leadership world of our denominations. If my own single experience feels this bad to me, so many years after it happened, I can only imagine how it feels and what the cumulative effect is on those women who have suffered such injustice repeatedly, in ways they cannot address."

In the last dozen years, Ned has had the opportunity to partner more directly with women who are his peers in leadership. Much of their work together has focused on forming collaborations among social service organizations. "Working in partnership with women has been a marvelously educational experience for me," Ned says. "To achieve the goals of bringing organizations together and forming new ways of working requires leaders who understand and share that dream; leaders who can be executives in their organizations while they share decision making and power with other executives in other organizations. Few men could have functioned that way very long and assured the time necessary to bring our collaborative dreams to fruition. My female colleagues did, and I am grateful beyond words for their leadership."

But, Ned adds, the women had some challenges to overcome in spite of their competence. "The women were doing the same work with the same people that I and other men were doing, were equally competent as—and sometimes more competent than—we men, but were treated differently. At times, others treated them as almost invisible. Early on, when they would draw my attention to the differing treatment, I confess I thought they were exaggerating. 'Couldn't be so,' said I. 'They must be excessively sensitive.' But they have kept showing me, and I now know that if I reflect on what they are saying, I often realize they are right. Their experiences in leadership are different than mine."

In 1998 things changed dramatically for Ned and one of his closest female colleagues, Sharon, who was head of a sister agency. "This is the most painful part of my reflective journey, because it is the most recent and represents a time when I failed to reflect as much as I should have," Ned says. It was a twist of fate that both he and Sharon experienced family tragedies at just about the same time that year. "For personal reasons that I respect and admire, Sharon took an extended leave of absence to be with her family. I reacted to my loss differently, choosing to pour myself into my work to the exclusion of all else. It was a time when we were just beginning delicate negotiations for another merger which, I believed, would be a bold and creative move in the social service world. It seemed to me this project might be the final and most creative act of my professional life.

"When Sharon returned from her leave, the merger negotiations had progressed so far that I could not really bring her fully on board—at least not as much as she seemed to want. I just needed her to get in there and be supportive," Ned recalls. "She needed something different from me, perhaps time to reconnect, and reassurance that I had not moved beyond caring about or valuing our partnership. After so many years of building a relationship, it seemed as though we were no longer understanding each other. I was grieved by this, yet I kept my focus on the project. I was in an activity phase. I was not in a place where I could be reflective."

Ned's activity did not mean "that I was not concerned about our partnership and deeply saddened by my own inability to repair our relationship," he says. He began to seek out other women who could help him understand what had gone wrong in his partnership with Sharon. "Of course, there are many complexities in any relationship, and I cannot enumerate all the elements of my relationship with Sharon," Ned says. "But I think I came to the truth of it when one of them told me I had put the merger project before the relationship, while Sharon wanted me to put the relationship before the project. This caused me to stop short. I remember when I heard this feedback. I was absolutely silent because I knew in my heart that it was the one thing I was not, at the time, able to do. I needed to attend to the task. I suspect Sharon did not understand this. And I did not understand why she needed me to put the relationship first, when this merger was so important to me. After all those years of working closely together, we just passed each other by, like ships in the night."

What does it all mean? What is the value of Ned's learning, based on his own personal reflection over the years? Ned reflects on this: "First, there's a lot to be done and to be done better if we learn to use the whole continuum of leadership styles. Second, no matter how experienced I am, I still have things to learn from reflection. Third, the issues revolve largely around power and authority and how each is understood and utilized. Fourth, the avenue to learning for effective change is not through the enumeration of principles; it is through our growing awareness, made possible by dialogue, candor, and risk. It starts with the reflective tasks. Our hope is for a time when we can position ourselves *with* each other rather than *on* the denominational totem pole."

The Call to Reflect

The call to reflect is not a call to inaction. We may interpret it so, but it is rather a call to inner action, as Ned's story illustrates. That inner action begins with prayerful acceptance of our ability to recognize the personal barriers that prevent us from truly knowing each other. This requires humility—the realization and acceptance of our own limitations. When we nurture humility in our hearts and lower our personal barriers, we become ready to understand and address this call. Only then are we capable of knowing one another better.

Then we must ask what it means truly to know one another, for we are not talking here about mere acquaintanceship. The deeper awareness and appreciation that comes from reflective activity goes beyond knowing one another for what we do to knowing one another for who we are and what we are like. This kind of knowing fosters acceptance of gender differences and of individual differences among people of the same gender. It also allows us to know ourselves better as we reflectively listen to "the other" at a deeper level. It takes time, perhaps time we have not in the past been willing to spend because we feel as if we're not doing anything.

Let us look closer at the reflective tasks to see whether we are indeed "doing nothing" when we commit to them.

Listening Comes First

In coming to know each other, we begin by listening. This requires much time and psychic energy. Women particularly say that they want men to listen to them. In fact, they ask above all that men take the time to listen. We want a place at the table, where the dialogue involves both men and women in leadership. "Men cannot know what we want and what the possibilities are unless they listen," says one laywoman in professional church leadership.

Men often wonder, Why all the fuss about listening? They take it for granted that they will be heard (Tannen, 1990). This is particularly true for white males, who are heard partly because they are white males and partly because they learn from childhood to *expect* to be heard. The difference for women is that they are not used to being heard, and they do not know how to expect it. A woman who became bishop in her denomination put it succinctly when she said that "the biggest shock for me . . . was that people actually listened and responded when I said something."

Men have some difficult hurdles to overcome in listening. First, they need to overcome resistance. Men don't like being challenged. Women joke about the male ego getting in the way. This egotism is part of growing up expecting to be heard and believed. The equally valuable skill of hearing others and considering another point of view is not so easy for men, who tend to approach conversations as opportunities to establish or exercise their independence and authority. They usually hear a "challenge," an attempt to belittle them, whereas women may intend to connect (Tannen, 1990). Thus men often resist what they perceive as the abuse of being verbally "beaten up" by women. In addition, men can learn to listen "almost as enemies," cautions a laywoman and theologian, who says it's dangerous for men to "pretend to be our allies." Men need to listen deeply, not pretending to know what women's experiences are like. They literally have to put aside their ability to banter, to challenge, to establish themselves in a conversation in order to hear women in this way.

A third hurdle for men is succinctly described in the words of a clergywoman who says that men should "hear our experience as valid, not as deviant." One woman who has benefited from this kind of listening by her partner said, "I always felt that Greg received what I had to say with a great deal of respect. He encouraged my ideas. I always felt listened to. After a very little while it became clear that Greg valued what I had to offer." This kind of listening requires men to put aside their tendency to enter into the conversation with their opinions, to provide answers, to be in charge. All of these hurdles may be difficult for men as they learn to listen.

Women too must listen, though we recognize that this is not a new task for us. Our challenge is to listen to men in a new way. First, this requires accepting the different ways men and women approach conversations. If we women truly want our male colleagues to engage in a conversation to get to know us (a connectional activity if there ever was one!), we are asking them to play by our rules. This requires patience and understanding, not criticism or pressure.

The converse is also true. Women need to learn how to listen to men more in the way that men listen to women—that is, without losing our own voices. Though women may be offended when men strongly assert their points of view in conversation (women often describe this as not listening), men are not so put off. On the contrary, they would be relieved if we women would enter into conversation with a bit more intent to establish *our* authority. To do this, we must not only understand our own feminine values but also articulate them. As we begin to know our own will, we women cannot blindly accept men's values as though they are our own (de Castillejo, 1973). It is difficult for women to do this in a world overrun by materialism, greed, prejudice, and violence—attributes foreign to the feminine essence. It is doubly difficult for women in denominations that are still patriarchal.

After We Listen . . . and Before We Act

If we can listen, then we are prepared to understand and engage in the reflective criteria, all of which are involved in acknowledging each other. They include *believing* in the leadership of men and women and in our work, *naming* each other as people, and *including* each other no matter how different we are from each other. These criteria demand that we know each other as unique persons, not as stereotypes, recognizing each other's skills and strengths, assigning value to each other, and the inevitable result: accepting that women as well as men have legitimate roles to play in the leadership of the church. These criteria ultimately take us into even deeper territory, where we get to know ourselves in new ways as we get to know "the other."

When we think deeply about ourselves and about our colleague of the opposite sex who is inevitably a mystery to us, we come to the core of our attitudes about the other. We confront what we least like to see in ourselves—that we too use labels in order to know each other without really knowing each other at all. And here we are called to examine the truth of the labels we use, the ways in which the labels hurt us as well as the other, and the things we can do to change inside ourselves.

Inevitably, if we take the reflective criteria seriously, we undo the "ungifting" that women have spoken about with so much pain. Women have "time and time again had the painful experience of the church ungifting our gifts. Our gifts are deemed undesirable because they do not match the ecclesial furniture or because they are not like anything anybody has envisioned. . . . This 'ungifting' is a denial of the giver as well as the gifts" (Yocum, 1991, p. 70). Ungifting affects men too, of course. But because men are in the dominant group, both men and women often overlook the ungifting they experience.

Our reflective work is a prerequisite to successful shared leadership. Without it, the increasingly active demands of *working* together, *communicating, influencing* for good, and *modeling* shared leadership cannot help us. We must start with the inner work, the reflecting. Once we start doing it, reflecting becomes a habit, providing fertile ground on which to plant the seeds of our activity.

Giving Ourselves Permission to Reflect

The call to reflect is above all a warning to us to pause and not act too quickly. Literally, it is a call to stop in our tracks and get to know ourselves and each other first. The inner activity required of us by the reflective tasks calls us to "being" time, not "doing" time. This is difficult for everyone, for our way in the West is to take action. Reflection seems like a waste of our time when in fact it is the only good use of our time at first.

The Call to Inner Action

Carl Jung once used the story of the Chinese rainmaker who was called to a village to bring the rain that would end a terrible drought. The rainmaker came and promptly withdrew to a small hut, asking only for bread and water. At the end of three days, the rain came. When the villagers asked him how he did it, he replied, "I withdrew into myself and put myself in order; and when I am in order the world around me must naturally come into order too, and then the drought must be followed by rain" (Jacobi, 1965, p. 95). This story presents us with a compelling picture of exactly what is required. Like the Chinese rainmaker, we must first withdraw to look inside ourselves. We must do so believing that when all is right within, the outer world will also come into order.

This truth Jesus knew as he withdrew into the wilderness for forty days, eating nothing and being subject to the most compelling temptations Satan could devise. The temptations were a test of Jesus' inner readiness for his work among us. They would indicate whether "all was right within" so that the outer ministry might commence.

This story of Jesus reminds us of another aspect of reflecting, for was not Jesus in dialogue with God while he sojourned in the wilderness? When reflecting engages us in a dialogue with God, we call it prayer. To be sure, prayer is most possible when we are right within and open to the voice of God speaking to us. Then we are ready to cooperate with God in our own transformation. Prayer, in this sense, fosters the spiritual basis for our journey. The nine criteria provide us with a structure for that transformation once we are ready.

It is the withdrawing that we so little understand. We think that action is required, but the rainmaker teaches us that action is useless unless we are prepared. The reflective tasks are what prepare us. Like the rainmaker, we literally deprive ourselves of outward stimuli; we go into the small dark hut. This is an image for putting aside the active tasks of the outer world—personal effort, dialogue, political action, and all the rest—until we ourselves are ready. For as Carl Jung (1966) reminds us, progress begins "with a single individual, conscious of his isolation, breaking a new way through regions hitherto untrodden. For this he must first reflect on the basic facts of his life—regardless of all authority and tradition—and become conscious of his distinctiveness" (p. 59).

What Happens When We Reflect

We may understand better if we look more closely at what happens when we withdraw and prepare ourselves. Some call this *centering*. Others call it *meditating*. In this time, deprived of outward activity, we do our inner work and in so doing engage in reflection. We are not deprived of all outward stimulation when we withdraw. It is still present within us; we are simply choosing for a time to live in a distinctive way, distanced from the hustle and bustle of our lives, so that we may find what is within. Here, we continually discover and accept who we are. We can grieve for our own losses and shortcomings and so break the cycle of projecting these onto others. We can experience our own boundaries and see others as separate and different. We have the opportunity to accept ourselves and prepare ourselves to acknowledge another who may be quite different. We can become comfortable with silence, which is a prerequisite for listening. We can literally become enchanted with the idea of the individual, and so begin our education ready to learn about and appreciate the unknown other.

Matthew Fox (1994) presents us with many images for this process. He says, "Facing nothingness can mean the beginning of a whole new life. The womb is empty before it fills with new life; our minds are empty before they see the world anew; the pupil of the eye is empty—as is the lens of the camera—in order to take in 'all things'; a mirror is empty before something passes before it and is reflected therein. When our souls are emptied, it may be the beginning of learning who we truly are, how original we are, how distinct from, yet deeply connected to others, we are" (p. 52).

Reflection prepares us to see each other as subjects rather than objects. Once committed to it, women are learning to see men not only as "those who have created barriers for us" but as individual men. Men are learning to see women as individuals, not as "those who shouldn't be here." This is the new wisdom we gain by reflecting. The world does indeed come into better order. The rains come to end the drought; the devil is cast out. But this does not mean that we make the world conform to our (old) ways of thinking, to our sexist attitudes, or to any of our other personal prejudices. It means that we, like the rainmaker, are each in our own way transformed and so brought into harmony with the world, so that the rains can fall.

Our Need for Reflection

The importance of letting go comes into focus when we realize that "it is not letting go of things that is important, but the letting go of attitudes toward things" (Fox, 1983, p. 160). When we can't let go of our negative attitudes, we literally project them onto others. Projection in the context of gender relationships is the refusal to let the other be the other. It comes from our inner refusal to let ourselves be or to be with ourselves. We are wise to remember that "life insists on being lived, and anything that belongs to one's life which is allowed to lie dormant has to be lived by someone else" (de Castillejo, 1973, p. 41). When we are dissatisfied with being ourselves and "so not at home with our deepest self" (Fox, 1983, p. 160), we tend to project onto others our own ways of thinking, acting, and living. Women are particularly affected by this human tendency because, as we shall learn more fully in Chapter Eight, women are the "embedded other" in our denominations, and indeed in most cultures in the world (Becker, 1996; Russell, 1993; Hearn and Burrell, 1989). Men are affected when women project onto them their own latent heroes. We women do this unconsciously when we are unable to complete our own acts of heroism, the courageous delving into ourselves to find and salvage our own feminine values (de Castillejo, 1973). Projection is deeply divisive because it "disrupts all authentic pleasure, all authentic communication, all authentic relating" (Fox, 1983, p. 160).

By contrast, a commitment to reflecting disciplines us to a different reality in which we have the capacity to approach ourselves and others in a radically different way. First, we will be freer to choose ourselves. This means "not just settling for what we are, but accepting ourselves in our own body, with our own abilities, race, sexuality, family, class and culture, as a gift of God. . . . For both men and women the choice is one of moving beyond particular assigned roles in the patriarchal culture, religion, family, or society and choosing to be ourselves in our own particular bodies, with our various limitations as well as our gifts" (Russell, 1993, p. 184).

Having chosen ourselves, we will be better able to reform our relationships every day because we understand relationships to be organic, living things, offering us unlimited possibilities (Fox, 1994). We will even be open to the possibility that our coworker, regardless of gender, and beyond our understanding of how or when or why in the politics of denominations, may be consecrated to God's work. We will be compelled, then, to choose the margin (Russell, 1993), that place where we can work with others to bring about a transformed society and a renewed church.

How Effective Teams Reflect

This may all be true, but we still may have the question: How to reflect? What do effective teams *do* that we may identify as reflective? Ned's story was one of lifelong reflection, which is important for all of us. But we also need to know the short-term strategies men and women use to reflect.

Structured Reflection Takes Many Forms

There are a number of ways that effective mixed-gender teams reflect in their practice. These include having regular meetings to "keep in touch" with one another, praying, studying, having fun or socializing together, scheduling retreat or recollection times, and talking to one another, as well as doing a variety of specific activities that are designed to build the team rather than get the tasks done. Effective mixed-gender teams report spending significant time—up to 20 percent of total time together—on these types of activities. The teams that report these activities do not necessarily recognize them as reflection, even though they do understand them to be "something more than getting the work done." Thus there may or may not be intent in their selection of some activity that builds the team or helps individuals get to know one another in a deeper way.

When reflecting is intentional, it usually takes the form of structured time set aside for team building of one kind or another. It may also be social time during which the team members get to know one another better, or informal time in the office during which people take time to talk to each other, pray, or study together. When reflection is unintentional, the team members report that they take little or no time to reflect; however, the interviews reveal that there is at least one identifiable activity that helps the team work on its effectiveness even though the activity itself may be done for a different purpose.

My interview sampling revealed that varied and imaginative activities help mixed-gender teams reflect together. They include very formal reflection: personality and work-typing inventories and discussions of the results, which are common among most effective teams; antiracism training, which team members say "makes all of our change and team building possible"; a structured process called "rethinking" that systematically helps team leaders in another setting understand and appreciate the different program areas supervised by members of the team and ultimately breaks down silos in the organization; structured discernment using Ignatian rules and formulas for decision making in a Catholic team; and cooperative method meetings in yet another setting, where staff are using a defined structure to build team communication. They also include less formal reflection: supervising students in seminary or other training, an active process that requires the supervisory team to reflect on their own work on a regular basis; writing together on an occasional basis, another activity that requires teammates to reflect together for the purpose of creating an article or book; shared Torah study, an activity that is formal in its own way but informally builds the relationship between teammates; and even a naming project, which one mixed-gender team created for the purpose of helping them name each other's gifts on a regular basis.

Team members report these activities with enthusiasm, whether or not they recognize their reflective qualities. "The article we wrote together," says one team member, "almost wrote itself, it was so easy. I wrote, then he wrote, then I wrote again, and pretty soon it was done. It just naturally seemed to flow out of what we were doing when we started to think about it." Learning the cooperative method has provided another team with the opportunity to reflect on and change its leadership style. The mentoring of seminary students, said a member of another team, "forced us to articulate our own understanding of ministry to each other. It gave us some time to look intentionally at what we were doing and how we were functioning." For yet another team, a rethinking project "systematically got every department talking to every other department about what we do and what would make our work lives easier."

Prayer is another activity that provides structure for effective mixed-gender teams to reflect together. One team reports starting a daily 11:45 A.M. prayer time for the pastoral team as well as "anyone else on the staff who wanted to come." They do: custodians, secretaries, other members of the extended staff join the pastors. People from the congregation may come as well, and "one day the Xerox repairman was with us." In this setting, the reflection of the immediate team reached out and embraced others in the wider community. Prayer, said another team member in a different setting, "is a guiding force as we go about the tasks."

The key to all of these very structured processes is that they are not done for the purpose of completing tasks but rather for the purpose of getting to know other team members or improve the team's leadership.

We can also distinguish those meetings that are reflective. They are not meetings that are held to accomplish tasks but rather meetings held to check in with the team. They may be a part of a longer meeting in which tasks are discussed. They have the distinction of being focused on the team rather than the work. One woman described the difference in her team's meetings once the reflective element was added as follows: "Before when we'd have a meeting, people would come with the attitude, 'Let's get right down to business.' We may have just come from a phone conversation or a meeting or a difficult situation somewhere else. We were not necessarily with the group. Also, there was a sense in which our meetings always felt competitive. Now we check in with each other first. We give all participants a chance to say what's going on with them personally and what's going on in their work. We even create the agenda together ahead of time so there are no surprises. During the meeting, we solve problems together and we share trends." This makes the meeting collaborative and a lot less competitive, she continued, if for no other reason than that everyone knows what's coming up in the discussion.

Engaging Constituents in Reflection

Some teams also engage their constituents in reflection. One pastoral team reports being "very intentional" by conducting a series of structured activities for listening in its first year as a team. "We spent a lot of time listening to people tell us about this church. . . . We heard some wonderful stories—people's perceptions of their history. We asked them where they saw challenges. We didn't do any tampering." In fact, this team didn't do anything right away. That's what made their process reflective. "This allowed the congregation to get to know us—and allowed us to know them. It allowed us to build the level of trust. Now, when we do suggest something we'd like to do, they understand that we come from a shared desire to do something good for this congregation."

Another clergy team designed a council retreat to teach spiritual quietness, focus on team building, and write a mission statement. "We went to a retreat center and began by spending three hours letting each person pray a particular scripture. Then we worked on team building the rest of the day, talking about visioning and where we wanted the congregation to go," recalls the former pastor, who was a member of one team in this study. "We got so many positive comments about what that meant for people to develop their spiritual listening skills. Everybody did it a little differently. Some people went off and wrote. Some sat and watched nature and prayed. We allowed everyone to do his or her own thing. That retreat is still a very significant event in my memory of that congregation and of what happened in the next couple of years with that particular council. It solidified that council as a team."

Yet another team uses mealtime reflection to help seminary students in a multicultural setting get to know one another better. They have created an event around naming, setting the dinner table with flowers and candles, using name tags, and building a program around sharing the meaning of names. This creates a particularly meaningful reflective time for students who come from eight different countries to receive their theological education in the United States.

Informal Talk Time Is Critical

"Looking back on it," said one team member, "the more informal ways we communicate and work on our team are hard to define and quantify." But overwhelmingly team members from all settings credit this time as the most important. Very different from structured reflection, it's mostly "talk time" that can't be classified or added up. Team members use the discipline of talk to check in with each other on how they are doing personally and professionally, to debrief recent activities or trips, to reveal their personal stories to each other, to confront one another honestly when they are hurt or angry, to discuss their ideas, and to share their values. They have learned to use "I" language in talking about themselves and "we" language in talking about the team. They are very committed to the discipline of informal talk time in someone's office, by e-mail, over lunch, during daily coffee hour, or in other settings, catch-as-catch-can. It may be informal but it happens every day, as part of the formal routine of teamwork.

"We have spent a lot of time finding out who we are, how we work, what matters and what doesn't matter to us," explains one laywoman who works in a parish setting. "The first few months, you have to be intentional. It doesn't just happen. People have a natural inclination to work well or not work well together, but you have to be interested in getting to the root of how the other works and thinks—how the other processes information. It takes a wise person to learn that."

Once started on this process, effective team members seldom give it up. "Our talk time," said a clergywoman, "is a time for nurture of the relationships, building of the trust . . . that allows our work to be so much more productive."

When intentional talking to each other is added to the other approaches we have discussed in this chapter, it adds up to a great recipe for reflection.

The spiritual formation team members, who tell their story in Chapter Eleven, combine the ingredients in this way: regular days of recollection, lots of talking together, frequent prayer together, staff meetings that include check-in time as well as work time, and regular opportunities to have fun together socially. The result: a strong foundation for all their work together.

It's "wasting time with each other in ways critical to our relationship," says one member of this team. He has a twinkle in his eye when he adds, "Others in our organization envy us because our team does it so well." This playful comment reveals a very serious contribution that effective mixed-gender teams in the church-related setting make to all teams, whether they are in the corporation or the nonprofit workplace. It reveals not only that mixed-gender teams use talking effectively as a reflective task but also that effective mixed-gender team members show all workplace teams how to work together as human beings.

"We thirst for a corporate admission that we are here in this life for more than work. Having a mixed team puts that on the table," explained one team member who is in international church-related relief work. His point was this: because mixed-gender teams have had such limited success, the effective teams have had to look deeper, work harder at teaming, get to know each other more completely to succeed at all. What they have learned about the value of talking to each other as a reflective task is a lesson for all teams. "It's also a cultural issue," he adds. "We play the theme in this country that we can do anything, that the clock is no object. And others around the world are imitating us. But the idea that performance is everything has the potential to blow our gender games right out the window. Giving 'value added' rarely means having coffee more often or sitting together in the shade." Yet this is the *very thing* the teams in this study say is so important for our working together. The danger this man points out is that we (both men and women) may be so captivated by the American way of working that we will forget—or perhaps not even notice—what these teams are showing us about reflecting with each other.

PART TWO

LEARNING

4

BEN, FREDRICA, AND KAREN

BUILDING A SHARED LEADERSHIP MODEL

BEN, FREDRICA, AND KAREN form the core of this mixed-gender, ethnically diverse administrative team in a small Episcopal seminary on the East Coast. Ben is interim president, Fredrica is academic dean, and Karen is dean of students and community life. These three professionals worked together for two years as peers until Ben became interim president in the summer of 1998. Before that time, Ben had been chief operating officer while Fredrica and Karen held the same positions they currently hold. Ben and Karen both joined the seminary in 1996; Fredrica has been on the administrative team since the early 1980s, serving as academic dean for two presidents who preceded Ben. Both Fredrica and Ben are lay and of Euro-American background. Karen, an African American, was ordained in 1996 after working as a laywoman in higher education for thirteen years.

When Ben became president, the team changed leadership style, placing the administration in the center rather than at the top. Before Ben's presidency the community had begun to work on antiracism, but it was done under the strong direction of the former president. The new leadership style of this team changed the way diverse groups were formed and the way the whole community worked together on the appreciation of diversity in the educational process. The challenge for this leadership team has been to create a shared leadership model in an institution that was formerly hierarchical, with a strong single leader who was an ordained Episcopal priest. Contributing to their transition is the several-years-long process to become a multicultural organization using a specific group process called the cooperative method, which is now valued in the community, not just by its senior leaders.

○

Fredrica: Leading Change

I worked with two presidents before Ben, one for seven years and the other for five years. Both tended to look at their administrative associates as their staff. They told us what to do. But before Ben came, we were already working on trying—through the lens of being much more antiracist and multicultural—to open up the system and clarify it. Over the long haul it has been tough, because the Episcopal model is pretty much "what the president says, you do." The first thing to recognize is that you do have power. I've got to name the personal, interpersonal, institutional, and cultural symbolic power I have. I'm much more aware of this now than I was. The attitude that "I don't have power" is a denial of what the institution has invested in me.

What we try to build here is a consultative model that holds people to the accountabilities that are stated . . . that allows us to make mistakes and move on, to ask questions of one another rather than level charges at one another. We have been using the cooperative method, basically, the notion that there is enough time and power and access and goodwill to go around so that you don't have to parcel it out to a few. I am more likely to ask a question of a colleague than tell him what I hear him doing. We are much more likely to give one another affirmations and say at the end of meeting where we are harboring resentments and concerns so that we can work on them with each other before the next meeting. In this way we can build a continuity of relationship that is a lot more cooperative.

The educational structure and philosophy of the school helps a lot. It places the students in learning groups from the moment they enter a degree program. It is designed to keep from producing lone rangers, a model we think "does in" many clergy. Our educational philosophy is adult-centered and driven by educational goals which shape the program and which are designed by a group. With that kind of structure in the school we already begin to address the building of community. Each entering student works with a faculty adviser, a student peer, and five others to design an educational program. We have distributed requirements, as guidelines. We assume that students are adults and can learn how to work in groups. We assume that as adult learners they can make mature choices when given enough information. We assume they will learn something about evaluation and differences when they work in groups. Every student enters a conference group like this.

A lot of our recent successes are in the area of antiracism work, guided by the organization Visions, Inc. We are now in our fourth year of trying to put the rhetoric and behavior together. Our prior president sent out an edict that everyone would do antiracism training, and it bombed. We had to undo the damage. Ben—who was then COO—and I got together to try to see how we could help staff get off the ground with this work and own it out of their own power. It has taken two and a half years. We formed a staff leadership team consisting of a variety of staff, and they designed the program. We started our work together by talking about what we were learning and what mistakes we had made. Now we have just put out a new request for people who want to do a four-day training, and we are swamped with requests.

Our model takes away the fear of being accountable. We need to be accountable to one another, to students and faculty. This is a fairly outrageous school in some of the stands we take. If folks aren't clear about who they are, they don't last very long and they aren't happy while they are lasting. We don't wear people down; still, we do have serious issues to deal with. Denial is the greatest enemy of leadership. What we are trying to do now within the leadership team is be clear about accountabilities and clear about how we like working. The secret of my working relationship with Ben and Karen is that we have access to each other, we appreciate one another's humor, and we genuinely care about each other. When Ben became acting president, I did not know how open he would be about criticism. It's a tender kind of thing. We went out for lunch and I said, "Let's talk about our egos in the job we're doing right now." We had a delightful lunch. Recently Ben and I did a sermon together about leadership and Karen celebrated, since she is the only one of us who is ordained. We are trying to be aware of our leadership explicitly and live it out.

○

Ben: A Different Kind of Leader

My predecessor as president was a priest with a model of parish in which the rector as ordained person in charge calls the shots. In many ways our group was very much like a board of advisers to the president. I don't work that way. I don't believe the best happens when an organization is run that way, particularly when the organization professes to be liberal. So I have worked very hard to develop a more collaborative style. It's not necessarily easy to do. It means a lot more responsibility on everybody—a lot more accountability. We've done some organizational things to make that happen better. People say it feels very different.

Part of it is in the way meetings are run. It sounds very elementary, but that's where it starts. My secretary and I go out and solicit agenda items. That in itself has been a liberating thing for folks. Before, my predecessor determined the agenda. I very often will prioritize the agenda because I am the leader and I am paid to do that, but we try to get everything in. We have sharing time—again, really elementary—but we never did that before. Then I try not to do all the talking. I try to let things emerge from the group. Or if I have issues that need to be dealt with, I try not to do that in a way that is directive . . . but to be solicitous of opinions from the group.

When a group goes from a hierarchical model to a collaborative model there is a lot of learning. At first, people often don't know what to do. A part of it is recasting the norms. You have to establish new normative behavior. Actually, when you're in a hierarchical model you don't even know you've got normative behavior. You just don't talk until spoken to. Normative behavior is even more important in a collegial group because people will unknowingly take advantage of the situation and not know how to make decisions together, check out assumptions, voice concerns, and so forth.

To address this, I called four of our leadership groups together for some specific training. We've been doing a lot of work on antiracism here and one of the things we've learned is that if you really want to be an open community, you have to be an open community—where people can find their way around clearly and easily. You can't afford to talk in code or group shorthand if you want to invite people in. Our consultants taught us the cooperative method so that as a community of leadership groups we could begin to use the same language about leadership and about interacting with each other. We're getting there.

One of the things I've learned is that in our organizations, we operate on a scarcity model. But when it comes to issues of human interaction, there really is no scarcity. There is always time to do what you need and want to do, and there is always plenty of praise to go around. The other thing I'd say about how we've been learning to work together collegially is that personal issues need to be addressed personally and organizational issues need to be addressed organizationally. Systems that operate on personal fulfillment aren't healthy. That's not what systems are for. They can help people fulfill themselves, but the system itself cannot be based on personality and personal discovery. I operate from the assumption that if you can get people doing and saying the right things, organizational health will follow. In an unhealthy system, all the talking in the world won't make a difference. If people experience the liberating power of a healthy organization, they will opt for it. But if you look them in the eye and tell them they have to change, they won't do it. They feel like they have to go a great distance in a short time, and it's very hard for them.

I am a great believer that we hire people for their talent and their gifts. Mostly I believe that people ought to do their own work. I think that now in many ways we bring fewer issues to the table. We don't have as many decisions to make together. It was very disconcerting at first when people would bring things to the table and want me to say yes or no to everything. I said, "I'm not going to do that. It's your job to do your work. It's my job to support you." Now when we do have an issue that we all need to have a say in, we try to do it together. We try to listen to each other. Every now and then somebody gets in somebody else's business and we have to apologize. I've had to do this myself. But I think we are more capable now of dropping the item that needs to be discussed onto the table and letting it be approached by the others. Before, people guarded their issues.

When I first came here, I felt that there was an incredible disconnect between what we felt, what we learned, what we were teaching spiritually, and how we lived out our lives organizationally. We were an incredibly liberal institution with an absolutely conservative organizational system. All of the things we've done to change have only been possible because of our antiracism training. One of the first things you learn is that if you're going to open your doors to a different clientele, you've got to be clear about who you are so that others can find their way around the organization. This caused us to systematically make clear who we are and how we work. As we did that, we found some things that were not very pretty. We had to begin to work on them.

○

Karen: Finding Her Place in the Team

Before becoming a pastor I worked at Ohio State, where things were very bureaucratic. The lines were clearly drawn. Here it is a bit more organic. Coming into a team like this has required a bit of finding my way. One of the things I've noticed is that different people have different gifts, and we shape positions according to those gifts. I have some gifts and talents that the person before me did not have and vice versa. For me, part of my journey has been finding my way within the system. As an example of that, I have a lot of responsibility for chapel, probably a lot more than a dean of students had in the past. The president is usually the person who organizes and coordinates chapel, but of course Ben is not ordained.

Now that we have Ben as acting president we have the more collaborative use of other people's talents, whereas in the past the leader might say, "This is what I want to have done." I do find that when there is an issue, we come together to talk about it as a team and then decide what step we want to take. We ask: Whose area is it? What does that person think? How does the decision that person might make affect the rest of the school? And we move from there. That's been different. At one time the three of us were on the same level. Now that Ben is president, it still makes sense for us to operate in this more collaborative way.

The thing that makes this institution different is the commitment to the emancipatory way of life, the covenant we have taken to do analysis along the lines of race, class, and gender. As we look at how we operate, we are always very self-conscious about what we are saying or doing with power. Often this slows down the process. But it gives us a very unique perspective on how we do things. That's why the collaborative method has been so important. It really does change the quality and process of decisions that are made. People feel more ownership and they have more commitment to what happens around here. In terms of power, I think it has been the philosophy of the school that has made the way power is used unique. People being people, we often fall back into the same patterns we have been familiar with in the past, but we really work at trying to deconstruct and change some of those. It has been interesting coming from a place where people speak of these things but don't really work at them. We tend to work very hard on it here.

Ben and Fredrica and I have very different leadership styles. This can be a challenge. I see Fredrica as being a very no-nonsense, let's-get-the-job-done person. She presents fully formed ideas. I am a circular thinker. The first thing that comes out of my mouth will not be a fully formed idea. A part of getting to the product will be hearing what other people have to say. Ben is very collaborative in his thinking and he has more strengths in organizational development than Fredrica or I. We each bring very different strengths to the process. We have learned to be very patient with one another and encourage each other's participation, given the gifts that each has. We try to value those gifts and see how they improve the product we arrive at together. Our different perspectives have really enriched our leadership.

We're successful as a team because we want to work well together. It's a spiritual value for me that I should work well with many different people. If we don't work well together, that affects the whole school. On the other hand, it's easy when people do work well together. We work with the belief that working well is a desirable goal, a positive end. From that, other things will follow.

O

5

LEADERSHIP IN
THE MIXED-GENDER TEAM

LEADERS AND TEAMS are the focus of this book. I have interviewed nearly two dozen teams. All of them include people who have been, at various times in the life of the team, leaders and followers. What does it mean to be a leader or a follower in a team? Answering this question is our *learning* challenge. First we need to know more about the challenges of leadership in our time. Second we need to know what it takes to build a team.

In the story of Ben, Fredrica, and Karen, we can see how leadership style works to influence the nature of the team. Ben, Fredrica, and Karen are intentional about placing the seminary administration at the center of the community rather than at the top of a hierarchy. Of necessity as they do this, they must ask questions about themselves as leaders and their group as a team. How do they each lead? How are they alike or different as leaders? How will they lead together? How do they communicate their leadership and their philosophy of leadership to others? All of these are important questions. Ben said that planning meetings is an elementary thing that makes a big difference. Indeed it does, for with that one activity he has the opportunity to interpret not only his style but also the style of the team. In this and the next chapter, we will use Ben, Fredrica, and Karen's story as a single example to look more closely at leadership and teams.

Leadership Today

What is a leader? How are women and men different as leaders? How are our prevailing notions about what a leader is like formed? Why are so many leaders today—including those who fit the norm—unsuccessful?

What will be demanded of us in the future? Do women really have the secret formula for leadership in the future? All of these questions arise as we begin to think about ourselves as leaders. To claim fully the label *leader* for ourselves, to know what is required of us as leaders, we must find some answers.

Many have recently defined leadership and done so well. Robert Terry (1993) and Ronald Heifetz (1994) give particularly good summaries of how leadership has been defined. What they tell us is that leaders have the ability to guide others in some kind of action. The debate about leadership today is all about how this happens (a question of style), why it happens (the leader's motivation), what role the leader plays in the process (the leader as a particular type of person), and what good or bad is derived from the activity (the ethics of leadership). But the fundamentals have not changed. *Lead* is a verb; it denotes action. No matter the definition used, leadership still refers to leading. Leaders, in all of their many incarnations, are those who inspire and guide us in this action.

With this basic definition of leadership in hand, I would assert that the real challenge is not just knowing what leadership is but knowing what leadership requires. We begin with a look at what we expect from our leaders.

The "Ideal" Leader

Our definition of a good leader matches the ways in which men are socialized to behave. We have also long held the belief that there is one way to lead that is best. (We may have changed our notion of what that one way is, but we still hold fast to the notion that there is only one way.) With these biases embedded in our leadership theory, we have long believed that the maverick hero male style is the most effective for a true leader. Without doubt, leadership theory is more complex than this. But leadership theory has not changed the fact that our culture reveres the strong male acting alone to control other men, women, children, animals, and environment to get the job done.

Jean Lipman-Blumen, an organizational consultant to political and business leaders all over the world, gives a thorough and convincing analysis of some of the trends in American business, psychology, and social development that have contributed to our preference for the hero-leader. She suggests that our leadership model is founded on "the curious American ménage à trois of individualism, cooperation, and authoritarianism" (Lipman-Blumen, 1996, p. 47), three values often in conflict with one another. She traces the roots of these three values to American social history in the eighteenth and nineteenth centuries. Perhaps the easiest to understand, if we look back at the frontier experience, is individualism. The task of taming the frontier and building the family farm forged leaders who took control, relied only on themselves, demanded the most from themselves, overcame enormous hardships, and succeeded against monumental odds. These are "the hallmarks of self-reliant American leaders" (p. 48). Yet cooperation, the second American standard for leadership, stands in contrast to our reverence for individualism. The Declaration of Independence and the U.S. Constitution are responsible for the value we place on cooperation. Although we assert the right of the individual to life, liberty, and the pursuit of happiness, we also elevate the rule of the majority. Thus we link the values of individualism and cooperation, values that remain in conflict in our culture to this day. The social history that enshrined authoritarianism, the third standard, is less self-evident. It grew out of the Industrial Revolution and the nineteenth-century immigrant experience. While waves of immigrants from Europe came to the United States determined to create a new life by blending in, American industrialists were coming into their own, creating fiefdoms in the factory where their rule was law. They were met by a multitude of willing workers. This period in our social history forged a leadership model that influenced the first wave of management theory, the scientific advancements that led to the assembly line, and the formation of bureaucratic organizations in the mid-twentieth century. Our military history is another cultural influence that elevates authoritarianism as a value, though Lipman-Blumen does not mention it in her critique.

Authoritarianism is characterized by the exercise of power over other people, decisive action by the leader, concern for status and authority, rationalism in decision making, legalism in resolving ethical dilemmas, establishing a comfortable distance from followers, and seeking advice or input from a few advisers who are of the same race, class, and gender as the leader. Strictly speaking, *authoritarianism* seeks power and position for personal gain, whereas *authoritativeness* is the individual's ability to be assertive regardless of the ends. We often confuse the two. We cannot assert, of course, that all men use or even desire to use the authoritarian style of leadership. But certainly it has been our ideal. Men who have not used it have not advanced as far and as fast as those who have.

Heifetz (1994) cites the nineteenth-century notion that "history is the story of great men and their impact on society" (p. 16) as the origin of the hero-leader model. Thomas Carlyle first wrote about this idea in 1841 when he wrote *On Heroes, Hero-Worship, and the Heroic in History*.

Women "were not even considered candidates for greatness," Heifetz adds. Women *have* largely been left out of our analysis of leadership until the recent generation of women became leaders in significant enough numbers to create a new critical mass and shatter our old notions. Women have demonstrated effective leadership using a radically different style. In so doing, we have enlarged our vision of the possible leadership styles available to all of us (Becker, 1996). Women consistently describe themselves as using a more participatory leadership style, which includes the following traits: focus on process as much as outcomes, concern for the whole experience or process as much as the individual task, working for consensus, win-win decision making, willingness and ability to negotiate, open sharing of information, skill at doing many different things at once, flexibility, willingness to take risks, and a close relationship with subordinates. Helgesen (1990) pictures women as weavers. It is not so much the goal reached that is the point of satisfaction for women in leadership, she points out. It is as much the connections and the process used to reach the goals. And in making connections, women weave a kind of web of inclusion in the workplace. Women leaders have, in fact, emerged in top management "not by adopting the style and habits that have proved successful for men, but by drawing on the skills and attitudes they developed from their shared experience as women" (Rosener, 1990, p. 119). They are succeeding, observers say, "because of—not in spite of—certain characteristics generally considered to be 'feminine' and inappropriate in leaders" (pp. 119–120; see also Russell, 1993; Nuechterlein and Hahn, 1990; Coger, 1985; Campbell, 1991; Hurty, 1991; Motte, 1991).

What Leadership Requires

There is no one right way to lead, any more than there is a single right way to manage people or run a business (Drucker, 1998). Nevertheless, it is becoming increasingly clear to all of us that we need new models for leadership. Much is said these days about the absence of leadership in our culture. Much can also be observed about our schizophrenic attitude toward our leaders. We complain about them often, turn them out of office regularly, and debate about what we want "instead." Still, often as not, we vote them back into office when we find their replacements wanting. Wheatley (1992) is so right in saying that "the search for new shamans has begun in earnest" (p. 26). At the same time that Wheatley was examining what quantum physics teaches us about how we run our organizations, Jean Lipman-Blumen and Sally Helgesen were writing about the need for connective leadership in the future, and I was writing on the contribution of women to a wider range of leadership styles (Lipman-Blumen, 1996; Helgesen, 1995; Becker, 1996). What is going on here?

Recent trends in our social history have compromised the effectiveness of the hero-leader. The labor movement was a strong political force that has raised our awareness regarding the treatment of workers. The rise of the human relations movement, aided by American psychology, helped us understand the worker's individual needs and motivations in a new way. Finally, the social revolution of the 1960s questioned the uses and abuses of authority, particularly military and political authority. Today, the increasing diversity of our population and the new demands of a different wave of immigrants have revealed some of the flaws of the old leadership values. The rugged individualism and determination to succeed that was a hallmark of our early leaders masked shocking disregard for the powerless indigenous people of this land, the early immigrants, the women, and the lower classes of all nationalities. Our rugged individualists created their reputations and their fortunes on the backs of many hardworking and unfortunate people.

Yet we still hold fast to the belief that the hero-leader is our ideal. Though tension still exists between authoritarianism and individualism on the one hand and cooperation on the other, it remains a fact that "we have raised individualism to its highest expression" for our leaders as well as for the followers (Wheatley, 1992, p. 30). The problem is that the model no longer works. Built into it were many traits not so laudable, traits that have come to haunt our national consciousness and call our leadership values into question as the demands of our world and our workplace change dramatically. We are thus left with some contradictions that we must examine in order to understand the leadership challenges of the present and future. We preach teamwork but we still hold fast to the individualistic ideal (O'Toole, 1996). Furthermore, our individualistic ego ideal is increasingly incompatible with our organizational lives (Lipman-Blumen, 1996; Helgesen, 1995). Realizing these liabilities, yet holding fast to the hero-leader model, we are increasingly ambivalent about leadership per se.

As the old models begin to lose their effectiveness, the demands on present-day leaders are increasing at a staggering pace. In our consulting practice in just the last five years, my colleagues and I find that we are helping the leaders of nonprofit organizations face a whole new set of challenges. Leaders today must make decisions faster, with fewer opportunities for a second chance if things go wrong. They operate on information that is readily available to everyone, not just to them and their close advisers. To make their situation even more challenging, the old ways of diagnosing problems often don't work anymore. Our leaders must find new and innovative solutions, sometimes reaching far beyond the boundaries of the organization to do so. They must also think for the long term, and they face staggering ethical dilemmas. Furthermore, because we expect leaders today to earn our support, they are often caught between pleasing the constituency and doing the right thing. Yet we still want the quick fix and the easy profit. We want to be assured on a daily basis that the United States is still—as of this minute—the reigning superpower in the world. We want to know that our nonprofit organizations provide a national safety net that the government doesn't. And we want to find meaning for our lives that has seemed largely absent in the past thirty years.

These are all signs that we are moving away from a "geopolitical era" (Lipman-Blumen, 1996, p. 8), when national boundaries and ideologies separated us and framed our understanding of who was enemy and who was friend. These boundaries helped us decide what to do to whom, when, and how. Now those boundaries are gone. We might look at the change scientifically rather than politically, and see the same trends. "At the end of the twentieth century, our seventeenth-century organizations are crumbling. We have prided ourselves, in all these centuries since Newton and Descartes, on the triumphs of reason, the absence of magic. . . . For three centuries we have been planning, predicting, analyzing the world" (Wheatley, 1992, p. 26). The boundaries we have created gave us "a sense of solidity, of structures that secure things, a kind of safety" (p. 28). They also gave us a strong sense of identity, and they made us lonely. But we don't live in a Newtonian world anymore. We live in a world defined by quantum physics, a world relevant to our present experience in ways that Newton never was. This is a connected world, one in which "connections between concepts, people, and the environment are tightening" (Lipman-Blumen, 1996, p. 8), aided by technology. We are exposed beyond our old boundaries to new people, ideas, environments; we are forced to see and experience our interdependence. And "even as technology and new understanding bind us closer, new groups and new identities, not yet comfortable with interdependence, increase overall diversity" (p. 9). As we move away from "the notion of the organization as a great machine—rational, static, compartmentalized, and closed—we are also moving away from . . . the belief that, to be efficient, organizations must mimic the design and workings of a machine" (Helgesen, 1995, pp. 16–17). These trends have changed the world as we know it and "drastically changed the rules of the leadership game" (Lipman-Blumen, 1996, p. 94). In our organizational lives—indeed, in every aspect of our lives today—"the issue is not control but dynamic connectedness" (Wheatley, 1992, p. 23).

The tension between diversity and interdependence, Lipman-Blumen (1996) predicts, will "create the backdrop of virtually all decision making" in what she terms the new connective era of leadership (p. 7). On the one hand, present-day leaders and their followers who largely still emulate the model of the hero-leader are ill-equipped for this new time. Connective leaders, on the other hand, will use the tension between diversity and interdependence to advantage in solving problems and inspiring people. They will operate from an ethical base. They will connect their vision with others, strive to overcome mutual problems rather than mutual enemies, create community, bring leaders together rather than divide them, encourage responsible action among their followers, create colleagues rather than adversaries, demand sacrifice from their followers and most often get it, demonstrate their own authenticity, and raise up the successors who will replace them someday. These connective leaders will understand and know how to be about the *reflective tasks* as well as the *active tasks* of partnership. In all these ways, they will be uniquely equipped for the connective era. They will use a range of styles including the direct, the relational, and the instrumental (Lipman-Blumen, 1996). Like Ben, Fredrica, and Karen, connective leaders "feel more comfortable being at the center of things rather than at the top." They "prefer building consensus to issuing orders" (Helgesen, 1995, p. 20). They get things done "by exercising *influence,* by being the servant leaders, the ones who design processes that enable people to think, know, feel, and decide" (McCarter, 1996, p. 80) about the serious matters before them. These new leaders will be right for a quantum world, in which relationships ultimately are *all there is* to reality (Wheatley, 1992).

Where will these leaders come from? Lipman-Blumen predicts we will find them in voluntary organizations where the followers sign up to do some good in the world; among entrepreneurs who always have had to use a wide range of leadership styles; among leaders in industries such as communication, entertainment, and the arts, where creative teams are assembled for each project; among dedicated activists, who sacrifice to achieve an altruistic goal; and among "the latest cadre of female leaders, who use leadership styles that are based on collaboration, networking, inclusion, and instrumental action" (Lipman-Blumen, 1996, p. 26).

The Debate About Differences

Do women really have something unique and important to contribute as leaders today? The most visible gender-related leadership dialogue of our day focuses on this very question. It is a debate about style. To be sure, we can note differences between women and men leaders. For some time women and men have been agreeing on this point: women coming into leadership in large numbers have, by their example, broadened the leadership repertoire available to both women and men (Becker, 1996). Yet I am not at all sure that we can leap to the conclusion that women are better leaders than men. It's a very complex question. It is more useful to understand with as much clarity as possible what women and men bring to leadership.

What Women Contribute to Leadership

We may begin to unravel the complexity by noting some differences in the ways women and men lead. Deborah Tannen's language analysis (1990) shows that the goal of men in conversation is power, whereas for women it is establishing relationships. In comparing the styles of women and men, Schaef (1985) describes male managers typically as "being in front," having the information and the answers, presenting an all-knowing image, and female leaders as facilitators—finding people, nudging them, encouraging them. If there is a style of leadership more characteristic of women, it may be called "embracing," whereas men may be characterized as "standing firm" (Nuechterlein and Hahn, 1990, p. 3).

Although the characteristic male style seems to fit our notions of what a leader *ought* to be like, it seems that the typical style of women fits what leaders really *need* to be like. This is the premise behind the notion that women are better leaders than men. To be sure, women make a major contribution by helping us all rethink leadership for the future, as Matthew Fox recognized in a letter to me. He predicted that "until women's wisdom . . . is infused in our cultural institutions . . . we will be bereft of the wisdom we need to change our ways" (personal communication, 1994).

Women are coming into the workplace in great numbers. We bring the expectation that we can and should work together. We ask the question, "Why not?" We also contribute different ways of working that show us much about how to work together. We do not accept the premise that competition is the primary value but tend to see the long-term benefits of working together. Thus women entering the workplace become a catalyst in helping us look more deeply at our leadership. Lipman-Blumen (1996) says that women are uniquely suited for leadership in a "Stage 3" or "connected" world.

> Growing pride in their "difference" and determination to demand their fair share of society's bounty have thrust women into the vortex of the social storm. Their quest for acceptance of their diversity has been the template for similar claims by other minorities across the broad spectrum of diversity. Women have frequently joined forces with other diverse groups to confront the pressure arising from their common position as "others." Consequently, women are no newcomers to the complications generated by independence and diversity. Their experiences, for better or worse, put them uniquely in sync with the complexities of a Stage 3 world. As such, women represent an important source of potential leadership [pp. 288–289].

James O'Toole (1996) makes a convincing argument for the importance of more feminine or embracing approaches to leadership in an age when so much change is upon us. "People become energized when they are included because they feel respected. In contrast, when they are ordered to do something, they become angry because they are being treated as inferiors" (p. 138). O'Toole's argument is simple. Women's leadership is teaching us better ways of creating willing followers. He emphasizes: "In a democratic world characterized by intense competition, in which organizations move quickly to cope with environmental turmoil, in which all members of the organization must be aligned with the vision of the leader, and in which all must be willing to lead the constant changes needed for effectiveness, the 'feminine' . . . style is almost without exception more effective and more appropriate than the 'masculine' . . . style" (p. 139).

Using the words of Ben Cohen, founder and head of Ben & Jerry's Ice Cream until his recent retirement, O'Toole suggests that this kind of leadership does not come very naturally to men, even those men who aren't authoritarian by nature. Cohen recalls that "it was not natural for him to ask questions of his employees when he felt he knew the answer, not natural to involve them in planning when in his gut he already knew what he wanted to achieve" (O'Toole, 1996, pp. 134–135). O'Toole even suggests that women should be unapologetic about the superiority of their approach to leadership. Perhaps because he is a man his suggestion can be heard not as political one-upmanship on the part of women but as a genuine judgment about what women are contributing to leadership theory and practice.

A Few Notes of Caution

There is significant evidence in the descriptions provided by women that we do have a different approach to leadership than men. We might assume that we can move very quickly from the description of "what women are like" to the many things women as leaders teach us about leadership in the future. Indeed, it's so simple, I believe, that it doesn't work. Despite all the evidence that we women provide about the uniqueness of our leadership style, we should be cautious about jumping to this conclusion for many reasons. We must be as reflective about leadership differences as was the man who said this to me about working first for a male and later for a female CEO in the same organization: "I don't think I would attribute the difference in our administrative culture to gender change. I would attribute it rather to the different nature of the two persons who were our leaders and the resultant changes in management style. Gender is a bit like race. It's obvious, so it's easy to try to tie something to it when in fact it may not be the heart of the difference." And yet, he added, "It is a difference that matters."

First and foremost in discerning differences in men's and women's leadership, we ought to remember our position. Women's identity as leaders in church and church-related organizations is still gaining legitimacy. We women are still searching for the attributes of our leadership and naming ourselves as leaders. This requires accepting our own authority and claiming our own voices. Men may take this activity for granted. But for those of us who happen to be women it is hard to do after so many centuries of being silenced. So at the outset we women may not yet know all there is to know about our leadership styles.

Men, ironically, may be in a similar bind for a different reason. They are beginning to catch on to the fact that the hero-leader model, to which they at least have had access, no longer works. They are therefore struggling to learn new ways of leading. They are observing women and trying out the more feminine styles available to them. They are reading and writing volumes about leadership. The range of leadership options available to them is growing, but they are cautious and feeling a bit rough around the edges as they try out new approaches.

Second, we should be very reluctant to stereotype. We don't want to be trapped in a new sexism, "the bleary-eyed idea that a woman's natural gifts . . . make her ideally suited to ministry" (Schaper, 1990, p. 5). We should be reluctant to say that women are one way and men are another, because we can always find the exception. The church has more than its share of exceptions to the idea that men are hierarchical and authoritarian in their leadership (Lehmann, 1993). There are also exceptions to the idea that women are embracing or collaborative.

Third, women particularly hesitate to claim their differences lest these be used against them. Certainly many women affirm their differences as leaders. But other women—and men too—believe that it is a threat to women leaders to name how they are different. Women have good reason to feel threatened about this. In her research, Lipman-Blumen finds significant evidence that women are in fact not consistently using the more collaborative styles of leadership over the direct style that is characteristic of the authoritarian leader. She suggests that a "status shield" must be in place to protect the leader before women or men can use these newer, less direct and aggressive styles without appearing weak. The status shield may be gender (maleness giving higher status) or position (Lipman-Blumen, 1996). Differences do get used very effectively against women leaders. This fact gives rise to a question that women ask about their leadership in relation to men's: "Can we be different and not be compared as one better than the other?" (Lindley, 1996, pp. 407–408).

Indeed, the prejudice that difference also implies better or worse comes from our tendency to dualistic thinking and remains the number one barrier to women and minorities in the workplace (Morrison, 1992). This should not be, says sociologist Deborah Sheppard (1989), who debunks the argument that affirming differences should jeopardize equality. It's an "implicit assumption," she says, that "evidence of a difference is ideological and discriminatory" (p. 141). Men too are affected by our dualistic thinking about leadership. Although they may recognize that authoritarian leadership no longer works, they may not feel free to try other, less direct methods. They too are accused of being weak, indecisive, and "feminine" unless they have the status shield (usually a high-ranking position) to protect them (Lipman-Blumen, 1996; O'Toole, 1996).

It should be obvious to us by now that the leadership styles available to us are culturally conditioned, whether we are men or women. This is the fourth and final reason for caution. In fact, if it were not so, I am quite certain that our leadership styles would vary more than they do. One way to look at this problem is to view how women's and men's styles have compared in the last few generations. A recent study of the accomplished women of the Progressive Era in U.S. history (women born between 1855 and 1865) reveals "a wholly different voice in the letters on the one hand and the autobiographical narratives on the other" (Heilbrun, 1988, p. 24). Their letters and diaries portray their own ambitions and struggles. "In their published autobiographies, however, they portray themselves as intuitive, nurturing, passive, but never—in spite of the contrary evidence of their accomplishments—managerial" (p. 24). These women lived and worked in an era when there was no socially acceptable place for women leaders. In the public sphere they were very cautious and deferential. Now skip forward a few generations to the middle of the twentieth century. By this time it was acceptable for *some* women to enter the leadership ranks, as long as they "did it like the men." The men and women I interviewed, who were in their prime in the 1950s, reported that women leaders of that era led much as men did, using the authoritarian style. Because so few women were leaders, they said, there was really no other acceptable way. These women were accepted as "honorary men" and so they could use a very direct leadership style with impunity. Jump forward again to the present. With more women leaders, we see the emergence of the embracing style described in this chapter. We also begin to see men experimenting with the attributes of leadership more characteristic of women. In the future, as more women become leaders, I believe we will see more styles emerge among both men and women.

Of course, we cannot know what our leadership might be like if our cultural expectations were different. But we can look at how our styles may be predictable based on the prevailing idea of what a leader should be like. A simpler way of saying this is that perhaps we women are relational, collaborative, process-oriented, informal, and problem solving in our leadership *because we are expected to be that way.* And perhaps men have been direct, fiercely goal-oriented, authoritarian lone rangers because *they were expected to be that way.* We cannot simply observe women's leadership and learn from it how to be effective leaders in the future. Nor can we observe men's leadership and say this is the way *not to be* in the future. We must realize there is much more going on as we look at the differences in the ways women and men lead.

Having come this far, perhaps is it best to stop the debate and turn our attention in another direction. Theologian Letty Russell (1993) challenges us "to look for clues about what feminist leadership gifts . . . might look like. We will most certainly not expect any one model or task to emerge, but it seems we could expect a particular style of leadership behavior with clues or indications that the empowerment of authority in community is already beginning to happen" (p. 67). As we consider how we might know ourselves as leaders and ultimately claim each other as partners in leading together, the significant question here is not whether women have a unique style or even whether women and men are different as leaders. Rather the question is, What can we learn from each about the leadership that is needed in a connected world?

6

CREATING EFFECTIVE TEAMS

OUR SECOND LEARNING TASK is to discover what it takes to build an effective team. Teams are so much a part of our working lives today that we take them for granted. Most of us have some experience working in a team. But what makes a team? And what does it take to build an effective team?

Karen, the newest member of the team with Ben and Fredrica, commented that "coming to a team like this has required a bit of finding my way." She came from a setting that was very hierarchical into one that was very relational. She had to learn what the team was like and discover her place in it. It wasn't just Karen who had work to do. The whole team had to rediscover itself when Ben became interim president. Essentially, they were a new team because Ben's leadership style differs so much from that of his predecessor. The process this team went through to discover itself and become effective in its work is one that every successful team must complete. The challenges of becoming a team are much more intense for mixed-gender teams because of the influence of diversity on teams. In this chapter we will review what teams are and how they work, the relationship between leadership and teams, and the influence of diversity in teams.

Understanding Teams

Some management analysts (Hill, 1994) assert that good decision making requires teams or that teams should be the basic "unit of performance in all organizations" (Katzenbach and Smith, 1993b, p. 15). Others believe that "almost everything we accomplish is the result of team play" (Jackman and Waggoner, 1991, p. 74). Yet those who study teams do not necessarily assume that every working group is a team. They are careful to define both what a team is and how a team works. We too need to know what makes a team. It's a reflective task to complete as we begin in earnest to consider ourselves as members of mixed-gender teams.

It's also important for us to have some benchmarks for understanding how teams work. We need to know this in order to discern how diverse teams, including the mixed-gender teams in this study, are like all teams. This knowledge will help us avoid the mistake of assuming that all our team issues are gender issues.

What Makes a Team?

What makes a team is the people in it and the way they work together, as we can readily see from Ben, Fredrica, and Karen's story, and indeed from all the team stories in this book. What constitutes "working together" is what constitutes the team. Although some analysts (Guzzo, 1995) do not distinguish between groups and teams in their discussion of effectiveness, most do identify clear criteria for working teams. These criteria include task-based interdependence of some kind (Guzzo, 1995; Jackman and Waggoner, 1991; Katzenbach and Smith, 1993a). To this basic definition, Katzenbach and Smith add considerable precision in defining teams as "a *small number* of people with *complementary skills* who are committed to *a common purpose* and an *approach* for which they hold themselves *mutually accountable*." Each phrase in the definition is "an explicit element of . . . the discipline of team basics" (Katzenbach, 1997, p. 84, italics in original).

Peter Drucker (1992) further delineates the different ways in which people work together in a team by using a sports analogy. He identifies three types of teams: *the baseball-type team, the football-type team,* and *the tennis doubles–type team.* In the baseball-type team, people "play *on* the team"; they do not "play *as* the team" (p. 16). Each person has a fixed position that never changes no matter how many times the team plays. The fixed role is appropriate to teams when specific expertise is required to play one's "position." Every person on the team can be a star in his or her own arena. People on such teams do not interact much with one another, yet they have a common purpose.

Drucker suggests that the interdependence among team members is low in such teams, and on this point I question his scheme. Even in situations where individuals play relatively independent roles, team members are dependent on one another if the team has a common goal for which they mutually hold themselves accountable. This interdependence is what being a team is all about. If the individuals do not have a mutual goal, we might

well question whether they are a team at all (Katzenbach and Smith, 1993a). Yet the baseball-type team is different from the more interdependent football-type team, in which team members play *as* the team. We may think of soccer or basketball teams here as well. Members of football-type teams still have fixed positions but there is more interaction among team members, more of a sense of give and take. As the team works together, the members' individual roles are subordinate to the agenda of the team.

At the other end of the spectrum is the tennis doubles–type team, in which "only the team performs and individual members contribute" (Drucker, 1992, p. 16). Team members cover their teammates, adjusting as necessary to each other's weaknesses and strengths and to the demands of the mission before them.

Although Drucker's definitions of teams do not address the duration of teams, they assume that teams can come and go as the purpose of the team dictates. Teams can be short-term or long-term, depending on the need for the team to exist. Katzenbach and Smith (1993a, 1993b) assume this. They exclude from their definition of teams those groups that work together continually because of their roles in the organization. They would not, for example, consider an administrative group of senior leaders to be a team unless they have a common goal. In contrast, I have included such groups in this study because I believe that in nonprofit settings they have a common purpose that is embedded in the mission of the organization as a whole.

Regardless of how loosely or rigidly we define teams, all the definitions in the literature presume a measure of effectiveness. Embedded in the very notion of team is the assumption that a group of people can be a team only if they are working together effectively. One man I interviewed suggests five criteria for an effective team: "Work above and beyond the call of duty, be creative, continue learning, take direction from the team, and maintain confidentiality." If the individuals in the team cease to be accountable to one another, fail to achieve their common goals, do not in some way share leadership, or do not make the most of everyone's skills, they are no longer functioning as a team. When our favorite sports team is losing, we say, "They are not really playing like a team anymore." When our local community organizing group is ineffective we say, "They aren't much of a team." The same goes for work teams.

Yet we can still ask what makes a team effective, for there are indeed some that are better than others at the art of teamwork. It is partly their work. Whether or not the team does quality work that meets the expectations and quality standards of their organization is the first test of team effectiveness. Hill (1994) suggests two other tests: how well the team experience contributes to the personal well-being and development of the members and how well the team experience contributes to the capacity of the team members to work and learn together in the future. Managers who neglect these criteria forget that team members must feel personally satisfied in order to contribute to the life of the team.

Although I would not hold such a rigid definition of a team as Katzenbach and Smith or draw the distinctions among types of teams as sharply as Drucker, in general the way teams are defined in recent business literature is largely applicable to the teams in this study. The mixed-gender teams I interviewed are all small groups of men and women who are mutually accountable for their work. Some are project teams, like the spiritual formation team described in Chapter Eleven. These members typically play *as* the team. Others, like the theological institute team or the Lutheran relief team, manage educational institutions or agencies. As teams, their work is relatively independent but contributes to an overall mission. Yet in my research among teams, I seldom found the team distinctions so clear. Most of these team members are skilled at changing their interaction based on what the project at hand requires. Sometimes they play on their team. At other times they play together as a team. And though I cannot identify any teams in this study that are characteristically the tennis doubles–type team, there are instances in which team members work together without any discernible role separation. In these situations, as with Drucker's tennis doubles, "only the team plays" (1992, p. 16).

Regardless of how they work together, all the teams in this study demonstrate their sense of shared accountability for the mission and ministry of their agency, school, or congregation. Some share leadership; others have a designated leader. Individuals in the team may (and most often do) have other work for which they are not accountable to the team. Finally, they measure their effectiveness as a team by how well they get that work done and how their work together builds the team.

Within these characteristics of all teams, gender plays a part, as we shall see in the remainder of this chapter.

How Teams Work

Teams just don't happen. They are formed by the hard work of the people in them. This book is about the formation of mixed-gender teams. Its premise is that mixed-gender teams require careful formation grounded in the reflective criteria. Yet we must not forget that mixed-gender teams are just one kind of team. Like other teams, they have cycles of formation. They depend on certain characteristics for their success. Their most basic ingredient is trust among the team members. Trust in the team is the mutually held opinion among team members that they can count on one another for an agreed-on standard of performance and discretion in handling both the tasks and the relationships of the team.

As teams mature they go through fairly predictable stages in development. Throughout these stages, team members learn to cope with the individual and group pressures they face (Scholtes, 1988; Heuser and Shawchuck, 1999). In its first *forming* stage, team members explore the boundaries of their work together and the behavior that is expected of them. This stage allows a transition from individual to teamwork. Team members may be uncertain about their tasks and their ability to work together. "While the individuals in the team may be highly competent, they have yet to learn how to work together as a team" (Heuser and Shawchuck, 1999, p. 16). Team forming may be brief if the team's goals are clearly defined and easy to achieve. It will be longer if goals are complex. Teams will get stuck in this stage if their goals are unclear or if they fail to learn about each other and embrace their differences (Heuser and Shawchuck, 1999). This is another way of saying that *teams members need to reflect with each other as they are forming* in order to complete this stage in their development.

The second stage is called *storming* because it is so difficult. Team members often panic at this stage as they begin to realize what is expected of them and how ill-equipped they feel to deliver results. Defensiveness, anger, arguing, and turf-protecting are all activities common to this stage. Even very skilled individuals with impressive work records may resist the team because, they suddenly realize, it requires new ways of working. At this stage, teamwork often seems like more trouble than it is worth. Some leaders get cold feet at this stage as they see their teams storming about, getting little done. If the leader of the team or the supervisor of the team does not recognize storming as a normal and necessary step in team development, and if the storming phase is not resolved, teamwork never really gets off the ground. A continuing commitment to the reflective tasks is critical in order for team members to complete this stage satisfactorily. Reflecting together will assist team members in overcoming competition, getting to know one another deeply, learning about shared goals, and developing commitment to the team.

Teams settle down to *norming* when they reach the third stage. If they have been faithful to their reflective work, team members will begin to reap the benefits in this stage of their development. Here team members reconcile competing demands and loyalties, accept the team ground rules (or norms), establish their place in the team, and become more cooperative. This shift signals that individuals in the team are becoming more comfortable with the idea and practice of teamwork. Time and energy become available for the projects at hand and team members begin to feel satisfaction in tasks accomplished. Because they are beginning to trust one another, team members can also recognize and address hidden agendas. Teams will complete this phase when team members acquire new skills for the tasks at hand, resolve feelings of dissatisfaction satisfactorily, value one another's different contributions, establish norms and practices for the team, and develop relationships with each other. Successful norming "is something far different than the maturing of individual group members. . . . Learning the unique contributions, patterns, and relationships of individuals in relation to one another and to the entire group are signs that a group has begun to take seriously its assigned task" (Heuser and Shawchuck, 1999, p. 56). Teams that cannot complete the norming stage successfully have three options: dissolve, stay in the storming stage indefinitely, or return to the forming stage.

Finally, in the *performing* stage, the team has settled into its relationships and expectations. If the team reaches this point with healthy habits and relationships (that is, as a team), it will be an effective, cohesive unit. Team members know each other and accept each other's strengths and weaknesses. They have negotiated differences and they know what it takes to reach their goals. They are also confident that they can reach those goals together. By this time, team members would rather work together than separately.

The literature commonly cites three essential criteria for an effective team that has reached the performing stage: commitment, competence, and a common goal (Billington, 1997). Good communication supports these criteria and is generally also accepted as vital. In this and subsequent chapters, we will see how the criteria for effective teams are realized in the ways mixed-gender team members maintain presence with each other and in their commitment to a common purpose. Like all teams, effective mixed-gender teams believe in one another's strengths, hold one another accountable, understand the benefit of the team, and share a common purpose for working together. They talk to each other. They can also readily cite the performance achieved by the team, though they will not typically do so in terms of profit, market share, or other business concepts. Instead, teams in the church-related nonprofit sector discuss their success in terms of hungry people fed; elderly people cared for in a healthy, holistic environment; young people educated to the faith; clergy ordained to the ministry; or some other people- or service-related outcome. This is not a difference based on gender. It is an environmental difference, based on the fact that my sampling was not from the business world but from a nonprofit, church-related world. It illustrates, as Drucker points out, that management is not just business management. Its principles apply in the nonprofit sector as well (Drucker, 1998).

Leaders and Other Roles in the Team

In Chapter Five we discussed leadership and what it means to know ourselves and each other as leaders. This is important because, in a sense, the teams we are in are leading the church. They are leadership teams. However, in our teams, as we shall see, we are both leaders and followers. Everyone in the team has a different but important role. Even these roles may not be static. At different times, one single individual in a team may play different roles. This too we need to consider as we think about our mixed-gender teams and our work in those teams.

Roles in the Team

The people in a team play many different roles. Team leader is a very visible role and one I discuss in greater detail later in this book. It will be clear in that discussion that I do not rule out teams led by ranking senior members. The teams in this study provide ample evidence to contradict the notion that groups led by such senior staff are not really teams at all. Katzenbach and Smith (1993a, p. 113) suggest that a "strong, clearly focused leader" is evidence that the group may not really be a team. Though they espouse team leadership, they consider it a shared activity, much different from the role of a senior leader guiding staff in the overall management of an organization or division. They run into trouble, I believe, by buying into the hero-leader model discussed in Chapter Five. In assuming that senior leaders (especially CEOs) have to be strong and individualistic in the hero-leader style, they miss a trend that is increasingly evident in the workplace. Leadership, even at the top, is shared. This makes teams possible and even desirable as we think of the need for partnership, collaboration, networks, and other connective strategies required to do business and promote mission today. The leader is important to the team, whether or not the leader shares his or her role.

Other roles are just as important as the leader's. The coach is a person who encourages others and helps the team work together. The facilitator takes on some leadership attributes but is not clearly the one to make decisions on behalf of the group. Instead, he or she will help the group to come to a decision as a team. The follower is also important to the team. Every team needs effective followers—those who do not wish to be the decision makers or do not have the temperament for decision making. Instead, they are gifted at raising questions for the whole team to discuss, taking instructions and carrying them out on behalf of the team, and bringing information and other resources to the team. Often I have found that the followers are the ones most attentive to the needs of individuals on the team and to the ways the team is working together.

The recorder is a person who keeps track, and this too is an important role in the team. Someone has to make a record of the activity of the team. In many teams this role is shared by different team members each time the team meets. We all have different memories of being asked to be the recorder "this time." What we all know from such experiences is that this role requires certain gifts that not everyone has. The role of recorder is one that teams ought to treat with much more care as they carry out their work together.

Yet another role is that of team sponsor. The team sponsor may not be an active member of the team but rather one or more individuals who advocate for, advise, or otherwise make the work of the team possible. Sometimes the sponsor is also the supervisor. This is a unique and important role that has not been written about very much. We shall return to the supervisor's role shortly.

Team roles are determined by a variety of factors. These include real or perceived rank, tenure on the team, communication skills of various team members, expertise, age, personality type, and gender (Guzzo, 1995). Roles are also determined by team norms, routines, and values. These set the rules for the team and determine how team members behave and go about their work (Hill, 1994). Teams develop norms for distribution of power and influence, communication patterns, agendas, expression of emotion or "team talk," how conflict is managed and more. Once roles are established, they may remain static. In some teams, defined roles that do not change are appropriate, as in the baseball-type teams where, as Drucker suggests, people play set roles on the team based on their expertise. For other teams, static roles are less appropriate and may in fact be a limiting factor.

Once solidified as norms or rules, roles in the team are often hard to change. Like all norms, they attain the status of basic assumptions and beliefs held by the team. They are soon taken for granted and may become invisible to the team members. They also profoundly affect team performance. In the mixed-gender teams in this study, roles in the team vary (or remain static) as much as in any team. How gender influences team roles depends largely on the type of team and how the team and the individuals on the team resolve gender issues, as we shall see.

Leadership in the Team

As teams go through the process of becoming teams, the leader plays a very important role. It's a role that changes as the team develops. The discussion of leadership in Chapter Five pointed out the need for modern-day leaders to have a varied repertoire for inspiring and engaging others in a mission. Here we will see how the team leader can use this repertoire to help teams through their various stages of development, using a scheme developed by congregational and denominational consultants Heuser and Shawchuck (1999).

In the first two stages—forming and storming—teams require more direction and structure from the leader. In the later two stages—norming and performing—teams want increased freedom and responsibility for the group. "The leader's ability to continually monitor the group's progress (or regress) and to match it with appropriate leadership behavior is a key factor in determining whether the group will tend toward greater levels of development" (Heuser and Shawchuck, 1999, pp. 62–63).

Obviously, teams in the forming stage require the most structure. Leaders of such teams will need to be task-oriented in their approach to the team, helping the team members get started, define direction and purpose, and become acquainted with each other. Structure is important, but control is a problem. Leaders are well advised at this stage of team development not to dominate the team or criticize individual team members.

In the storming stage, team leaders can add relational skills to help the team members get to know one another better, manage differences, and discern common tasks. Although the team still requires structure at this stage, the addition of relational skills to the leader's repertoire is critical. Above all, the leader must be able to help the team address conflict as it moves through storming.

In the norming stage, the leader can reduce task-oriented behavior as the group develops its own ability to work together. The leader can now become more people-oriented, remaining available for support, ensuring that communication is healthy throughout the team, and building cohesion among the team members. One note of caution for the team leader in this phase: building cohesion in the team does not mean building allegiance between team members and the leader. It means "working toward a team commitment to a team effort" (Heuser and Shawchuck, 1999, p. 60).

Finally, as the team enters the performing stage the leader can withdraw somewhat, allowing the team to take over as it demonstrates ability to be responsible for tasks and relationships in the team. The leader's role at this stage is delicate. It requires a significant amount of discernment to know how to lead a team of high-performance people who are working well together but still have their differences and conflicts.

Team Supervision and Evaluation

Before we conclude this discussion of roles in the team, we return briefly to consider the supervision and evaluation of teams. I mentioned earlier that most teams are accountable to someone or some group that governs the organization. Some teams are directly accountable to an individual outside the team who created the team and sponsors it. This model holds when a CEO forms a project team. Other teams are accountable to persons specially designated for this role, such as a district superintendent in a denominational region. The most senior teams are usually accountable to a board of directors. These persons or groups to whom teams are accountable are the external supervisors of the team. They have a role in relation to the team, but they are not on the team.

Many supervisors consider only the individuals in the team when evaluation time rolls around. In some cases this includes only the team leader. In others, it includes each individual in the team. But seldom does it include the team as a whole. I believe it is necessary also to evaluate the team *as a team*. In addition to evaluating leaders and other individuals in the team, it is the supervisor's role to monitor the effectiveness of the team by the criteria suggested earlier in this chapter: performance by the team, satisfaction of team members, and capacity of the team to be a team. This might be done by meeting with the team at the beginning of the evaluation period and establishing benchmarks against which the team will be evaluated in these three categories.

Team evaluation also ought to be done internally, by the team itself. Some of the teams in this study do this in a retreat setting once a year. They also accomplish it more informally in the ongoing conversations they have about their effectiveness. I suggest that mixed-gender teams engage in structured evaluation of their effectiveness according to agreed-on benchmarks, just as their supervisor does from an external perspective. Then, together, supervisor and team ought to engage in dialogue about the team's effectiveness.

The Influence of Diversity in Teams

Diversity affects teams, there is no doubt. Because this book is a study of one type of diverse team—the mixed-gender team—it is important for us to review some of the known ways in which diversity of any kind affects a team.

Little research involving actual diverse teams has been done (Jackson, May, and Whitney, 1995), though more has been done to study the impact of diversity on the workplace in general. This study is one of few to research gender-diverse teams that have been together for extended periods of time in the real workplace. Studies of diverse teams have favored team composition and cognitive decision making. The following summary includes highlights from recent research, including my own.

Positive Influences of Diversity on Teams

Recent research reveals four major benefits of diversity in teams. These suggest that diverse teams are good for the organizations that have them and the people who are in them.

• *Diversity consistently correlates with superior performance.* Diverse teams make better decisions and thus perform better (American Management Association, 1998). This is a direct result of having more experience on the team. In addition, results from twelve studies of problem solving suggest that mixed-sex teams outperform same-sex teams (Jackson, May, and Whitney, 1995). Of course, for the team to benefit from its diversity, it has to have a process that allows different voices to be heard (Hill, 1994). The anecdotal feedback from mixed-gender teams in this study verifies these findings, as we shall see. Without analyzing how men and women think differently, we can readily observe in practice that teams including men and women are better at problem solving. If the evidence of the teams in this study is indicative, they also enjoy it more. As one woman observed, "I think teams come to better decisions. It may take longer sometimes. But as

---

Exhibit 6.1. Benefits and Challenges of Diversity in Teams.

Benefits	Challenges
Diversity correlates with superior performance.	Effective communication is more difficult.
Team members learn more from each other.	Roles in the team often persist once established.
Team members establish social relationships.	Team members must address power issues in order to succeed.
People in the team report higher levels of satisfaction.	Trust development requires attention to reflective tasks.

much as I like to make important, concrete, quick decisions, some decisions are better slept on. I do think it's good to talk with others about a particular way to solve a problem."

• *People in successful diverse teams learn more, establish social relationships, and achieve satisfaction* (Jackson, May, and Whitney, 1995). These findings bring to mind one woman's comments about the satisfaction she derived from working in a successful team: "Having been a lone ranger for so long in my work, I was hungry for a team. I see the strength there is in many minds. Deeply enriching things can happen when you are all working together."

Challenges of Diversity for Teams

In order for diverse teams to realize the benefits of their makeup, they have several challenges to overcome. Recent literature, as well as my own research, suggests these four:

• *Effective communication is more difficult in diverse teams.* We shall see in Chapters Fourteen and Fifteen how hard mixed-gender teams work at communication. The research indicates that there's a reason for this. Diversity decreases communication overall in organizations. Access to informal communication networks seems to be hardest for team members who are in the minority (Jackson, May, and Whitney, 1995). It's easy to see, then, why homogeneous teams find it easier to build relationships, because "homogeneity promotes trust and ease of communication" (Hill, 1994, p. 7). Thus although homogeneous teams initially have an easier time becoming productive, the greater breadth of experience in a diverse team ultimately leads to better decisions, as I have already pointed out.

• *Team roles often persist once they are established.* Static roles are more likely to be a limiting factor in teams that are diverse by age, gender, culture, ethnicity, or any other criteria. A diverse team "will often adopt the social structures (norms and roles) established during performance on a prior task as the baseline when beginning a new task" (Jackson, May, and Whitney, 1995, p. 225). We've all seen this happen. In a diverse team, the members are less likely than in a homogeneous team to know one another well and have common ground for understanding one another. If the diverse team does not complete its formation period successfully, team members usually fall into roles that are comfortable, safe, and socially acceptable. Sometimes even when a diverse team completes its first tasks effectively, team members keep the same role configuration as they go into new tasks. They thus avoid the risks of re-forming into new roles in the group. The risks of re-forming are lesser for homogeneous groups where individuals in the group can assume a lot of knowledge about one another at the outset. To understand the difference, we need only to think of the difference we have all seen between an all white male (or all white female) work group and a diverse group including men and women of different ethnic groups and different ages.

• *Diverse teams must address the power issues in the group in order to succeed.* This is a finding from my own research with mixed-gender teams that I suspect is true of diverse teams in general. The importance of addressing power issues does not emerge readily in the management literature on diverse teams. It may be a hidden influence. But in mixed-gender teams, it is an obvious factor that emerges quickly. Mixed-gender teams must address the power issues, first in order to deal with the power issues that exist between men and women (and between ethnic groups in racially mixed teams) and second because of the pressure from external sources that attempts to break down the team. By definition, of course, all teams must redistribute power in order to be true teams. But they do not necessarily have to reexamine all their attitudes about power to succeed as mixed-gender teams do. Thus addressing the power issues in the group is not a make-or-break factor for single-gender teams in the same way it is for mixed-gender teams. We shall learn more about the complexities of power in Chapters Nineteen to Twenty-One. For now, it is instructive to observe how mixed-gender teams enlarge our view of what it means to work together by *raising the power question.*

• *Trust development in diverse teams requires attention to the reflective criteria.* This too is a finding of my research with mixed-gender teams that I suspect is true for all diverse teams. Past studies have shown that trust in teams evolves in three stages. First, teams exhibit deterrence-based trust. They agree to trust each other enough to get the work done because they were directed to do so. Second, as team members get to know each other, knowledge-based trust develops. Finally, identification-based trust emerges. This is trust based on empathy and shared values (Coutu, 1998). In contrast, mixed-gender teams tell us that trust will not necessarily develop along this continuum unless the reflective criteria are taken seriously. It's harder to get to shared values and empathy because gender barriers trip us up unless we are very careful. In this respect, mixed-gender teams enlarge our view of what it means to work together by *causing us to reexamine how trust is formed between us.*

When we compare diverse teams with what we find in the management literature on effective teams overall, we can readily see how diverse teams, including mixed-gender teams, both affirm and enlarge our view of how we work together. With this wisdom in hand, we turn our attention to the remaining criteria.

PART THREE

BELIEVING

7

ERIN AND WAYNE

ADVOCATING FOR WOMEN IN CHURCH LEADERSHIP

THE STORY OF Erin and Wayne's partnership begins with Erin. In her early life she showed leadership potential. Here's what happened.

○

Erin's Story: Affirming Her Own Call to Ministry

I did not grow up in the church. Because we moved a lot and I was always new at school—and I was very bright—I always felt alienated. As an adolescent in Southern California, I was influenced by the Jesus movement. The church I came into was very fundamental, but love and caring were the norm in the group. By the time I got to tenth grade, I was at church five nights a week. On my own I ran a junior program for disadvantaged girls who attended a school across the street. I cooked for the junior high fellowship, attended the senior high fellowship, and was invited as a high school student to attend the college fellowship. I also taught Sunday school and was codirector of Bible school before I even had a driver's license. This church was very proud of all the men they had sent to seminary, but it never once occurred to them to suggest I might have a call.

In college I majored in elementary education and assumed I would be a teacher. When I was a junior, a new chaplain came in midyear—a woman—the only person they could find on short notice. Liz was an American Baptist, the first ordained woman I had ever met. Here I was, twenty years old before I even knew women could be ordained. She was the first person to say to me, "You have a clear call. Why hasn't anyone ever told you this?"

Immediately I changed my major to religion and English literature, and I entered a new world—a world where women were battling for a position in church leadership. At the time I was president of our Intervarsity Christian Fellowship chapter. I refused to sign their doctrinal statement and wrote my own instead. The discussion about whether this was OK went all the way to the top of the Southern California organization. I was permitted to stay in leadership, but I was suspect from then on. The combination of having clear leadership gifts that the church wanted and used and at the same time remaining suspect as a leader always made me examine the practice of ministry with some suspicion of my own.

I went on to graduate from Earlham Seminary, a Quaker school in Richmond, Indiana. I joined the Presbyterian church because my husband, whom I had met in seminary, was Presbyterian. My first call was in the congregation where I was working as the director of Christian education. I was permitted to be a candidate for the position. While I was DCE, the pastor who was the head of staff and I were really close. Soulmates, I'd say. The congregation was very hierarchical. All previous ministers had been male. I'm not sure, looking back, that they really approved of women in ministry. At the same time that the congregation was engaged in the search for the associate pastor, I unexpectedly became pregnant. The vote on whether to call me to the position fell on my due date. The congregational meeting became embroiled in a discussion of whether to offer a paid maternity leave. I heard later that conversation was circulating over whether a woman can be a minister and a mother without "shortchanging" both.

As it turned out, they did vote to extend me a call, but more than 10 percent of those voting were opposed. Normally in these circumstances, the presbytery Committee on Ministry recommends against going forward with the call. But for some reason this COM permitted it. I was never officially informed about the vote results. I accepted the call. After maternity leave, I was ordained and my baby was baptized at the same service of worship

As I began in the ordained position, there was increasing pressure on the pastor who was head of staff to make sure that we did not appear as equals. As things deteriorated, the personnel committee told me that my job was to keep my mouth shut, do what I was told, and not rock the boat. In that environment much of what I did was interpreted as undermining the pastor. We could not confront the problem constructively. He was trapped in it, as I was. It destroyed our friendship and collegiality. We were not able to step back and say, "Let's look at what this working relationship means to us. We need to deal with the power asymmetry between us, and if we can't, let's part ways."

At that time I was also in school, working on my doctorate in women's psychology and feminist theology. I had to give up my studies when we discovered that our son had life-threatening asthma and severe food allergies. Finally, we reached a crisis. On one of the several occasions when our son almost died of anaphylactic shock, I missed a preaching assignment. The pastor had to fill in for me with only a couple days' notice. My alleged lack of "reliability" contributed to the congregation's decision to hire another associate pastor. They stipulated that they wanted a male over fifty-five years. Although they kept my position, they transferred many of my duties to the new position, making it clear that my "place" was Christian education. By the time I'd been in the ordained position for two years, the conflict between the personnel committee and me was intense, the issues ambiguous, the situation unresolvable. I had to leave. It broke my heart.

When we moved to Pennsylvania, where my husband accepted a call, I was very wary of church hierarchy and how it deals with power.

o

Wayne and Erin Form a Team

Wayne had been executive presbyter (head of the presbytery) for about a year when Erin and her husband moved to Pennsylvania and Erin began serving on the Committee on Ministry as a volunteer. In the Presbyterian church, the presbytery oversees a number of congregations in a particular region, providing guidance to pastors and support services to congregations. Pastoral relationships are handled by the Committee on Ministry. After Erin had served on the COM for two and a half years, Wayne sought her application for a new part-time position in the presbytery, that of associate for Christian education. Recently, Erin's position became full time and was upgraded to presbytery associate for congregational ministries. Erin did not share her past experience with Wayne when she began working with him. Altogether, Wayne and Erin have worked together for nearly nine years.

o

Erin Continues . . .

I came onto the Committee on Ministry very wary about how our COMs typically deal with power. Sure enough, I found much of what the committee was doing disturbing. At that time Wayne had been in the presbytery a little over a year. He had inherited a typical Committee on Ministry and was just beginning to look at the underlying power issues. With his pushing, the presbytery had just elected the first woman head of COM—a pastor of some of our smallest churches. But Wayne is a strong *J* on the Myers-Briggs Personality Inventory. From my perspective it seemed he was waging oversight of the presbytery like a military campaign.

When the staff position opened up, Wayne demanded my resume. I wasn't a shoo-in by any means, but in the end I was selected. I came on staff and suddenly was responsible to Wayne as my supervisor. I backed away from controversy and began working hard on programming. When I became pregnant with our second child, I was very ill and in danger of losing the baby. I was not able to fulfill all my responsibilities for a time. Wayne became a shield for me with people in the presbytery who were frustrated with lack of services. It was a new role for him. He is often not perceived as an empathetic person. Yet I was getting a great deal of empathy that I did not expect. . . . He not only supported me through a very difficult pregnancy but was also remarkably tolerant of all the things my husband and I have to do to ensure the safety and health of our older child.

Wayne also made me his partner. He created an office for me, including the space, the secretarial help, and the equipment. He downgraded his own computer purchase so that I could get equipment too. This was significant, because the position I held was new. Gradually, we were moving into a new understanding of my position and of our relationship. At the same time, we were moving into a much deeper and more vulnerable relationship with each other.

Then the first Reimagining Conference was held. The topic, female spirituality, was very controversial in our denomination. Although no one in our presbytery was directly involved, it brought life as we knew it to a halt. Because of the controversy the conference generated, every presbytery was required to have a dialogue on human sexuality. At this time I was about to go on maternity leave. I was also assigned staff oversight for this dialogue. The activities we planned included a discussion of homosexuality. This decision was controversial, and it provoked an unfortunate misunderstanding with a congregation in our presbytery over an invited participant. I was at risk. Here I was, having another baby, trying to deal responsibly with reactions to the Reimagining Conference and the fear of female sexuality that was coming out, and dealing with reactions to our decision to include homosexuality as part of our dialogue on human sexuality.

This was the turning point in my relationship with Wayne. He took complete responsibility for the communication oversight. When I came back from maternity leave, the whole situation had been defused. He presented it to me as a done deal. It completely floored me. This was the point at which I decided I could trust Wayne and tell him about my past work situation. But the point is, Wayne did not support me because of my past experience. He did it because he valued the partnership.

I'd say we have developed a real ability to move around the hierarchy. We have to work at it. We are very different. I am more permission-giving. We are constantly looking for a different perspective from each other. We've developed an integrated style, where Wayne, as senior, does not dominate. An example of our successful teaming is the Commissioned Lay Pastors' Program, which we developed. We had a long, intense dialogue about whether the program needed to be nurturing and permission-giving or controlling and gatekeeping. I really pushed for the former and eventually won Wayne over. Now we have one of the preeminent Commissioned Lay Pastors' Programs in our denomination. We have truly become partners and colleagues in what we do.

○

Wayne's Turn

Knowing Erin's spirit as I did from working with her on the COM, I was determined to work with her professionally. We are night and day in our styles and I knew we needed that here. Also, I was intent on modeling male-female leadership in this presbytery. Erin really razzles and dazzles folks. She is very well spoken, very well written, and she has a good up-front presence. She is also strong enough to challenge me. When Erin's position went full time, I wanted her title to be associate executive presbyter. She is the person most capable of stepping in as acting executive presbyter if anything were to happen to me. But the presbytery wouldn't agree. I had my fallback position and my bottom line. If they had not agreed to elevate her position some, I had decided I would leave. We were satisfied with the outcome. In the end, we don't let title bother us, though. We act as coequals.

Erin is in many respects my opposite. I tend to move quickly to a decision and am damned convinced it is right. Erin looks at a broader picture and considers more options than I would. More often than not, I recognize the wisdom she brings and modify my position. We are a great tag team. We work very hard to model partnership. We talk a lot—all the time—in person and by e-mail. There is very little I know that Erin doesn't, and vice versa. People are coming to know that. We never cross each other in public (and seldom in private), and we show up to support each other.

The issues around our human sexuality dialogues and the Reimagining Conference were a real turning point in our relationship, I agree. I didn't see myself as covering for Erin. It was very simply a situation in which I had more power than she did, and I didn't want her to get chewed up. I took the responsibility for handling it. There are some situations in which I can be more effective and others where Erin is more effective. In fact, sometimes I think Erin has more power than I do. That's OK with me. The bottom line is that we make an effort to be partners in the team regardless of how we have to act externally. And it works. It is fun working and serving together. I feel we are a good team and want to do all I can to continue to develop our partnership.

When I look at my role in the relationship, it's more important for me to show up in a support capacity than vice versa. At our recent youth event, I came to do the step-and-fetch work. People see that, and it's very important. I go to her office as much as she comes to mine. I work to give her visibility, experience, a chance to be published. People never challenge me to act the senior because they know I would not respond. I don't do this to "help the women out." I do it because I firmly believe that Erin belongs in governing-body work, writing, and publishing.

Some men would look at Erin's difficult pregnancies and the stresses of her son's allergies and asthma and say, "See, when things get really tough, you can't count on the women." But I don't agree. We are a team and cover for each other. In fact, it's unfortunate that we have not in the past provided the encouragement to fathers to be more involved in child care. If we had a different model it would not be considered "disruptive" when women, who still carry the primary child-care role and have a career, need to have time for those responsibilities. As a matter of fact, in my experience it has often been the women whom I have been most able to count on when things get tough.

Early on I saw great gifts and potential in Erin for significant service in the church. That's the most significant thing. I understand part of my responsibility is to nurture the gifts and potential of those with whom I serve. I like to think this would be no different with any other person serving in Erin's capacity. In fact, I have been instrumental in identifying and enlisting other women into leadership roles in the presbytery. From the very outset I have been committed to modeling mutuality in this ministry, particularly with a woman as associate. We have several women serving congregations as pastors. By supporting Erin and intentionally working to develop and be visible as a partnership I hope to lift up the potential of women serving as pastors.

But my motivation is selfish too. I know I cannot meet the "counseling-support" needs of everybody in the presbytery, particularly women serving in the pastorate. There are some things that I do not, and never will, understand about the varying stresses for women in ministry. Erin's ministry extends far beyond the limits of her position description. Erin provides another person on the staff, with her own particular understanding, ways of responding, and experiences, with whom ministers and members can unload or seek counsel. I know I see and understand from a very particular perspective—white, male, now over fifty. I know there are other perspectives. Erin brings a different perspective. Erin brings a different set of analytical gifts. Together we are stronger and better able to serve the presbytery than either of us would be able to alone.

Working with Erin has changed me light-years. It has softened me up. She is constant at helping me develop a deeper spirituality. It is God's grace that she is able to challenge me and I am open to it. I am not sure I would always be as open to the challenge from others. Erin has a real gift that way.

---

o

8

BELIEVING WOMEN
SHOULD BE LEADERS

MIXED-GENDER TEAMS will not work unless we believe in them. This requires believing that women as well as men should be leaders. It also requires believing that women can be equal partners with men in leadership. If we believe this, we can change an environment that has historically been very hostile to women leaders. In Erin's early career, we can see how she was discouraged in her quest to become a leader. Later, we can see not only how Wayne encouraged her but also how he accepted her as an equal. This is what it takes for both men and women to be present in church leadership. Obviously, the presence of men *and women* is a prerequisite for effective mixed-gender teams. But Erin's story enlightens us about the hidden attitudes and practices that still prevent the full partnership of women.

The feedback of team members in my study also enlightens us on this point. Although my interview subjects self-selected as members of successful teams, I was struck by the number of people who volunteered unsolicited information about other teams that are not successful. They mentioned teams in their workplace, in their denomination, or among their circles of friends. They also mentioned teams they had been a part of in their past professional lives. Thus I was aware from the start of my project that successful mixed-gender teams are not only hard to create and sustain but also hard to find. This is not necessarily because men or women do not want to work together or cannot learn how. Indeed, we've already discussed the motivation and the hope that women and men have for shared leadership in the church. First and foremost, such teams are few because the church as an environment still has embedded characteristics that counterindicate the effective leadership of women.

Let's take a closer look. First we will examine the barriers to women's leadership in the church. Then we will discover how to break down those barriers and bring women into full partnership with men. In the course of this examination we will see why it is so important for men to be involved.

The Mixed Message

The simplest way to look at the question of women's participation in church leadership is to look at experience, as we have done with Erin's story. The first thing we can observe from her story is that women who are already in church leadership get a mixed message. This is particularly true in the patriarchal traditions. On the one hand, women are made welcome—by the churches' intention to have growing numbers of women in leadership, by quotas that make sure women are present, by invitations to speak and in other ways be visible, by men who advocate with us for the ordination of women in more and more denominations, and by many other individual and denominational actions. On the other hand, women are made unwelcome, either explicitly or implicitly—by language that excludes us, by hierarchical models of management that tend to exclude us, by exclusively male origin theology that has for centuries dominated the church's official decisions and attitudes, and by an enduring fear of women's sexuality that is characteristic of most religious traditions in the world (Becker, 1996). What women are experiencing, says one clergywoman, is "the creaking of an ancient, heavy door, slowly opening, with some pulling it open and some pushing it shut" (Schaper, 1990, p. 69).

How the Mixed Message Goes

In practical terms, Erin's story illustrates how the mixed message goes. Her story is one of many. During the writing of this book I heard from one woman who had been called to a congregation only to be criticized, tricked, trapped, and physically harassed by her male partner until, only months into her assignment, she resigned to protect herself. This may be an extreme case, but it illustrates the problem. Another incident also reveals that the problem is real. I was asked by a seminary student if I would share the first chapter of this book in manuscript form so that he could use it to report preliminary findings to a class. After his report, he shared this feedback with me: "The women in our class did not agree with your assessment that 'women have found a place at the table alongside of men.'" The women said two things about my assertion: First, if women are at the table, they are invisible (that is, men speak right through them), and at times men do not even acknowledge their presence or ideas. Second, the only reason that women are at the table is that it makes men in the room *more visible* to the world. Women in leadership, they said, "are just window dressing that makes the organization look better in the community's eyes." It is clear just from these examples that the debate about women in leadership is not over.

Women as a group also hear a mixed message. By way of example we may consider Lindley's account (1996) of women who in the past dozen years have become rabbis in Conservative Judaism. Jewish law as defined in *halakhah* and modern influences on Judaism clash to create a powerful and confusing mixed message for these women. *Halakhah*, which is really more than Jewish law, defines what it means to live a Jewish life, and for traditional Jews, it is binding. *Halakhah* codifies women's role as secondary and subservient to men. It creates a powerful but entirely separate sphere of influence for women in the home. The separation of men's and women's responsibilities contained in *halakhah* is explicitly adhered to in Orthodox Judaism, where women to this day have no access to public life, consistent with Old Testament legalism. Conservative Judaism, however, strives to integrate age-old tradition with modernity. Thus since the mid-1980s, women in Conservatism have been granted some access to public life, including the right to be ordained. Women wishing to join the rabbinate in Conservative Judaism must, of course, uphold and transmit *halakhah*, the very tradition that defines their proper role as limited to the private sphere. One can hardly imagine a more explicit example of women dealing with a mixed message than this. They are, in the words of one woman, "confronting the terrible choice between their identities as women and as Jews." And when they enter rabbinical training they must recognize that they "can help create a new tradition, but will always be straddling two worlds" (Lindley, 1996, p. 322).

These examples from real life and from history reveal at least three mixed messages, all of which are confusing to thoughtful women. First, of course, is the compelling message that women long to hear from the church: "We want you here. We know you have something to contribute." The second message is a bit more problematic and goes something like this: "If you are going to be here, we want you to act in a way that will be comfortable for us men." The implication of this second message for the intelligent woman is, of course, that at least some men aren't really sure they want us there after all. This message is frustrating to women and embarrassing to men who strive to affirm the leadership of women. But the third message is the real clincher. It's simple: "This is the way things are (in the examples mentioned here, women aren't supposed to be aggressive or too powerful or too visible) and you have to fit in." This message makes no sense to women because it does not fit our worldview (Becker, 1996).

The Influence of the Prevailing Worldview

To understand how confusing this experience is for women, we must understand how deeply our attitudes and behaviors are influenced not by our own worldview, whatever it might be, but also by the *prevailing worldview*. First, some definitions. A worldview (popularly called a *paradigm* in recent business literature) is a set of deeply held rules and regulations surrounding the way a person or group of people see and do things; it provides boundaries for us. We rely on our worldview to filter information, to make sense of our world, and to help us decide how to do the things we do (Shawchuck and Heuser, 1993). Often without even knowing it we rely on our worldview as individuals, as groups, and as entire organizations. Denominations and organizations, as well as individuals, have their worldview.

The prevailing worldview of our culture is still defined by white men. Like any other worldview, this one can be changed. Still, as the prevailing worldview of our culture, it's hard to remember that it is only one way of viewing the world; that is the nature of a prevailing worldview. "It is the system by which we live, and in it, the power and influence are held by a few select white males. It controls almost every aspect of our culture. It makes our laws, runs our economy, sets our salaries, and decides when and if we will go to war or stay at home. It decides what is knowledge, and how it will be taught" (Schaef, 1985, p. 2). From one clergywoman's point of view, the prevailing worldview "tells me over and over again that men are different from me, that culture sides with men in what it values, and that sometimes it is willing to be extremely mean, if not violent, towards me and other women to get what it wants." She adds, "I, of course, have this theory packed in my bags when I approach ministry and the doing of it" (Schaper, 1990, p. 16).

Schaper's comment illustrates how the mixed message affects one clergywoman. Her point is clear: women get mixed messages because the prevailing worldview promotes the interests of a few at the expense of many. Letty Russell reminds us that the white male worldview is patriarchal and "places everything in a hierarchy of domination and subordination, accepting the marginalization of the powerless as given." It "is a manifestation of a social system that changes form but continues to define women as marginal to the male center" (Russell, 1993, p. 35). Nine-tenths of the law of patriarchy, says Carolyn Heilbrun (1988), "is the desire [of men] to have all the fun" (p. 20). But I believe patriarchy also excludes many white males who do not fit the limited definition of what a man should look or act like. We all work within these patriarchies in our denominations and other church-related agencies. And as we all know, "there is a direct correlation between buying into the white male system and surviving in our culture" (Schaef, 1985, p. 5). What the prevailing worldview misses is that outsiders (women, African Americans, Hispanics, and others) are not "additions to" or "defections from" the standard but elements of that life, with their own contributions that invade the prevailing paradigm (Rhodes, 1987; West, 1993). We shall discuss this point in greater detail in Chapter Thirteen.

How the Prevailing View Affects Women

I have said that our worldview helps us sort and interpret information. It also helps us make judgments, including judgments about women in leadership today. We judge women competent or incompetent leaders based on the prevailing models for leadership. The challenge for women as we search for and articulate our own styles of leadership is that the white male system is still the norm in management and church leadership circles. If we accept the white male system as our worldview (and because it is the prevailing one, most of us do to some degree), we women are likely to be found wanting in our leadership, no matter what we do. Here's how it works. A woman who is assertive, goal-directed, firm, even authoritative, is adopting the hero-leader model we discussed in Chapter Five for her leadership. She is not, however, following the worldview in her behavior *as a woman*. She cannot do both. Even though new models for leadership are emerging, the white male worldview still expects women to be caring, relational, gentle, and silent, whereas leaders are supposed to be tough, decisive, authoritative, and outspoken. In Chapter Five we discussed how this stereotype puts pressure on men to be one way and women to be another as leaders. Here's the dilemma it creates for women: If we women are aggressive leaders in the white male style, we will be criticized for being "bitchy" or tough or unfeminine. But if we behave "like women," we will be judged indecisive, weak, and unfit for leadership.

As leaders caught in this dilemma, we women have historically tried to honor the expectations of the white men in power positions, either by being "proper" women or by trying to be like men. Increasingly, women have forged a leadership style that transforms attributes acceptable for the proper woman into a collaborative or embracing style that is effective in the workplace. I described this style in Chapter Five. Essentially, women have demonstrated a new leadership style acceptable (to a point) in the prevailing worldview. We still get criticized, of course, for being indecisive and weak, even though we are not. Women know all too well that "men are graded on how well they do ministry the masculine way, and women are graded on how well they do it in the masculine way *as long as they also remain feminine*" (Schaper, 1990, p. 10; italics added). In the dilemmas created by this mixed message, women must have a strong partnership with and assistance from male colleagues who can understand— and interpret—that there is a different worldview operative for women leaders. We can see at least one example of what this strong partnership is like in the story of Erin and Wayne.

Virgin, Whore, Mother . . . and Leader?

Why do women get a mixed message about their leadership? More specifically, why did Erin have such a difficult time achieving a leadership position in spite of her obvious leadership skills? In answering this question we will come to understand better how the very nature of our denominations as organizations undermines the leadership of women.

Women get mixed messages from the church because the embedded characteristics of organizational life in the church that reject women's leadership contribute to our attitudes and behavior without being fully known and understood. They include a view of God as male; a view of women as not only second class but also unworthy, and in fact, responsible for evil in the world; and finally, the idea that women should play only limited roles in our culture and our faith traditions. We can observe the effects of some of these beliefs in Erin's story. As we look at these characteristics of our organizational life we must ask: When women are viewed as wife, mother, virgin, or whore, how is it possible that we can embrace them as leader?

The Sexuality of Denominations

A laywoman who has served widely in ecumenical circles for many years has said: "To gain respect you have to stick around long enough, and of course, a lot of women are rejected out of hand in church circles, especially global circles, where there are very few of us. But if you stick around long enough, and if you are tough enough, and if you are nice enough, and most of all *if when they look at you they don't think about sex,* it will be all right" (Becker, 1996, p. 74). Her comment graphically illustrates the most limiting embedded characteristics of religious traditions that counterindicate the effective leadership of women: in an ardently masculine sexual environment, women stand out as the "unknown other," a source of fear and temptation. This is true not only in the Judeo-Christian tradition but also in most religious traditions the world over. One has only to watch modern-day news footage from Iran or Iraq to see the results of this worldview in the culture. The strands of historical and cultural development that have resulted in the fear and hatred of women are varied and complex, but now so intertwined with our way of viewing our moral universe that we can hardly separate them anymore. They are at the heart of what we might call the sexuality of the denominations (Hearn and Burrell, 1989).

Admittedly, sexuality is a difficult thing to define, and its interplay with gender is complex and variously interpreted by sociologists, psychiatrists, and theologians. Furthermore, both sexuality and gender are largely ignored as concepts of any concern to the workplace. They are, nevertheless, deeply embedded in the nature of most religious traditions.

It is obvious to even the most casual viewer that the denominations—mainline and fundamental, Christian, Jewish, Muslim, Hindu, and others—are deeply antifeminine and fundamentally masculine in their sexual orientation. All faith traditions to some degree (except perhaps the Quakers, the ascetic Shakers, and the marginal disciplines of New Thought and Theosophy) still rely on biological essentialism to assert the supremacy of the male gender. They assert that it is in the nature of man—in his sexuality—that he is superior to woman. What sociologists call biological essentialism, feminist theologians call the doctrine of fixed natures, which dictates a proscribed destiny for women based on our biology. It is precisely this argument that was (and in some traditions still is) used to keep women out of the priesthood, pastorate, or rabbinate, and as we shall see, still underlies our understanding of the church and the way in which we construct our faith in a most fundamental way (Becker, 1996).

Out of this framework grows the habit of *sexual zoning,* a sociological term that describes how organizations create a geography of access to certain types of experiences for one sex only. In traditional Judaism, women have been denied full access to worship. So as not to distract the men, they are traditionally seated in a balcony behind a screen, or in some other separate area. Mormon women are also restricted to certain areas of the temple that keep them from the "inner sanctum." In the Christian denominations, certain types of religious leadership experiences are still largely reserved for men because of men's physical nature. In many denominations that still do not ordain women, access to the pulpit is denied to women. The Roman Catholic Church, in fact, adopted this argument in 1976, in Pope Paul VI's *Declaration on the Question of the Admission of Women to the Ministerial Priesthood.* The church's old argument, based on the idea that the order of creation dictates the headship of men, was already at this time largely discredited. The new argument "claimed that although equal to men in dignity, women do not bear a natural resemblance to Christ and so cannot represent him sacramentally" (Ashe, 1997, p. 107). More recently, in his 1994 apostolic letter *Ordinatio Sacerdotalis,* Pope John Paul II emphasized that the church has no authority to ordain women.

The denominations' predominantly male sexuality is constructed in a larger environment of sexual negativity or denial. In most traditions, the historical weight of religious, intellectual, and moral opinion has accumulated against sexuality. We consider sexuality frightening, uncontrollable, illegitimate, chaotic, unpredictable, and even evil. It is something we strive mightily to limit, control, and keep private (Hearn and Burrell, 1989; Rhodes, 1987). Men are victimized in a unique way by this view, living as they do as preeminent embodiments of the favored sex in an environment that would rather we all be without sex, if that were possible. They are forced to suppress their sexuality, and we now see the dark side of this suppression emerging in an overwhelming abundance of cases of sexual misconduct. But women have much more to overcome as individual persons living and working in an environment sexualized to be masculine (Becker, 1996).

To begin, some definitions and clarifications are in order. First, in our everyday discourse, we often confuse gender and sexuality. *Gender* is the sex we are—and we are each still one or the other. *Sexuality* is our quality of being sexual, and this takes many forms. Intertwined as they are, sexuality and gender are different. Furthermore, it's not only people who are sexual. Sexuality can be attributed to organizations just as it is to individuals. It is therefore not just a distinct feature of our private lives or our private selves but also "an ordinary and frequent public process" (Hearn and Burrell, 1989, p. 13). In applying the notion of sexuality to the denominations, I do not mean to imply that sexuality can be organized. In fact it is diverse and diffuse, defying organization.

Woman as the "Unknown Other"

In patriarchy, woman is always "the other," the antithesis over against which men define authentic (male) selfhood. This worldview, first articulated by Simone de Beauvoir in *The Second Sex,* defines the sexuality of our denominations as male. As early as the first century, male philosophy aligned the masculine with transcendence, the spiritual, and the intellect, and women with nature and the physical. Our tendency to dualistic thinking added that male was better; female inferior. The Aristotelian version asserts that women are biologically defective males, merely the vessels that hold the potency of men. They symbolize the passivity and inferiority of nature.

The Christian church fathers solidified this view in the fourth century when Augustine put it theologically, attaching the inferiority of women to the creation stories. His view went beyond the simple woman-is-inferior theme, adding that God *intended* her inferiority. It was a short leap from that view to the Christian concept of woman "made only for procreation; a helpmeet for man in the only area where he cannot be served better by a male" (Tavard, 1973, p. 125). The church fathers assigned women secondary biological status, but they could not agree about her soul. Augustine rejected the idea that a woman's soul was inferior. Other theologians argued that Eve bore the primary responsibility for the fall of humankind. Her actions relegated her soul to secondary status, requiring the abasement of all women and the covering of their shameful female nature for all time. Later in his life, Augustine added his view that spontaneous sexual desire was the proof of and penalty for original sin, and the indictment was complete. Woman was responsible for the de facto existence of evil. It was in the nature of woman—in her sexuality—to be evil. The Christian church fathers thus achieved both a theological explanation and a practical justification for male dominance and female subservience (Prusak, 1974). This theme has been repeated in the literature, theology, and language of the Christian tradition, and women have been consigned to an inferior status ever since.

By now we have forgotten that a sexual interpretation of the creation stories in the Judeo-Christian tradition would have astounded the Christians of the first century and their Jewish and pagan contemporaries (Pagels, 1988). In fact, the early Christians interpreted the story of Adam and Eve as having little or nothing to do with sexuality or carnal knowledge, a historical fact that may be surprising to us. To the extent that it is, it indicates how we have been captivated by the moral implications of Augustine's view of the creation stories, even though we may not read the stories themselves literally (Becker, 1996). Theologians today may say that theological justifications for male dominance based on women's moral inferiority are largely passé. Yet these ideas are so deeply embedded in our subconscious that they still have a profound effect on our values.

Jewish tradition does not have the same spirit-matter dualism characteristic of Christianity. Sex is largely viewed positively. Yet many of its traditions, still practiced in Conservative and Orthodox Judaism, belie a negative view of women and female sexuality. Nothing could be more explicit in this regard than the traditional morning prayer of the Jewish male, in which he thanks God that he has not been born a woman. In general, a strong tradition enjoining female modesty "lest a woman tempt a man to lust or distract him from worship or study" suggests a negative view of female sexuality (Lindley, 1996, p. 229). The traditional dictum *kol isha irva,* which translates "a woman's voice leads to sexual excitement," holds women responsible for their own and men's sexual behavior and further reveals some fear of women's sexual power. Laws of ritual purity required of women provide further evidence. *Niddah* requires women to visit the ritual bath seven days after each menstruation. In the meantime, it is the woman's responsibility to make sure that neither she nor her husband violates cultic purity by having sexual relations. This law has continued in traditional Judaism long after other laws about cultic purity associated with sacrificial worship have became inoperative (Lindley, 1996).

In the major religions of the East we can also find evidence of the typical denigration of women even in traditions that assert the equality of the divine masculine and feminine principles. The Hindu tradition provides a specific example. The Upanishads, foundational texts of the Hindu tradition, define the material world, *maya,* as the impermanent source of human suffering. *Maya* is a feminine word, and throughout the Hindu tradition women and *maya* have been seen as one and the same. Furthermore, and much to the point here, they are defined as seductive temptresses that cause the true self (often referred to in the masculine) to forget its (that is, his) true nature. Even though Hindu theology stresses the unity of the universal masculine spirit with the universal feminine energy as the source of creation, Hindu tradition is sexist; women are forbidden to study or even read the Vedas, or sacred scriptures (Wessinger, 1993). American Buddhism provides another example. Like Hinduism, its theology includes ancient ideas about egalitarianism. When combined with the Western idea of equality of the sexes, the traditional Buddhist identification of women as the source of evil begins to be mitigated. Yet a significant portion of the Buddhist tradition has viewed women as sexual temptresses who embody—in their sexuality—"the limitations of the human condition, the continual process of suffering and rebirth" (Paul, 1985, p. 3). A common Buddhist attitude has been that birth as a woman is bad karma. Buddhist folklore includes the story of Mara, ruler of the realm of desires, who sends his three daughters, Lust, Aversion, and Craving, to tempt the Buddha and thus prevent his enlightenment. This story symbolically communicates the traditional Buddhist view that women are the source of evil and a threat to man's attempt to eliminate desire (Wessinger, 1993). In Islam, the subservient status assigned to women is often characterized as part and parcel of the tradition's concern for family. Women in Islam are defined by the Koran as a step below men and in need of male support. Yet the religious laws that require the veiling of Muslim women are not only for the women's protection against promiscuous males but to protect males from their own temptations.

Classical mythology is also full of stories of the devouring mother. These are stories of woman's power, which is considerable but smothered. It is she who gives us all life and nurtures or withholds from us when we are helpless infants. And in growing up, it is the ultimate task for the male to define himself as different from her. In a patriarchy, woman's power must be suppressed and her mystery must never be known. It is in the nature of the known (male) to wonder about and fear the unknown (female). Ancient mythologies play on this theme. The Phrygian myths of the great earth mother Cybele tell the fate of her son-lover Attis, who was castrated for secretly observing women's rites and being unfaithful to her. Ishtar, a major goddess in the Assyro-Babylonian pantheon, emasculates and slays a new son-lover every year. In the Hindu tradition, Kali is the great mother and benefactress on her right side and the fury and ogress, devourer of her own offspring, on her left side. Almost every tradition has its mythology of the emasculating or devouring mother-lover (Jobes, 1962). These stories remind us that woman is indeed the unknown other (Becker, 1996).

Since most faith traditions are still uncomfortable with the physical, and particularly the sexual, the very presence of women remains deeply troubling for them. The fact that sexuality is a major identifying characteristic of the white male world (Schaef, 1985), combined with the fact that church systems and theologies are so firmly grounded in white male thinking, exacerbates this problem. We are left, as a result, with three limited images for women: whore, mother, and virgin (Ruether, 1975).

The Imperative to Be a Mother

The secret that we women know about ourselves is of course found in the mystery of Incarnation. Woman is as divine as man, privileged to share with God the reenactment of birth cycles, over and over, with every moon. The image of the feminine in God is a representation of immanence, symbolic of the value of physical power that comes from within, rather than the power over. It calls to memory all the power and even the violence of creation and birth, growing, changing, living, and dying. Our natural world demonstrates these powers to us every day, and we each carry a hidden knowledge of it in the forgotten memory of our birth. Having forgotten it, we fear its return—if not before, then surely at the moment of our death. Whatever images we carry with us of the feminine holy, they are images of connectedness, sustenance, healing, creating. They are earthly and physical, and indeed these feminine aspects of God do represent feminine power, the power of the dark womb. It is a power that most religious traditions have not embraced (Becker, 1989).

The problem is that we women are imprisoned by our sexuality when the church limits our proper role to mother or celibate nun. It's a catch-22 for us. When we are not demonized for the power of our sexuality (including, of course, the power to become mothers) we are limited by it. This is the second characteristic of most religious traditions that counterindicates the leadership of women. Several faith traditions that are divergent theologically have in common the emphasis they place on a woman's primary role as mother or guardian of the family. These include (but are not limited to) Roman Catholicism, Judaism, Islam, and Mormonism. We may look briefly at each of these traditions as examples of attitudes about women's roles.

Injunctions against birth control and the reverence for motherhood are well documented in Catholicism. Attitudes and views toward women's role in the twentieth century remain much as they were in the nineteenth. "Women were by divine decree subordinate to men; except for religious sisters, their natural place was in the family as upholders of piety and purity; women who did not thus emulate Mary were to be regarded as dangerous and rebellious daughters of Eve" (Lindley, 1996, p. 360). These were the images promoted by the Pope and the patriarchy of the Roman church.

Until the Protestant Reformation, Catholicism offered Christian women an alternative to motherhood in the cloister. Here women could become leaders based on their charisma. During the Middle Ages, when monasteries were the source and standard for Christian ministry, women achieved levels of prominence in their own spheres, apart from men. However, the Protestant Reformation closed convents and thus removed the alternative of cloistered life for many women. Some did eventually find opportunities for service in teaching and evangelizing primarily in the more liberal Protestant traditions, but these were not part of the Protestant Reformation in the Middle Ages. Those who remained in the Catholic tradition had their ministry concentrated largely within the convent walls until Vatican II, when more varied opportunities became available to women religious. Still, with the exception of the very early Christian period, when women seemed to enjoy a significant (though largely undocumented) role among the disciples of Jesus, women's roles in the Christian tradition have been limited by social convention that proscribed not only what work they could do but what roles they could play. The long and short of the story is that women's roles in Christianity were, until the nineteenth and twentieth centuries, limited to mother or celibate nun.

The rise of the Reform and Reconstructionist movements in Judaism have, of course, mitigated the imperative somewhat for women in the modern era. Yet even in the most liberal circles of Jewish life, motherhood is still expected. There is real pressure from the Jewish community to follow the injunction of Genesis 9:5 to "be fruitful and multiply." Although the technical commandment to continue the survival of the Jewish people is directed at men, it is women who "have internalized the sense that to be complete as Jewish women they must have children" (Alpert and Milgram, 1996, p. 308). There is less support in the community for the idea that women can strengthen the community through their professional contributions.

Muslim concern for the family and for family life dictates women's roles in Islam. They are subordinate to men and considered to be in need of male protection and support. They play a traditional role in the family and in support of the religious activities of the community. To varying degrees they follow traditional Islamic dress code and observe strict Islamic law. In the West, we understand the rights of Muslim women as severely limited more from what we read about the Middle East than what we observe in our own countries. Nevertheless, Muslim women do not play a leadership role in their mosque apart from the concerns of family and community.

Mormonism offers one of the most radical theologies of motherhood. Curiously, though the Mormon church in many ways avoids the limitations placed on women by other patriarchal traditions—including in its theology the concept of a Heavenly Mother as well as Heavenly Father, rejecting the doctrine of original sin, and holding that both men and women can achieve equal divinity in the eyes of God—it still circumscribes women's role both in the church and the world. Women are barred from the priesthood, and motherhood has been elevated to the highest office a woman can hold. Polygamy, which was practiced by Mormons even after it was outlawed by civil society, contributes to the belief that women ought above all things become mothers. The basis of the Mormon argument for this organizational bias is that priesthood and motherhood are "ontological categories of parallel function" (Bednarowski, 1993, p. 213). Furthermore, Mormonism asserts that gender roles are a matter of choice made by each individual soul before taking on the physical body. Women, therefore, have before birth chosen to be mothers rather than priests. Women's role as mother in Mormonism is not limited to temporal life. Explicit gendered roles for both sexes are considered an intrinsic part of eternal spiritual reality. Biological motherhood continues for women in eternal life where the highest station is reserved for married men and women (Lindley, 1996). This view, like so many others that limit women's leadership in the church, also limits men. It eliminates the value of fatherhood.

Leadership Beyond Motherhood

In spite of the injunction to motherhood, women do become lay (and sometimes clergy) leaders even in conservative patriarchal traditions. Our roles may be circumscribed, but we women are present. Later we shall examine how the social expectation of equality for women contributes to the possibility that we may break out of limited leadership roles and therefore be more available for true partnership with men. Before doing that we shall consider how women achieve leadership roles in traditions that remain conservative and patriarchal.

A summary of women's changing leadership in the neoevangelical traditions provides a good example. [I use here Margaret Bendroth's definition of fundamentalism and its neoevangelical offspring (1993): those denominations that are culturally and theologically conservative and include denominations as diverse as the Southern Baptists, the Missouri Synod Lutherans, the Christian Reformed Church, the Assemblies of God, the Evangelical Free Church, and others. There are also many predominantly black denominations that have conservative views of the leadership of women. Some may be considered a part of the neoevangelical tradition; others are in the Pentecostal tradition. They include the African Methodist Episcopal, the Church of God in Christ, and others (Gray, 1992).] Women have long been able to hold influential roles in leadership by claiming a direct calling of the Spirit (Ruether and McLaughlin, 1979). Thus a historical look at the leadership of women in the nineteenth century actually reveals more women in the conservative, neoevangelical movement than in mainline traditions. Denied the authority of office (of clergy) in most denominations, women could in these traditions claim the authority of direct spiritual gifts. The women put to death as witches in Salem had made similar claims, but to no avail.

The mystical tradition in Catholicism and the Quaker doctrine of Inner Light are examples of trends that supported women's charismatic leadership outside the neoevangelical stream. But Pentecostalism provides the most fertile ground for women's leadership as a direct spiritual calling.

This tradition, after all, "is soundly based on the premise that Spirit-filled encounters can and do happen to everyone who seeks them." Furthermore, "Pentecostals are generally not in the habit of questioning other believers' testimonies of a personal spiritual encounter with God" (Lawless, 1993, p. 44). A summary of Pentecostal women's call-to-preach narratives in central Missouri verify the women's sense of personal calling from God, a calling that they resisted, tested, and finally accepted in a denomination that is otherwise conservative, Bible-based, Bible-inspired, and patriarchal. By virtue of the way in which these women claimed their public role, they, like so many before them, "were unable to write exemplary lives: they do not dare to offer themselves as models but only as exceptions chosen by destiny" (Heilbrun, 1988, p. 25).

Women have historically achieved successful leadership in neoevangelical traditions for a sociological as well as a theological reason. Women are more likely to be accepted as leaders in a movement when it is young and needs leaders, and again when it is old and in decline (Carroll, Hargrove, and Lummis, 1983). Women gained a foothold in the leadership of charismatic movements in the nineteenth century because the movement was both young and antihierarchical. Because fundamentalism is a neo-ecclesiastical, market-driven popular religious movement that is built on a foundation of independent, entrepreneurial, special-purpose organizations, it was initially easier than in mainline denominations for women to gain entry at most levels. Authority in fundamentalism tended to work from the grassroots upward, rather than downward through a male-dominated hierarchy as is typical of the mainline denominations. In addition, there were many ministry roles available in fundamentalism, where women staffed a massive missionary movement, taught Christian education, became Bible translators, and the like (Hamilton, 1993).

Today, as these movements mature, we see more and more of them restricting the leadership of women. The reasons are complex, related to other considerations that the denominations could afford to respond to once the movement became strong. Backlash against the leadership of women is one factor. Another is the neoevangelical retreat to a theology based on a "biblical" universe, in which women are subservient to men. Furthermore, the neoevangelical traditions do not espouse a social gospel definition of sin (Lindley, 1996). They view sin as disobedience rather than injustice. The influence of this theological stance is that neoevangelical traditions do not embody the social expectation of equality for women that is so important for overcoming the negative influences of patriarchy on the leadership of women. Thus whereas mainline Protestant denominations began providing greater equality for women, rising fundamentalist organizations segregated or excluded them (Bendroth, 1993).

Expecting Women to Be Leaders

Our analysis so far should cause us some alarm. If the patriarchal traditions do not welcome women leaders, the likelihood that we will have many effective mixed-gender teams diminishes. It's simple. If women are not present, the mixed-gender team is not possible. We can see by the foregoing analysis that discouraging women—and sometimes barring them outright—from becoming leaders is a limiting factor. It limits the number of women who are available to be partners in mixed-gender teams. It also limits the leadership repertoire women can use when they succeed in becoming leaders. We can see this in the story of Erin's early career, and perhaps even more clearly in the story of Erin's partnership with Wayne.

How then can we change these embedded characteristics so that our denominations are more welcoming of women leaders? In seeking the answer to this question we will discover a critical role for men. We shall also see how our future can be very different from the past. Finally, we shall discover a new possibility for mixed-gender teams.

Catherine Wessinger has shown that there are certain features of a religious tradition that positively correlate with the ongoing leadership of women. She states that these characteristics include a view of God that is not solely masculine, a view of human nature that does not blame women for the fallenness or limitations of the human condition, and a view of gender roles that does not insist that marriage and motherhood are the only roles available to women (Bednarowski, 1980; Wessinger, 1993, 1996). When these characteristics are absent, the tradition is not conducive to women's leadership.

The embedded characteristics that counterindicate the leadership of women in most religious traditions are, in fact, conversely related to Wessinger's criteria. We have discussed two in this chapter: the patriarchal view of woman as not only second class but also unworthy, and in fact darkly evil by nature, and the limited roles we assign to women in our culture and our faith traditions. The third—the view of God as only male—deserves some mention by way of introduction. All of the patriarchal traditions present God as masculine. Debates about the use of inclusive language in most of these traditions reveal ambivalence, even refusal, to name God other than male. Language that attempts to name God in other ways thus becomes a critical factor in opening these traditions to women's leadership. We shall examine this point in more detail in Chapter Fifteen. Suffice it to say here that we are currently limited to a few traditions outside the Judeo-Christian mainstream that provide nonmasculine images of the divine. Even some of these do not provide effective leadership opportunity for women when other criteria are considered.

Our analysis brings us now to the critical question: Do we write off the patriarchal traditions as infertile ground for effective mixed-gender leadership simply because women will be unavailable? The answer is no, with qualification.

The Social Expectation of Equality

Wessinger (1993) adds a fourth criterion when she stresses that "the social expectation of the equality of women is crucial for women's equal access to leadership roles in any religious tradition" (pp. 6–7). A dozen years before Wessinger, Ruether (1981) recognized the importance of this criterion, calling it "a definite theory of female empowerment in the ideology and structure of the community" (p. 51). Here the Judeo-Christian tradition along with others both mainstream and marginal fare somewhat better (at least in the United States) when we consider the factors Wessinger enumerates for the social expectation of equality: girls' and women's access to education, women's ownership and inheritance of property, women's significant economic earning power and their freedom to pursue activity outside the domestic sphere, parents valuing daughters as much as sons, women's right of self-determination apart from fathers, husbands, and sons, and finally, women's ability to gain status in their own right. If the social expectation of equality is present in the culture, Wessinger (1996) emphasizes, women will seek out or create religions that have the other three characteristics. Furthermore, she has observed that women who are attached to a patriarchal tradition will begin to introduce the other three characteristics into it, particularly as they gain access to leadership roles.

This point is critical, revealing—ironically—a critical role for men. *If women can influence the patriarchy by introducing these criteria, men can do so more quickly and more effectively.* Men who work actively within the patriarchy for the leadership of women become more sensitized to the issues and experiences women confront in entering church leadership. They can also be more effective than women in introducing Wessinger's other three criteria into the patriarchal traditions. Ideally, of course, we would like to see men and women working together to open the patriarchal traditions to the leadership of women and therefore to the possibil-

ity of more men and women working together. But right now in the patriarchal traditions, men have a primary role. I would assert, in fact, that
unless men do their part, what women do alone, or what men and women
do together, will be slow to produce results. As architects and beneficia-
ries of the patriarchy, *the men* must confront its age-old characteristics
that prevent women's presence and participation as equal partners in leadership. Then we shall see an increasing number of *effective* mixed-gender
teams in the leadership ranks of the denominations.

My own studies as well as those of others support this view. Men's
voices are heard and their words believed. As long as the patriarchy pre-
vails, men are in control of the workplace in both church and secular settings. They have the power and the influence. They make—and therefore
know—the rules of the prevailing culture. In his 1997 study of the history
of women's ordination, Mark Chaves points out the critical influence of
those inside denominational systems in bringing about greater equality
for women (in his study, specifically ordination). His point: there is greater
likelihood of change when insiders as well as outsiders who stand to benefit from the change are involved in social action. This is precisely why
we say that the men must be involved in changing the patriarchy. In my
interviews with teams, in fact, one of the most important "secrets" of
team success was the commitment of the male in power to being a part of
a successful mixed-gender team.

Challenging the Patriarchy

In challenging men to a primary role in changing the patriarchy, I do not
mean to dismiss the importance of women's work. We women have done
much to open our faith traditions to our leadership. Women scholars have
for the past two decades been offering alternative views of theology.
Indeed these are feminine theologies, but each is its own. These theologies are well documented, carefully conceived, and respected in their own
right in religious circles. We should not overlook the fact that many of the
most prominent women theologians of our time are members of a faith
group—Roman Catholicism—that remains stubborn in its unwillingness
to allow women leadership posts alongside men, particularly as a part of
the ordained clergy.

Women in the Roman Catholic Church are also serving as parish ministers in locations where priests are not available. Their leadership is striking in its persistence. Most know that their church will cast them aside
when and if more priests become available, yet they continue to serve. A
major study of Catholic laywomen serving as parish ministers points out,

in fact, that "what is striking . . . in the career paths of many laywomen ministers is the number who initially experienced a strong call and desire for ordained priesthood yet who have moved forward, steadily and sensitively ministering and exercising leadership without attaining that ideal." Despite the "tepid encouragement and even veiled discouragement" from those in positions of power in the Roman Catholic hierarchy, these women ministers "persist in aspiring to leadership *in order to enflesh a vision of a collaborative church within American Catholicism*" (Finn, 1996, pp. 260–261; italics added).

Many women in many religious traditions are similar to the Catholic women we have used as examples here. We are all working to capitalize on the social expectation of our equality. We are becoming better educated, serving in a wider variety of lay (and where possible, clergy) positions, providing new models for leadership, demonstrating that women can be responsible to family as well as work, asking that our spouses join us in caring for family so that we *can* work, affirming the value and place of traditional roles as one choice for women, mentoring each other, and throughout it all maintaining a sense of humor. The most important thing about all these examples is that we women are present, making a significant contribution every day. Women in church leadership will not go away. By our presence, which is often accomplished at great personal cost, we women provide impetus for change in the patriarchy. Apart from overcoming our ambivalence about power, which we discuss in Chapter Twenty, and carving out our own leadership styles, as noted in Chapter Five, maintaining a presence is the principle task of women.

While we women are about these tasks, there is an imperative for men. The difference that men can make might well be illustrated by the work of Mordecai Kaplan, the founder of the Reconstructionist movement in Judaism. Seventy-some years ago, Kaplan called on women to demand their equal rights, claiming that equality could only come through women's own effort and initiative (Wessinger, 1996). For his time, he was prophetic. In our own time, we can look back on his work and say that it was a perfect example of the contribution men must make. Today, when women *are* demanding equality, we wish for more men with Kaplan's commitment. He worked tirelessly to create the expectation of equality for women within traditional Judaism. He passionately opposed the patriarchal view, reinterpreted *halakhah,* created the first *bat mitzvah* so that his own daughter might mark her entrance into adulthood by pronouncing the blessing and reading from the Torah, supported other creative approaches to Jewish ritual that would be more inclusive of women, and backed up his innovations in women's roles with the idea that Judaism is a constantly evolving civilization rather than a static religious system. Kaplan's energy and commitment did much to further the equality of women in Judaism specifically because he was a male with access to power in the tradition.

Many men since Kaplan have done their part to further the leadership of women by taking action that brings women into leadership in their denominations. They work to get women elected to top administrative posts; advocate for inclusive language; work with women as peers in the parish; promote women; attend workshops to learn about how women work, think, and feel; step aside when the job they want is given to a woman; call women to their parishes; and accomplish a host of other things. They do all these things because, said one clergyman, "many of us believe the traditional interpretation of male-female roles, the equality taught in the scriptures, has been skewed in the hierarchy and needs to be corrected." Other men have advocated for women for exactly the opposite reason: because they consider the traditional inequality taught by their denominations to be wrong. All the men who take such action on behalf of women are demonstrating that they are willing to move beyond life in the white male system (Becker, 1996).

Achieving Parity in Leadership

Although we recognize that we must seek equality, we women are cautious about parity with men in leadership for at least three reasons. First, we do not want equality with men to override the values, concerns, and interests we have long held. We wonder if it is possible to step out of our traditional roles and still affirm the causes and concerns of our mothers and grandmothers. If so, what happens to the concern women have long had for relationship, inclusion, and the welfare of those less able or less fortunate?

Second, women are not willing to buy the white male ideals of individualism and competition hook, line, and sinker. Feminist theologians warn us about "being diverted from [our] own concerns to support privileged models of leadership that have little to do with the gospel idea of a 'discipleship of equals'" (Ashe, 1997, p. 109). Women and men who already work in successful teams are, in fact, keenly aware that authentic partnership in church leadership requires more than "gaining leverage for women in an essentially unchanged patriarchal system" (p. xv). Something new will be required. It is already clear that we need changes that will "move us beyond not only the cultural but also the sexual colonialism" of the present (Glaser, 1983, p. 45).

Third, women are still asking the question Helen Barrett Montgomery asked in 1910 about the men who potentially could be (or already are) their partners: "Are men emancipated from the caste of sex so that they can work easily with women, unless they be head and women clearly subordinate?" ([1910] 1987, p. 269). This is one question addressed and successfully answered by every effective mixed-gender team. Those teams that are not successful are often run aground by the problem this question suggests: the men are not ready for team parity, and the women don't know what to do about it.

If we can create a new kind of church where women and men have the possibility for mixed-gender leadership, both men and women would exercise their right and ability to "join in the human and religious activities of symbol-making, becoming not only consumers but creators of religious culture" (Ashe, 1997, p. xiii). Women would add their voices to those of men in the discourse on ethics. The church would recognize women's as well as men's existence, experience, and value. And finally, our criteria for effective leadership in the church would value relationships, inclusiveness, participation, and flexibility as much as order, achievement, and power. We would, in fact, re-create in our time the "flexible, egalitarian, inclusive, and charismatic model of ministry" (pp. 93–94) that was characteristic of the early Christian church and indeed of most other religious traditions in their formative phases.

We can create this new kind of church and workplace environment if we believe it is right and important. But where do we start? It's one thing to know what we need to change and why we need to change it. But how do we do it? The next two chapters tell the story of one mixed-gender team that answered this question and provide specific guidelines for other teams who wish to work for gender equity.

9

THE LUTHERAN RELIEF TEAM

BUILDING A MODEL FOR GENDER EQUITY

THE LUTHERAN RELIEF TEAM heads an organization that serves the poorest of the poor by partnering with local organizations to provide aid to
refugees and people affected by disaster in Africa, Latin America, Asia,
and the Middle East. The team's work is an outreach and community
development ministry of the Lutheran denominations in the United States.
Kathryn heads this team, which includes three program area supervisors
(Joe, Susan, and Jeff), two finance office staff members (Mike and Lisa),
a communications director (Jonathan), and a supervisor of grants, emer-
gencies, and material aid (Kenlynn).

As a part of becoming a learning organization, the Lutheran relief team
has addressed gender equity as a "crosscutting issue" that should influence all areas of their work. The result is a formal theology of gender
equity that has influenced organizational policy and practice. The process
of creating a gender equity statement was part of a new program coordi-
nation effort they named Rethinking the Organization. In addition to
addressing crosscutting issues including gender equity, this team's Rethinking project includes a structured process to lower the internal walls that
have existed between their three program areas, says Jeff, who is in charge
of the effort. Before having the structure of the Rethinking project, "we
had no way to integrate our crosscutting issues," he adds. Now the team
is at work on another crosscutting issue. They are examining how their
work can and should create capacity (for self-determination and change)
among the countries and peoples they serve as well as in the organization
itself. This effort is, by the way, an excellent example of how one team reflects together.

Similar values and a strong belief in the mission of the organization sustain this team as they work very hard to integrate their programs and become explicit about shared values. I spoke to them about believing in the organization and in the right of both men and women to serve the mission of the organization equally. The strong connection between mission and gender equity comes in part from the fact that this organization serves poor countries where the suffering of women and children caused by the limited lives of women is shockingly apparent. It's something to be overcome in order for this organization to achieve its mission.

○

Kathryn Frames the Issues

On the gender issues and working toward a gender equity statement, this group really did work as a team. Some deep thinking went into it. We're the cheerleaders for gender equity in the organization, both with our program partners and internally with our staff here. It will be interesting to see how much we have internalized the gender equity commitment.

The gender equity statement itself went through a whole process. It was written in 1994 and revised in 1998. It all started with our program partners, because we always have had this focus on working with marginalized women in our projects overseas. Because of that we've always been aware of the extra burdens of women in the countries we serve. We wondered how we could address this, and possibly move some of our women's projects to be more gender-balanced. Because of this process, we also said, "How do we apply gender equity to ourselves as an organization?" We looked at board issues and staff recruitment. We keep on evaluating every so often with a checklist to see how we are doing, what the weaknesses in our own program are, and what the strengths are too. It has been a fairly participatory process, again, more among the senior management than among the whole organization.

We have achieved some gender equity in the numbers of staff we have in senior management. That's a real shift. When I came here, I was the only woman who reported to the then-executive director out of six senior managers. Now we are pretty much even as men and women in senior management. Among the support staff, it's ironic that we had a much better balance before. Now you walk around this office and it's predominantly female. When we advertise for assistants or for secretarial positions, we just do not get male applicants.

We want to keep testing how we are walking our talk. How does our commitment to gender equity play out in orientation of staff? How do we explain to people how we even got to this commitment in this organization? Why is it about us and not just about our overseas partners?

Now that we have this mixed team, I'd like to think we are doing pretty well at issues like inclusive language, recognizing different people's gifts around the table, and other things that make a difference. Sometimes these things come out jokingly around the table as we talk to each other. I never know how much is gender and how much is other personality issues, or just our different ways of doing things. I look around and see a real diverse groups of gifts in this senior leadership team. There's really a nice blend—for the most part complementary. And the conflicts that come up are usually substantive and not personal. I'd like to know how much is because we focus on the gender differences and how much is some other influence.

When I became president, this was an incredibly well-managed organization. People knew what their jobs were and were very focused. It was great at maintenance. I was excited about the possibility to say, "If everything is running so well, what's the next step?" Gender equity and capacity building as issues that cut across all departments came out of our first strategic planning process, but were not applied so much internally until recently when we started this Rethinking the Organization project and began working more across departments. We're changing the culture. The walls between departments are still up, but it's much more open. There is less of a sense of "my department" and "your department." Instead, people see that they have a set of tasks and skills, but they can't do those tasks or use their skills well unless they coordinate with others. In that sense there is much more identification with the mission than there was in the past. I attribute a lot of our success to the professionalism and the passion for our mission. Those are two key elements that would characterize everybody here.

○

The Team Comments . . .

JEFF: Our work on gender equality began with training, laying out a few concepts, discussing those concepts, describing the rationale for gender equity including both the efficiency and the equity arguments, then formulating a draft statement to see where we were. Then we said, "Now that we know about this, what is this organization going to do about it?" The result is the gender equality statement we wrote and adopted.

Speaking of the specific gender equity steps we have taken since then, we've had changes in our personnel policy related to family leave. In the personnel manuals for our field staff we have provided input on gender equity issues. We had implicit sexual harassment policies in those manuals, but now we have explicit policies. That's formally how I would see it present in how the organization works.

SUZANNE: Kathryn has created discussion groups on different topics—one being gender equity—to which she is very committed.

JONATHAN: There are so many blessings that help us to see beyond gender, and also to see what a team requires of us, to be to each other one fraction of what we know we need to be to people outside, to our partners overseas. Remember the partnership theme we have, whereby the mobilization, consensus building, and all that we do is done through the methodology of working with overseas partners. This organization does not have staff overseas, it has overseas organizations that we view as equals.

KENLYNN: Because gender equity is a crosscutting theme in our strategy, the men here are very sensitive to gender issues. Our partner organizations overseas also know it's a priority. If they want to be funded by this organization they have to work on gender equity. The sad thing is that, while gender equity is a value in our overseas projects, the men and women in our partner organizations who work with other interfaith groups experience the same old thing. The men in the project teams are assumed to be the leaders. If the men do not bend over backwards to give the women a chance, the women are not heard.

JOE: The much greater emphasis we have now on gender as a program issue as well as an issue that has to do with how we deal with staff, and the kinds of jokes we don't tell . . . certainly arises in part out of Kathryn being a woman because she feels gender issues in an existential way that her predecessor—both being a man and being from a very different generation—never felt. But I think the generational change and the changing context in which we all work—both culturally and legally—have had as much to do with our openness and ability to work in a mixed-gender setting as the fact that Kathryn became president.

SUZANNE: It has been helpful to identify the two themes of gender equity and capacity building. Those two themes are woven through the proposals we get from overseas partners now in a more consistent way.

KENLYNN: We all have a commitment to the work of the organization. That means helping the poorest of the poor no matter what country they live in or what race or gender they are. Our own diversity goes far beyond gender. We try to have a diverse staff so we can learn from each other and serve our constituents better. If we were all Anglos trying to work in the Southern Hemisphere, our integrity would be lacking. Even the Anglos have a background of being born or having lived in the countries we serve. Our mix of experience comes out in so many wonderful ways.

JONATHAN: At the same time, I think the gender issues are overrated. I don't think gender is the defining thing on a mixed-gender team. In a sense, to be a good team, you've got to go deeper. The threshold that I think makes this work here is that you've got to have people on the team for whom gender is not the issue. To put it more positively, you've got to have people on the team who are gender-blind, who are relating to each other on the basis of shared criteria that are larger than gender. We're here to do the kinds of things that organizations try to do together, and those things, at the end of the day, are better with a mixed-gender team. There is an inescapable added value, if you like. And that's where gender is significant. The symbol I like best after the cross is the yin-yang.

JOE: The gender tension—or I guess what I would call the gender magic—is generally a positive thing here. It isn't talked about or flaunted. It's just here.

○

10

ACINGCO —

ACTING ON OUR BELIEF

THERE IS A SENSE with the Lutheran relief team that time is a-wasting. There is not a moment to lose. People in Africa, Asia, the Middle East, and Latin America are hungry, homeless, and poor. They need partners to help them reach self-sufficiency. Why then be concerned about gender equity? The answer is that gender equity is critical to the team's mission, and these people care about their mission.

The Lutheran relief team is a standout example of a team dedicated to mission, yet it is not unique in this regard. All the teams in this study care deeply about their mission. It is one critical thing that team members have in common, and it is a driving force in their success. They also believe that achieving that mission requires them to care about and advocate for gender equity. Taken together, these two beliefs represent the second way in which effective mixed-gender teams apply the criterion *believe*.

In this chapter, we'll look at what teams say about their mission and the importance to the teams of believing in a mission. Then we will return to the Lutheran relief team to see both why and how it created a gender equity statement.

The Importance of Mission

We start with the idea that there's no time to waste. It's true not only for the Lutheran relief team but also for all the teams. There are people to feed and clothe but also money to raise, good news to communicate, students to educate, couples and individuals to counsel, meals to deliver, congregations to staff, converts to baptize, children to confirm, sick to visit, older people to care for, dead to bury, youth to encourage, brides and grooms to bless, and on and on. The mission work of our nonprofit organizations is *all* so urgent. These various missions are the "shared criteria that are larger than gender" that Jonathan talked about in Chapter Nine. One man, agreeing with Jonathan's view, told me that "believing in the need to do something important together takes us beyond our gender issues." A deeper look at the teams will help us see how profound is their sense of mission.

The Lutheran Relief Team

We can begin with the Lutheran relief team here as well, because their profound sense of mission and their urgency about it drives their work and their commitment to gender equity. I noticed in the individual interviews that, unsolicited, they all brought up the value of mission. They verified Jonathan's perspective.

"We all want to do good," said Suzanne. "Everybody here wants to help the people out there—some for religious reasons, some for reasons of common humanity. That's what makes the team."

Joe, who has been with the agency the longest, agreed. "Primary to our success as a team is an honestly held and generally practiced commitment to what the overall purposes of the organization are. I don't mean that in an overly idealistic way, and we wouldn't all express it in exactly the same way, though most of us can probably quote the mission statement or come close to quoting it. But I think that honest commitment to enabling poor communities is known to be commonly held, and that's why we can work together."

They also share a commitment to the organization because they believe it is effective in achieving its mission. "There is a tremendous amount of commitment to the underlying principles and to what this organization is and does. You absorb it," Jeff said. "This is the underlying factor in our success." It's no small task for a relief organization these days to succeed. More and more, relief organizations are challenged by almost insurmountable problems worldwide (Rieff, 1999). This behooves them to "keep looking out for the good of the organization," Kenlynn added. "I wouldn't suggest anything, do anything, or try to make a recommendation that did not have the organization and its mission in its best interest. To me that's the test. I wouldn't want to waste time doing anything but what's best for this organization in carrying out its mission."

A third factor is their commitment to each other. "I never feel that my department has to take on more than another. I feel that we share accountability," Lisa said. "We are accountable to each other every day. We don't want to let each other down," Mike emphasized.

Other Teams Confirm the Commitment

Both the literature and the other teams confirm the emphasis on mission and the sense of urgency as critical for an effective team. Establishing urgency is one strategy for building team performance (Katzenbach and Smith, 1993a). A profound sense of mission galvanizes a sense of urgency for many teams. Over and over with these teams, I had the experience of people on the team bringing up a sense of mission as a factor in their success. It seems that they all understand shared criteria beyond gender issues.

The secret of our success, said one man who works in an educational institution, "is the idea that we are servants. We are doing something beautiful for our church, our world, and especially our students. We are helping them grow in their spiritual lives and discern their vocation. We have this perspective for each of us personally, for the team, for the students, for the church, and for the world. That creates a foundation. Our goal is not to make money or gain prestige." A woman in this team agreed. "We all believe in our project. We believe in trying to provide the best possible guidance for the students here. We all believe in a team approach to doing that rather than that any one of us should get to do more, or could do less. There is a high level of ownership for whatever we do and for approaching it as a team." A third member of the team emphasized "our commitment to something that is outside of ourselves and outside the team, to our God and to our relationship and to building that. We don't put onto the experience of the team unnecessary expectations for our own gratification, our own need to be fulfilled, or our own affirmation. That allows the team to function freely without trying to meet everybody's needs."

For the people who don't necessarily think about themselves as team players, the mission of the team is a compelling factor. One woman commented that she "never had a conscious thought about being part of a team. I'm not a big a team person, but this team has the potential to change people's lives." Al, a member of the theological institute team presented in Chapter Sixteen, said, "Each one of us is dedicated to the mission of the school and it becomes our personal drive. I feel a personal responsibility to doing my job well. I'm basically not a team person. Sometimes it's very stressful for me to work with a team. But I realize these other people, their talent and ideas, are necessary for the work I do. I can't imagine another way of doing it."

These teams believe in what they do so strongly that the internal integrity of their teams matches the integrity of their missions. The next step is to believe that gender equity is important to mission.

Gender Equity and Mission

The Lutheran relief team is a particularly good example of a team that connects mission with gender equity. There are two platforms for doing this. First, gender equity in poor countries around the world is critical to the team's mission. Second, gender equity at home will allow the group to work as an effective mixed-gender team in partnership with poor communities. To understand the relationship between gender equity and mission, let's take a closer look at both these platforms.

Gender Equity in Our World

The disproportionate way women are affected by inequality all over the world prevents the Lutheran relief team from fully realizing its mission. They key to understanding why is in recognizing that this organization does more than give direct relief aid. It also works with overseas partners to develop the capability of poor communities to help themselves. To do this, it encourages "the active and equitable participation of both men and women in decision-making processes that affect their lives." But as long as women represent 70 percent of the 1.3 billion people living in poverty worldwide, they will never be equitably represented in decision making that directly affects their welfare. They cannot reap the full benefit of programs aimed at helping them develop their own resources. That's the first platform for a gender equity statement for the Lutheran relief team.

It should be instructive for other teams to consider what a similar perspective might mean for them in their own contexts. All they have to do is ask the question, "How does gender equity in our external world matter for our work?" Each answer will be different, but I suspect each will be important in helping us enlarge our view of the importance and urgency of gender equity. It's more than a matter of principle, though that is important. It's more than a matter of changing a patriarchal system. It's a matter of mission.

As I think about the teams in this study, I can see how they might answer this question. In the Roman Catholic Church, gender equity would mean the end of a shortage of priests. For millions of women who sit in the pews in churches all over the denominational spectrum, gender equity would mean hearing the faith professed in their own language more often. It would also mean that more little girls, as well as little boys, would consider the ministry a vocation. Gender equity in our culture would mean less domestic abuse, fewer babies born malnourished or drug addicted, fewer children growing up in poverty, fewer young women affected by eating disorders, and fewer teen pregnancies. It would also mean higher self-esteem among teenage girls and more highly educated women in the workforce receiving equal pay for equal work. It might also mean less war in the world as men and women work together more effectively on peaceful solutions to conflict. It would certainly mean the blossoming of more, many more, effective mixed-gender teams.

In these examples I am answering the question, "What is the benefit for our world?" not "What is the benefit to the women who wish to have better access?" I am making the efficiency argument. Too often we make only the equity argument, which shows the benefit to the women but not the benefit to society. We would do better to remember, as Jeff pointed out, that it's important to consider both the equity and the efficiency arguments.

Gender Equity in Our Teams

The Lutheran relief team members also believe that gender equity is important *for them*. They emphasized this point in their story. Why? Because men and women are both required. The work can't be done as well as it needs to be done unless men and women are about the tasks together. This is a perspective clearly held by the Lutheran relief team, but not only by them. All the teams in this study hold this belief in common: *they cannot do their best work unless men and women are free to work together in settings that allow both men and women equally to make their unique contributions.* In terms of mission, this is the reason gender equity is important for our teams. Effective mixed-gender teams see equity as an opportunity to learn more, establish wider social relationships, make better decisions, and achieve higher levels of satisfaction from their work.

Several years ago a friend in a conservative church, which bars women from many leadership positions, said the same thing to me in another way. He was struggling with the position of his denomination because he wanted to hire more women for the current job openings in his organization. He said, "I am not free to hire the best person for these jobs unless I am free to hire women as well as men."

To be sure, the teams in this study have experienced the value added that women and men working together can create. "It's not always easy to work together, but it's the only way to go," said Diane, a member of the theological institute team. "We enrich one another. As men and women we often approach things differently. We can have similar strengths and weaknesses, but I think as men and women we bring some ways of doing things that are proper to our gender. I don't want to go back to an all-woman world in terms of working. We [men and women] learn too much from one another."

Many others made the same point. The men and women in these teams have very different gifts, and they even have very different approaches to leadership. Some of those differences are related to gender. This adds an edge, a constant way in which teammates interpret for each other, a continuous churning of the ideas, the insights, the solutions to problems. "We do a lot of processing of thoughts, ideas, plans, issues, and questions. There is this sustained conversation between us," said one woman of her work with a male partner. "We have very different gifts," another man said of his relationship in his team. "At the same time, because we have a fundamental core on which we agree and also because we have worked together for so long, we know each other. The communication between us is very hard to put your finger on." Members of a clergy team said, "We model many more dimensions of God on Sunday morning when we do worship together than when one of us does it alone."

Team members also find that they grow as individuals in a mixed-gender team. This makes each person more skilled as a result of the teamwork. Remember Wayne's comment about his partner Erin, in Chapter Seven: "Working with Erin has changed me light-years. It has softened me up. She is constant at helping me develop a deeper spirituality. It is God's grace that she is able to challenge me and I have been open to it. I'm not sure I always would be." Barbara, whose partnership with Neely appears in Chapter Nineteen, said, "For him, I became very much an ear, a person to whom he could vent and articulate what he was thinking. He gave me a lot of freedom to develop my own corner of the world with faculty. As I look back on those years, I grew. I was nurtured."

When men and women see their gender differences from this perspective, they have moved beyond gender issues to the "gender magic" that Joe talked about in the last chapter. Effective mixed-gender teams are alike in seeing gender in this way. To put it simply, they see the possibilities and not the problems.

Creating a Gender Equity Statement

The Lutheran relief team chose to make its commitment to gender equity explicit in a written statement. This statement is not only practical but theological as well. It frames what they will do in the context of what they believe and why they believe it. A closer look at what they did can be instructive for others who wish to write a theology of gender equity.

Principles of Gender Equity

The first segment of the statement sets down the principles. It describes what the organization means by gender equity and tells why the organization should focus on gender equity.

> We strive to incorporate awareness, attitudes, and measures which promote gender equity through all aspects of the life of [this organization] and its partners. By gender equity we mean the pursuit of policies and actions that are just, impartial, and fair to both men and women. We strive to ensure that projects favorably impact women. Addressing the particular needs of women as well as men in their respective communities and strengthening their voices in planning, implementation, monitoring, and evaluation enhances the impact and sustainability of development efforts.

Notice that the statement of principle does four things. First, it states a purpose for the whole document. This purpose includes not only "awareness" of gender equity as an issue but also "attitudes and measures." Thus we should understand the statement as attempting not only to inform those who read it but to enlist support and ultimately change behavior. It is also important that the statement apply to the organization and its overseas partners, even though those partners are independent. We shall see in the implementation section how the organization *will relate to its partners* in terms of gender equity.

Second, the statement of principle defines what the organization means by gender equity. In its definition, gender equity includes both men and women. Thus although practical applications of the statement will focus on women's position in the world because of gender inequities, the statement itself concerns both men and women as well as policies and actions as they affect both men and women. The third sentence clarifies the emphasis on women, stating that the organization will implement this policy by "ensuring that projects" through which the organization achieves its mission "favorably impact women."

Finally, the last sentence in the statement of principle tells why the organization is creating this document. The aim is to enhance both the impact and the sustainability of the organization's development efforts. This is another way of saying that the organization cannot achieve its mission without greater gender equity, at least in the countries where it serves. This final sentence also identifies four ways in which the women and men in development programs will have a role in implementing this policy.

They will have stronger voices in "planning" programs that meet their needs as well as "implementing, monitoring, and evaluating" those programs. This is what the policy is intended to help the organization *do,* and it is for the purpose of achieving their mission that the organization does this.

Theological and Sociological Framework

The second section sets down the theological and sociological framework for the gender equity statement. There are eight paragraphs in this section, beginning with the phrase: "[This organization] holds to these principles of gender equity because . . ." Each paragraph then addresses a different element of the context for a statement of this kind by this particular organization. In a sense, each defines the organization's policy relative to a different issue.

> Men and women are equal in the sight of God, and both are created in God's image (Genesis 1:27). Jesus makes no gender differentiation with His love and saving grace. He commands us to treat all with dignity and justice as an expression of our Christian love.

In this paragraph, the organization states its theological position. It is a Christian organization and it establishes a biblical context for its views on gender equity. Other Christian organizations might disagree with this simple theological statement. Volumes have been written on this very subject. However, the theological statement wisely does not attempt to prove its position. Putting this statement first creates a theological context for all that follows in this section.

> We maintain a commitment to social justice and equity in development. We believe all people have a right to live in dignity and in control of their lives with equitable access to natural resources, economic resources, and basic services such as education and health care.

This paragraph states the organization's social policy. It follows naturally from the theological position. This organization believes in the rights of all people. The sentence further suggests what those rights are. In the American context, it seems hard to argue with a social policy that places the equal rights of people front and center. But not all societies would agree with this either. Wars are fought over issues like this. But again, the organization wisely makes no attempt to justify its position.

Women and girls suffer disproportionately. They represent 70 percent of the 1.3 billion people living in poverty worldwide. Violence, illiteracy, malnutrition, overwork, injustice, and access to health care and education are generally worse for women than they are for men. Women are also underrepresented in decision-making structures and other positions of power. We encourage the active and equitable participation of both women and men in the decision-making processes that affect their lives.

This paragraph summarizes the environmental conditions. It provides very important information as context for a gender equity policy. First it provides the relevant statistic, and then it explains the meaning of the statistic. With this information in hand, one can hardly wonder why the organization will put emphasis on the needs and concerns of women in the world. Again, this section draws conclusions about the meaning of the statistics but wisely makes no attempt to justify those conclusions. In a closing sentence, this paragraph says what the organization's response to the statistics will be. It is the aim of this organization to place women in an equitable position with men, relative to self-determination. It is not the organization's aim to concern itself with women alone, in spite of the statistics.

We want to uplift the current and potential contributions women bring to the world as leaders. We seek to help women empower themselves so that they may more fully develop their capacities as agents of positive social change in their families, communities, nations, and the world.

This paragraph states the specific concern of the organization relative to women. It might be called the organization's women's policy. It explains the intent of the gender equity policy as helping women to empower themselves. It follows from the last section, which explicitly discussed the need of both men and women for self-determination and the limited opportunities women have for self-determination.

Men and women need to work together to learn more about each other and their relationship to one another. Each of us needs to learn to truly respect each other's contributions in the household, community, workplace, and nation. Both men and women should be fully incorporated into the reevaluation of our current power structures. We seek to encourage the empowerment of women and men so that each may exercise power in equitable, though often different, ways.

This paragraph tells what needs to change. It might be called the organization's change policy relative to the social relationship between men and women. It is significant in defining a role for both men and women. It identifies multiple arenas appropriate for the contributions of both men and women, addresses the power imbalance between men and women, and acknowledges that men and women are different in how they use power and personal influence in the arenas of "household, community, workplace, and nation."

> We recognize that there are different understandings of gender and we celebrate the equitable aspects of traditional customs. However, we can neither condone nor take part in practices which violate the rights of either women or men. The full realization of all such rights is essential for the empowerment of individuals. We do not seek to minimize the value of traditional customs and practices. However, we do seek to eliminate oppression in all of its forms, and to create awareness when customs and traditions become obstacles to the life and dignity of human beings.

This paragraph might be said to describe a policy toward cultural differences. Given the scope of this organization's work, this is a crucial element of the overall gender equity statement. Because the organization works in cultures that do not promote the equitable treatment of women, it must state its position relative to these inequities. Although honoring cultural differences, the organization clearly states that it puts the rights of individuals and the need for empowerment first. Again, this is a position that many cultures around the world would not espouse. The organization does not try to justify its position but simply states it as a context for the action steps to follow.

> We assert that local leadership must play a key role in order to genuinely affect the lives of women positively and sustainably.

In this short paragraph, the organization states its policy relative to local participation in achieving gender equity. Notice that it concerns itself not only with affecting women positively but also with providing for a "sustainable" difference. Achieving sustainable change is especially dependent on local participation.

> We recognize the need to learn more about gender equity in our organization and in our relief and development efforts. We will continue

to work toward the goal of gender equity recognizing that gender integration is a process.

At the last, the organization takes a learning stance, stating in this paragraph that it intends to continue its own effort to learn about gender equity. This is its organizational policy relative to the issue. This section prepares the way for change in the overall statement, should conditions or information about gender equity merit such change. The process approach to gender equity stated in this final segment also allows the organization to remain open and flexible.

Throughout this document, we can note how carefully the authors have *balanced* the issue of gender equity. Never is the concern only for women. Yet because of the statistical evidence against equity for women, the implementation will emphasize the needs of women. This point is made in eight places in this document in the first two sections.

Action Steps

In the final section, the statement outlines action steps for the organization and its overseas partners.

> [This organization] confirms its commitment to promote the equality of women and men as an ongoing learning process by:
>
> 1. Adopting gender equity as a crosscutting and organization-wide issue
> 2. Constantly examining our governance and management to identify, eliminate, and prevent gender inequality and bias
> 3. Striving for balanced representation in our board and management positions
> 4. Requiring gender training for all staff members at headquarters and in the field
> 5. Maintaining a commitment to an annual institutional review of how far we have progressed in gender integration
> 6. Focusing on advocacy, education, and communication with our constituency
> 7. Accompanying our partners through exchange and training as they seek to deepen their understanding, commitment, and competence regarding gender equity

8. Engaging in dialogue with our partners at planning, implementation, and evaluation stages of projects

9. Gathering and disseminating gender assessment tools, methodologies, and approaches to our partners

10. Sharing with our partners particularly effective practices regarding gender equity that have been developed and applied

11. Gathering sex-specific data for all phases of a project

The eleven action steps in this final section are divided into two parts. The first five deal with the organization itself and what it will do to promote gender equity. The next six deal with the relationship between the organization and its partners around the world. Points five and eleven are significant in indicating how outcomes will be measured internally (point five) and among partner organizations (point eleven).

A comparison of the verbs in the first five and the last six points show that this organization has *control* internally and *influence* externally with partner organizations through which it provides service. It can require gender training and commit to annual review and adopt gender equity as a crosscutting issue. In relation to external partners, however, it will advocate, educate, communicate, accompany, disseminate, and share. This difference does not mean that the organization is unlikely to be successful in the field. More and more organizations are crossing their own boundaries to work with partners and even former competitors on issues of mutual concern and benefit. It's actually a good sign that this organization has positioned itself to implement a policy with flexibility, using collaborative practices with its partners around the world.

Guidelines for Other Organizations

For each organization, of course, a gender equity statement will be different, depending on the environment in which the organization works, its issues, its scope of influence, and a number of other factors. Organizations wishing to learn from the example provided here might consider the following elements in a gender equity statement:

• *What is our purpose?* A statement of purpose ought to begin the document. As with this example, this section should cover both the purpose of the statement itself and an explanation of why a gender equity statement is needed. The need should be congruent with the organization's mission. In the example here the need is to improve the impact and sustainability of development efforts. This need is congruent with the organization's mission, which is to alleviate suffering, enable marginalized people to realize their God-given potential, and promote a peaceful, just, and sustainable global community.

• *How do we define gender equity?* The definition also ought to come in the first section. It's important for each organization to say clearly what it means by gender equity. Taken together, this and the previous question constitute the *what.* They identify *what issue* the organization is addressing and *to what purpose* the organization addresses it.

• *What do we believe?* A gender equity statement ought to be based on the values of the organization writing it. It's a matter of defining what the organization believes as a framework for the statement. In the example we have critiqued, the values have a theological and a social justice framework. They are outlined in the first, second, and fifth paragraphs of the second section.

• *What is our scope?* In order to write an appropriate gender equity statement, the organization will have to determine its scope of influence. The scope addresses where or how the organization works based on its mission. In the example, the scope of influence for the organization is covered in the fourth paragraph of the second section. If this scope of influence makes sense in light of the organization's mission, it is appropriate. Each organization will have a different scope of influence based on this test.

• *What is our context?* To answer this question, the organization must know its external environment. Factors in the environment drive the need for a gender equity statement. The important factors for any given organization will depend again on the organization's mission. In the example, worldwide statistics about the condition of women (paragraph three) are the key, because the organization is concerned with development around the world. For a congregation, the relevant statistics might be the number of women clergy relative to the number of women in seminary. In addition to statistics, there may be other contextual issues relevant to gender equity that the organization should address in its statement. In the example, these include cultural differences, local autonomy, and the limited information that is available to the organization on gender equity in its programs (paragraphs six through eight).

The three foregoing questions—addressing values, scope, and context— are the *why.* Taken together, they summarize why the organization is writing a gender equity statement.

• *What will we do?* Because action is much more concrete than purpose, definition, values, scope, and context, it's easy to understand this part of the statement. This is the *how*. It tells how the organization will respond. It's important for each organization to consider all the arenas in which it ought to act. In the example, the action steps cover U.S. response at the headquarters office as well as response with partner organizations around the world. In order to determine arenas of response, an organization needs only to look at its structure for answers.

Finally, the order of presentation in the statement ought to flow from *what* to *why* to *how,* as in the example, though it need not necessarily be divided into three parts. Ultimately, the commitment of the organization to the statement is as important as the statement itself. There is a delicate counterpoint here. A written statement helps make the commitment real simply by virtue of the fact that it is there in black and white. Nevertheless, without the commitment of real people to the real work of gender equity, the statement is meaningless. As an example of this point, consider action step two in the example. One might criticize this step as not very measurable. The Lutheran relief organization might do just about whatever it pleases here, and it might do nothing. To be sure, this action step could be more concrete. Yet because of the commitment of the people to gender equity, it works as it is. This team clearly demonstrates a commitment to "constantly examining their governance and management to identify, eliminate, and prevent gender equity and bias." This commitment is the reason they contacted me, wishing to be interviewed to examine how they are doing on their own gender equity.

PART FOUR

NAMING AND INCLUDING

11

THE SPIRITUAL
FORMATION TEAM

DEMONSTRATING THE COMMITMENT
TO KNOW EACH OTHER

IN THE ROMAN CATHOLIC TRADITION, the human, spiritual, pastoral, and intellectual formation of seminary students are all concerns of the seminary. At one seminary in California, a mixed-gender team is responsible for the spiritual life of seminarians. This spiritual formation team has been in existence for six years. Its duties include preparing and executing all activities that support the spiritual readiness of seminary students and faculty, including retreats, workshops, days of recollection, and other activities. This assignment is only a small part of the job of each person on the team. Among their many other duties, the priests on the team provide spiritual direction for individual seminarians. Women are barred by Roman Catholic polity from this role in a seminary.

Sister Cecilia, a Dominican religious, is the only woman on the team and one of four women faculty members in administrative positions at the seminary. In addition to serving on this team, she is the director of formation, coordinating the development and evaluation of students in the four areas listed earlier. After six years on the team, Cecilia will be leaving the seminary this year to return to life with her own community. In addition to Cecilia, there are four priests on the team. Rick has just joined the team as supervisor, replacing Austin, who supervised the team for its first five years. Other team members are Jack, Binh, and Jorge. Both Cecilia and Jorge are Mexican, Binh is Vietnamese, and Jack and Rick are Euro-Americans. The diverse team was built intentionally to serve this seminary, which has ten different ethnic groups (including Hispanic, African, Asian, and Pacific Islanders) represented in its student body of eighty-six seminarians.

I interviewed each team member individually, and then we gathered for a discussion about the challenges of working in a diverse team in a male-dominated institution.

○

Who Is This Team?

CECILIA: I was raised in a traditional Mexican family where the mother was the heart of the family but the father was definitely the head. Women were respected and their opinions were expected, but so was obedience and acquiescence to men. I attended Catholic schools and saw women in leadership roles there. Although encouraged by my parents to get a higher education and a profession, it wasn't until I became a Dominican sister of Mission San Jose that I had an opportunity to work with men as an equal.

I was trained by my community in the areas of spirituality and human formation. Because of my background in spirituality I was a good person to be part of this team. Being in an all-male environment was totally new. If anything, I'm used to an all-female environment because I live in religious community and I've worked with women. But in the few times I have worked with men, I have found it very easy to relate to them. In one teaching experience in my past I was vice principal working with a male principal. That taught me a lot about communicating with men, dealing with the male ego. That was the first time I had to figure out how to communicate with a man in a way he can hear it and we can get the job done. That was good training for me. I hadn't thought about it that way until now.

JORGE: I was an architect until the mid-1960s when I began my journey to the priesthood. I was born in Mexico City in 1930, part of a large middle-class family. There were nine of us—my parents, my sister, my five brothers, and myself. We always had a lot of discussion over meals. We had the Hispanic tradition and also, in a way, the French tradition from my Swiss grandmother. We talked a lot. There were no sharp distinctions between men and women. That background served me a lot. I studied architecture in Mexico and Europe and then practiced architecture and taught at a university. Then I was commissioned to travel around the world to research the teaching and learning methods in architecture in thirty-six different countries. Through these opportunities, being in touch with different cultures, my horizons expanded and I started to ask myself deep questions about the meaning of life in general and meaning of my life. With all this turmoil in my head and in my heart, my sister, who was studying to become a nun, suggested that I have a retreat with Thomas Merton. He put me in touch with the Missionaries of the Holy Spirit. I now belong to this order, which was founded in Mexico City in 1914 by a French Marist priest under the influence of a Mexican laywoman, a great mystic, Concepción Cabrera. The order came to the United States originally to help the *braseros* (migrant workers).

I have worked with many mixed-gender teams, in the university when I was teaching and in our architectural firm in Mexico, and in the firms from the United States that we worked with on projects. I also worked with mixed teams in the parish, when I was a parish priest. It is not something new for me to work with women, but this is my first experience in an all-professional mixed-gender team in the church.

RICK: I am a diocesan priest. I grew up in a Catholic family in Southern California. Both my parents were active in church life, and I suspect this gave me an early lesson in church as a place where men and women worked and ministered together, although (unfortunately) not with equality. I was ordained in 1978 and served three parishes in the Los Angeles diocese before coming to St. John's. I have the fewest academic credentials but the most parish experience of anyone on the team.

I am here specifically to head the team. The rest of the team sought me out as their new leader. I had given a retreat about eighteen months ago, and they must have liked what they heard! I took three months for prayer and consultation to make the decision to join this team. Prior to beginning my last parish assignment, I had studied spirituality with a specific focus on spiritual direction at Washington Theological Union. This experience confirmed in me the need for and the richness of collaborative ministry, especially in the area of men and women working together for the good of the church. Coming here was a chance to do it. I came here in June of 1998.

BINH: I was born in North Vietnam. My parents moved the family to the south when the war started. I entered the seminary of the Congregation of the Missions (Vincentians) when I was twelve years old. In 1975, when I was eighteen, I left Vietnam on a boat with other refugees. From my family, only my one brother was with me. We were at sea for two months, a part of which we spent on an island. We went to Thailand, Malaysia, and Singapore looking for safety. Eventually we ended up in the Philippines. There were twenty-eight of us on the boat when we started out, and three more were born by the time we landed in the Philippines. I delivered one of those three babies. I finished my seminary training in the United States. I feel more American in my church context than Vietnamese. In Vietnam the church is still very conservative. I work part time at the seminary and am also superior of my local community.

JACK: I grew up in a Catholic ghetto and entered the seminary when I was fourteen. In those days you couldn't even go to another denomination's church—even for a funeral or a wedding. Thank goodness that's changed! I went into the Jesuit order for two years because I wanted to develop my own spirituality. It was a very intense formation, both spiritual and personal. I had gotten ordained because in my family, in that ghetto, the best thing I could be was a priest. I wanted to do what would be respected. When I started living from inside that changed. I did not need the external motivation and affirmation, but I stayed in the priesthood even though I did not stay in the Jesuit order. It has been an interesting journey. The capstone to my openness to diversity was my experience in Berkeley at the Graduate Theological Union. We had what all of us dream about—real people, all different kinds of people in my classes. Working with women on the gender relationships in six very diverse parishes also contributed. I served in several large parishes, with over five thousand members, and have worked with many mixed-gender teams in that setting. Then in 1987 I came here and was the spiritual director until 1991. I actually led spiritual formation without a team. Then Austin came and we decided to work together. We both thought it was impossible to do it alone. The team evolved. It happened intentionally, but out of our talking about it over time. We said at that time that we really need to get a woman's perspective. Cecilia came. And then Jorge came. And Binh became available more recently.

○

What's Involved in Knowing Each Other?
JACK: My first reaction is that it's a process and it happens gradually. We never sat down and said, "Tell me about yourself" to each other. A lot also happens in our praying together. Another way we get to know each other is by the perspectives we bring to the work of the

team about certain issues. Lastly, when we go off and have fun together monthly. In these interchanges we get to know each other.

CECILIA: The fact that we are a spiritual formation team means that we are talking about spiritual topics, which we may not talk about with just anyone. That's a way of knowing each other that moves us into deeper levels of conversations than would be typical with other members of the faculty.

JORGE: We get to know each other through the conversation that goes on in our meetings—the way we look at the projects or problems we have to deal with.

BINH: By the way we react to each other when we talk. Different team members have different reactions. But we are on the same boat. In that way our relationship develops.

RICK: One thing that helps us get to know each other perhaps better than another group might is that we are all spiritual directors. We all have the skills of listening which we bring with us. We don't leave them somewhere else. We use them all the time. We are able to listen at a different level—I think by intention.

o

How Much Is Knowing Each Other Dependent on Knowing Yourselves?

JACK: A lot.

RICK: I've only been here since June. It's a two-way street. I have found a very welcome environment in this group, where I can be me. As I get to know myself better, I can be as accepting of the others as they are of me. It goes back and forth.

JORGE: Because of our work with our own spiritual directors we have more awareness of who we are in this kind of collaborative work. We know how we feel about working in this way, with our team and with our colleagues in this team.

RICK: One of the things that helps us in that sense is being in a formation center. Our focus is helping men here understand who they are.

You can't ask that question without having the question rebound to yourself constantly.

BINH: When we work with the men here, they help us to know who we are by their reaction.

CECILIA: As a woman in this team, I was surprised by how much I had to reflect on what it meant to be a woman in this setting—as well as being myself. I have found that the environment in the team is very conducive to that kind of reflection and honesty. We give each other permission to be authentic. There is a lot of freedom in the group. This group has helped me to be in the larger environment of the seminary.

JACK: I would underline what Cecilia has said about how easy it is to be myself in this group. Because I am more of an introvert, it's harder for me to be the same in the larger community as I am in this group.

○

How Does This Team Work?

RICK: I'd say of all the people I've worked with in ministry, the members of this team are the least possessive of their own ideas, very willing to adjust, to build on what I do or on someone else's idea. It's the first real team I've worked with. It's a difficult experience to come by in parish work. Through the crucible of experience with each other, we have come to trust each other. We have the freedom that comes from trust. What I find surprising is that the others included me in that from the get-go. There was no testing period.

JORGE: This team works very hard. We meet twice a week together and once a week with our rector. But in fact, we are working continuously together. We share many things together. We have our own days of recollection; we celebrate a lot and we take time to pray together. I've never had that kind of experience with a team.

CECILIA: In our team meetings we often start with brainstorming and work to specific ideas that have energy for the group. Then tasks are assigned to specific people. Our former director would often ask someone to take an assignment. He would tell us why he was asking that person. Sometimes this comes from others in the group too. Because we work so closely together and meet so often we can really talk to each other about any topic that comes up. We have some very painful conversations about things. In decision making, we tend to be pretty like-minded and come to consensus. We don't take votes. If we don't have good clear consensus, we keep working until we do. Everything takes longer this way, but there is a high level of ownership. Whatever we do, it's all of us doing it. The men on the team are not impatient with the fact that it takes longer. They are totally committed to the process because it produces results.

RICK: We prepare ourselves by meeting regularly even if we have no business. Once a month we get away for an afternoon and evening, to relax and have fun. That's the basis of it. We build our relationship with each other as people, and from that we do our work together. A lot of it is simply being around each other. The presence of this team challenges the faculty to avoid getting caught up in their academic life of constant study and preparation for class and becoming isolated. We make a conscious effort not to do that. Apart from our scheduled times together, there are times when we will gather together to relax and just unwind. We could always do that by ourselves, but we choose to do it together.

After everything we do, we have some kind of evaluation or assessment. We are able to acknowledge, celebrate our successes, and seriously look at problems without becoming morose. If there is a shortfall on the part of any one person, the others rally instead of isolate. There is no finger-pointing, and I find that particularly unique. I've been in situations where that's all there was. It goes back to a distinct lack of possessiveness. Everything belongs to everybody on this team.

BINH: What we do is so effective because we share with each other. We talk with each other before we do anything. So we learn from each other, help each other. Last year I was new and the people who had been here longer helped me. They want me to have some experience. They could do it easily without me, but they want me to have this experience.

CECILIA: The secret of our success is the commitment of the members that it be a success, the willingness to share our "whole selves" in the team, the willingness to be vulnerable and honest about what we think and feel. This year we see evidence of this willingness to be vulnerable, but it's not at the same level for those of us who have been in it the longest. We have deeper trust to build with new team members.

○

What Does Diversity Mean to You?

JORGE: The most obvious is diversity of race. There is also diversity in life experience. One of the other elements of diversity that is very important for me is the way that people understand God's presence in their lives in unique ways. Some are very much aware of God almost in mystical ways. Others are very unaware. They are not introspective at all.

JACK: A lot of our diversity has to do with our formation, like Father Binh coming from Vietnam and Jorge coming from Mexico and living in many places in Europe and all over the world. Even my own Anglo background makes me different from them. One of our projects here is multiculturalism. We have to be real careful that we don't look at it as, "Here are Asians, and here are Hispanics, and here are Anglos," but at the whole question, including women and men, differences in sexual orientation, and all of it. Diversity is so much deeper and so much subtler than just race.

CECILIA: For me it's a matter of the uniqueness of each person. If you have two people you have diversity. Being mindful of that requires being conscious of the diversity and respecting it. We have a common humanity, but in each person it's going to be expressed differently. That's not a threat to me but an enrichment for me. The ethnic diversity of our community here at the seminary is just the tip of the iceberg. There are all kinds of ways we are diverse. As a woman here, I find myself in a culturally different environment. A missionary once told us that the gospel requires multiculturalism. Because Jesus dealt with everyone as a unique individual, there is no way we can impose one culture as a standard for everyone. That was a profound statement for me. We have a long way to go in understanding the implications of multiculturalism. It's an extremely important topic for us in the church today. Maybe because cultural diversity has caught our attention enough, we're willing to broaden the topic to look at diversity in general and to realize that we're just beginning to explore it. Sometimes I get uneasy with people who say, "We're all human." Yes, it's true we are all human, but if we are going to understand one another accurately, we need to connect with one another in terms of the cultural groups we see ourselves identified with.

○

Has the Diversity of the Team or
the Seminary Influenced Your Work?

RICK: From my perspective, in the seminary community I'm not sure we've gone very far in letting it impact us. There is a lot of leveling the playing field, saying, "We are all human." There is a nod to diversity and the differences that exist, but then a retreat into "our common humanity" and "let's not deal with it." I think there's a tremendous amount of work that still needs to be done to open people up so they can find a space in their own lives to let diversity in, to challenge them. The recognition is there, but the reality has not penetrated. On the team, it's not something we dwell on but we're very open to the different perspectives people bring. We really do listen to each other and find ourselves pushed, challenged, and enriched.

BINH: Our students are multicultural. We have Anglo students, students from Africa, students from the Pacific Rim. We also have a lot of Hispanic students. Because we have different ethnic backgrounds on the team, this helps us deal with the students better, especially as we help them with their spiritual formation. We are better able to understand how each ethnic group experiences God in their lives and how their culture has had an effect on that. I think having different ethnic backgrounds represented on our team helps a lot.

CECILIA: I think it's valued on the team. Before we had any non-English-speaking members, we talked about the value of having somebody who was Spanish-speaking and who would bring that perspective. I was hired because the team wanted a woman. There is a value to having different experiences and points of view represented. When there was a possibility of adding Binh, the value was that he comes from a different culture and could bring a different perspective to our work, a sensitivity to students who come from that culture and that part of the world. In this sense, we place value on diversity. We value having a mix in the group.

BINH: For myself, I have been here twenty years. A part of my education was in Vietnam. A part of it was here. I react differently from people who have recently come from Vietnam. I also react differently when I work with Vietnamese than when I work with Americans. That diversity is in myself. Then when I see the different people on the team and realize they can contribute in different ways, it helps me to see that everybody has some good things.

○

How Has Gender Diversity Influenced Your Work?

JORGE: I was used to working in a plurisexual environment (that is, it included, in addition to heterosexual men and women, people who are homosexual or bisexual). In my experience as a layperson I was very much used to the presence of women in my life. I don't feel any discomfort with Cecilia in our team. In fact, I would like to have more women present and work in a more open setting. This would make the presence of women more enriching for me.

RICK: There was no change for me—to work in a situation like this. Twenty-two years in the parish involved a lot of work with women. The change for me is to work mostly with men. To be immersed again in a largely male environment is a step in the opposite direction.

JACK: We thought it was very important to have a woman on the team, not just as a token but because of the gifts she could bring to the spiritual arena, to the formation of the students. I feel almost a panic inside now that Cecilia is leaving, and coincidentally the other sisters who work here are leaving us too. I would hate to see this become more and more a male bastion. As they leave us, we see the diversity they have brought. There are so many gifts that Cecilia brings to the group, a whole different perspective! And yet it's one I can relate to.

Her presence gives me permission to access the feminine in myself. . . . That's one of the incredibly valuable things Cecilia brings. Not just because she is a woman but because of the particular unique woman she is. Her understanding of spirituality, her own commitment to prayer, her work on herself—she has been very careful not to make them political. For example, with inclusive language, she has been very understanding and patient—even though she feels very strongly— not to make these things "Cecilia's issues" because then they would be dismissed.

RICK: There is great value to the church and to this seminary in a mixed-gender team. Everyone sees a group of people working together as a team, no clergy dominating, no strong feminist trying to forge her way and creating strife in the process, women and men responsible to each other in an all-male environment. It's a challenge to the students, I know. They see that women have as much to offer as any man. But there are students who struggle with the idea of a woman in leadership.

CECILIA: It is part of our mission at this seminary to both have a collaborative approach to formation and teach the men collaboration. The only way we can model that is by having a variety of people be part of their formation experience. So there are laypeople and religious on faculty as well as priests. This has been true for a long time. At the time I was hired, they were just creating the spiritual formation team. Jack and others working in spiritual formation at the time felt that the seminary very much needed a feminine presence. The area of spiritual formation was another place we could have someone join the faculty who didn't have to be a professor. This opened the way for a woman, for me. But it is very hard to attract women to the seminary. It's not a university; we have a small number of students. But most significantly, it's the all-maleness of the institution.

JORGE: It is a real privilege for me to be on this mixed-gender team. Cecilia is a very special person and a very important addition to our group. But I wouldn't be uncomfortable working with another woman. My experiences working with women is that they are brilliant people and they bring their own sensibility and way of looking at things, which is different from a man's perspective. We are complementary.

CECILIA: I deal with the other team members as individuals first and not first as men. Second, I apply the same rule to myself. I try not to think that everything I am thinking and feeling is because I am a woman but because I am a person. Third, I believe in the need for good priests and I want them to be well formed. Fourth, I let go of the expectation that I can change the world. I am making a difference just being here and being a part of the students' formation. This would be true if I were a man, but more specifically because I am a woman it is true. The male faculty seem to feel that very strongly and I get it from students too. They tell me what a difference it makes to have women here because we see things from a different perspective. Finally, I have to be willing to be prophetic. Sometimes I am whether I want to or not, because I see things so differently.

BINH: It's good for our students today. Later, if they become parish priests, they will know what women can do for the church. In the Catholic church in the past, men dominated officially recognized ministry positions. Now women can hold more positions in ministry.

○

12

NAMING EACH OTHER

KNOWING EACH OTHER DEEPLY is a prerequisite for working together effectively. I call this *naming*. It seems like a simple thing to know someone's name, but it is not. We are not concerned with acquaintanceship here but rather with the deeper knowing of one another that is necessary for us to work effectively together. Naming, as we can see from the story of the spiritual formation team, covers a lot of territory and includes many reflective tasks that help us know one another better as individuals and as men and women. Learning to respect each other, building trust, understanding our differences as men and women and as leaders with a variety of styles, seeing and acknowledging each other's skills and strengths, accepting each other's legitimate calling to leadership in the church environment, and assigning value to each other are all a part of *naming* each other. We can hardly complete these tasks satisfactorily without at some level confronting our own personal prejudices and striving to overcome them. Thus we will address these final two reflective criteria—*naming* and *including*—in this and the next chapter.

In this chapter, as a foundation for understanding the tasks of naming each other, we will consider the importance of naming in knowing ourselves and each other. We will look at the difficulties that women have in knowing themselves and writing the script of their own lives, a difficulty largely misunderstood by men. Finally, we shall consider what it means to name each other as leader, follower, and partner.

Naming Ourselves and Each Other

Knowing ourselves prepares us to know each other. The story of the spiritual formation team teaches us this vividly. Here are five people who have come together from places all over the world. Here are five people whose life experiences have been very different in fundamental ways. Their team success is based on the commitment of each individual to know himself or herself, and then to know the others in the group. It starts, for each of them as for each of us, with knowing our own names, which at a deeper level really means knowing ourselves.

What's in a Name?

My husband's profession is finding people. He is a genealogist. Most of the time he is looking for ancestors—those who have gone before in the history of a family and whose personal histories give meaning to the lives of present generations. He tells this story to illustrate how important it is to have a name and to be known by that name.

In England as in many other countries, children have long been registered by the state at birth and registered again by the church at baptism. It is usually the civil registration records that genealogists search to find ancestors or to prove the existence of an ancestor known only by word of mouth in the family. But in the British Isles, Church of England registration has for centuries taken priority over civil registration, a fact that has caused problems for genealogists since 1837. Since that date, the church has allowed parents to change the civil registration name of their infant at the time of baptism, so long as the baby is baptized within one year of birth. When they choose this option, parents are required to correct the civil registration records, but some do not. It's possible, in such cases, that the child cannot be found and charted in the family history. The family member is literally lost because civil records do not "know" the correct name. My husband documented one case in which the child, a girl, was named James at birth and later renamed Mary at baptism. It took some detective work to find this woman and document her existence for her family.

With apologies to Shakespeare, there is much in a name. In the names we are given or the names we give ourselves, we identify who we are. We distinguish ourselves from others. We define our characteristics and our tribe. We may even carry in our name some description of what we look or act like. Any investigation into the history of naming reveals all these and more meanings that we find in our names.

A pastor friend of mine tells a story that illustrates this poignantly. With other pastors, she was engaged in a project of collecting feedback from children about what they would like to see changed in the world. One young African American boy said, "I would like to change my name." When my friend shared this feedback with her colleagues later they asked her what the boy meant by his response. "I told them it means he does not like who he is, where he is, and what he is. It was all about his identity. If he had a different name, he would have a different identity," she said.

In the Native American tribes of the North American continent we can find many beautiful names that tell us in a few words about some trait of the person whose name it is: Little Bear, Turtle Woman, Cloud Dancing are simple examples that come to mind. I have always thought the names of the Native Americans so beautiful for the very reason that they reflect a deep knowing of each person in the tribe, a sense that all are endeared to the others by the traits that make them an individual and by their connection to the natural world. In *The Last of the Mohicans*, Nathaniel Hawthorne gives a fictional representation of how the tribes gave even white men and women names that spoke of what they were like or what they did. Hawthorne's character Nathaniel is called Hawkeye by the Delaware Indians and Long Rifle by the Iroquois. He is given these names because of what the tribal people observe of him. Both names speak of his bravery.

My father tells a story that illustrates this point in another way. When he was in Umpumulo teaching in the Zulu seminary in the early 1970s, his African students gave him—and indeed each of their professors—a special name. We would call it a nickname. But unlike the nicknames we give each other, the special name my father's students gave him described a special personality characteristic that was unique to him. It was a name that described my father as his students knew him. "This name was never revealed to me," my father recalls. "To this day I do not know what they really called me."

We can go back even further in human history to the advent of the poll tax in Europe to observe another significance in names. Here we find the beginning of surnaming. When there were only a few persons living in a place, there was little purpose for a second name. As villages grew in size, residents needed more than one name to identify people who had the same first name. The use of second names or surnames was the solution. In patriarchal traditions, surnames usually identify a person by the father's lineage or profession so that people in the same family have the same or similar surname. Thus John, Mary, and Elizabeth might all have the surname Baker because they were the baker's son and daughters. Henry and Charles might have the surname Peterson because they were the sons of Peter. In medieval Norway the surnames not only identified the individual in relation to the father, but also indicated gender. Sigrid who was Lavran's daughter would be known as Sigrid Lavransdätter, and John who was Lavran's son would be known as John Lavranssön. Most of the surnames we have today are variations or modernizations of the old ways we were named to identify us as belonging to one family or another.

Faith communities also recognize the meaning in names and name giving. Why else would name giving be so significant a part of baptism in the Christian community or the ritual of circumcision in the Jewish tradition? Baptism is one of the first things to identify and include us as member of the faith community in the Christian tradition. Circumcision is one of the first things that identifies a male child as a member of the Jewish community, and beginning in 1975, a different kind of naming ceremony for baby girls has become part of Jewish religious life in the liberal traditions. It makes sense that these ceremonies both claim the child as part of the religious community and give the child a name.

With a heightened awareness of naming and its importance, based on writing a first draft of this chapter, I went to visit the spiritual formation team for a second round of interviews. I was keenly aware of my responsibility to know the names and pronunciations of names for each person in the group. It was not acceptable, in my mind, that I should pronounce Jorge or Binh with any more difficulty than Jack or Rick or Cecilia. I owed them the honor of knowing their names, and this included knowing how to pronounce them.

In many ways we who are Euro-Americans have lost connection to our names. We are given names, or we change our names, to fit in. Among other things, this makes the challenge of acknowledging each other all that much greater. My friend Sue recalls her naming in this way. "I came from a family that always had Italian names," she explains. "But my mother wanted us to have 'regular names.' Her name was Annabelle and her mother was Arabella. She always told us, 'I don't want you to have the *burden* of a name like mine.' We were really giving up our cultural identity in giving up our names."

Sue's new daughter-in-law Shontashone is Vietnamese. Shontashone gave up her name when she came to America because it is hard for Americans to understand and pronounce. For many years she went by the name of Thenn because it was easier for *us*. As an adult, she has reclaimed her real name and her identity and heritage. Many young immigrant children are summarily renamed in our school systems in just this way because it is convenient for the rest of us. Their real names get mispronounced, forgotten, and lost. We give them names that are convenient for the rest of us and think we have done them a favor.

Shontashone's story is a reminder that when we lack connection to our names, we lack connection to who we are, where we came from, and where we are going. This loss makes it harder for us to acknowledge ourselves and, ultimately, each other. Perhaps the brightest sign that we may be strengthening our connection is in the popularity of genealogy, which is the fastest-growing hobby in the United States today. I hope this trend is one sign that we want to know more about our names and therefore about ourselves. If so, we will be better equipped to know each other in the future. For if we lack any knowledge of ourselves and have no interest in deeply knowing ourselves, we will be ill-equipped for the task of knowing each other in our teams. In contrast, if we have thought deeply about who we are and have done so in the context of understanding our own names, we are equipped to name each other as leader, colleague, and partner.

Writing Our Scripts

A part of knowing ourselves is knowing where we are going and why. People of faith often express this as a question of one's calling or vocation. "What is my calling in life?" they ask. One's calling may change, as Jorge's story illustrates, but it is always to a role that represents congruence between the individual's gifts and the work that needs to be done in the world. It may not, however, be congruent with social convention or with what we think we want. So there is challenge as well as possibility in knowing and taking up our calling. I recently received a letter from a dear friend, a doctor who has retired after a long career in family medicine. "It will be interesting to see what God has in mind for me next," he said. He is waiting and watching for his next calling. But we don't just wait and hope that the blinding flash of God's insight will knock us off our old path, as it did for the Apostle Paul. We must engage in our own story and our present place in life and society to discern what is right for us. Carolyn Heilbrun (1988) calls this "writing our own scripts."

Our own scripts are much more than the autobiography we all had to write in high school or college. In addition to life experience, our scripts include our hopes and dreams for the life ahead, our memories about our lives past, and our reflections about the meaning of our lives. Ned's story in Chapter Two is a good example of a portion of one person's script. Our life scripts are not literally scripts, either. Unless we are intentional about writing things down, our scripts most often take the form of a dialogue we have—with ourselves, God, others, and our world—about who we are and what we want to be and do in this life. This dialogue not only helps us acknowledge ourselves but also helps us know what we want to be a part of. Thus it helps prepare us for partnership, the task of becoming a part of something, with other people.

As we mature, our scripting should include our thoughtful consideration about the meaning of our name. It should cause us to think about
our childhood experience of our particular parents and what it has meant
to have or not have siblings. Especially in reflecting on our adolescence,
our script should include the discovery and working out of our sexual
identity, including the cultural forces and the individual role models that
have influenced us. It should also cause us to ponder our religious experience, our loyalties, and our values. As we think about our calling, our
script should ultimately inspire us to think about what we want to be,
what we are good at, and what action we want to take in the world.

The stories of the people in the spiritual formation team vividly illustrate the importance of scripts in our lives. It's easy to imagine Binh as a
young man on the refugee boat, seeking safety and asylum somewhere so
that he might continue his theological studies. Binh's script included a
hoped-for vocation as a priest. The war in Southeast Asia changed his
script somewhat, but eventually he was able to pursue his calling nonethe-
less. It took bravery and courage for him to follow that script. He has
now been safe and resettled in the United States for twenty years. Still,
how many of us here can imagine what it is like to be separated from
one's homeland forever?

Jorge's story too is poignant. A successful architect with an interesting
and challenging career, he realized after a decade in that profession that
he needed to change his script. He listened to the voices deep in his heart
and discovered from them that he was destined to live a very different life.
He went in search of the meaning of those questions and eventually
became a priest. There was much about Jorge's life in a secular profession
that he liked, even some things that he misses today. Yet no one talking
to him would ever doubt that he is living the right script. In coming to this
change, Jorge came to know himself. That personal work has also prepared him to know and greet others in his team.

Cecilia too has asked many questions about herself and her life. How
was she, as a particular woman, suited to work at an all-male seminary?
What could she contribute and how could she make her contribution? In
her own words she has told us about some of the challenges and some of
the ways the experience has caused her to reexamine herself and her leadership. This is the personal script work that has helped her know herself
and has prepared her to work as the only woman in a mixed-gender team
of five people.

Rick's and Jack's stories may not seem so unusual to us if we too are
Euro-Americans. This may be because they are quite like us. It does not
mean they have not had script work to do in their lives too. When Jack

said he grew up in a Catholic ghetto, he did not mean that he was poor. He meant that he grew up in a neighborhood where everyone was very much alike. Because of this, Jack has had to spend some time getting to know people and ideas that are different from his own. Jack also spoke of his questions about remaining a priest. In answering these questions, he had to discover many things about himself that ultimately prepared him to be a team member. Rick too has had questions about his life script. He left many years of parish ministry to come to the seminary as the leader of an already-established team. Why was this important to his life script? What did this decision mean for him? How was he equipped to take on this leadership role? Rick had to answer all these questions.

Because the members of the spiritual formation team understand the value of examining their own lives, they require the seminarians to do so as well. The activity of sharing their stories with each other "heightens their awareness and is a level of disclosure that helps them bond with one another," one team member pointed out. Students continue to work on their stories throughout seminary. At the end of the first year, they are still doing weekly sharing in groups. Personal sharing is also built into their days of recollection and their spiritual direction.

Another thing we can learn from the spiritual formation team is the way change forces us to look at our life scripts. In fact, we are most likely to think deeply about our scripts when we face a change. One woman in the interview sampling shared her decision to leave a more traditional nursing job and become a parish nurse. The change required a great deal of thinking about what was right for her and a decision to leave a teaching position after over a decade in nursing education. The journey took five years from the time that the "idea first clicked with me," she said. The parish nursing position is "very much a calling for me," she added. "I have not felt so strongly about doing something since I went to nursing school." Now, a part of her life script involves meeting new challenges in a setting where she is part of a team but has no colleagues in her own profession. This disadvantage is offset somewhat by the opportunity to have longer-term relationships with people, she said. "You move in and out of people's lives as things happen." This is part of what made it right for her. In this new role, she will be in a position to help others examine their own life scripts, as they come to her with problems, concerns, and questions.

Many other people in these mixed-gender teams shared their own life scripts. A male pastor shared his struggle to leave a difficult parish and find a new type of ministry that would better suit his gifts. He is now in campus ministry. A woman shared her decision to find work with a good team when she had always in the past preferred to work alone. A man told of his desire to promote the work of women and his decision to seek successively more challenging positions for doing this work. Examining our own lives in this way is something that we all must do if we are serious about knowing ourselves. A laywoman who has been a mother, grandmother, career woman, and wife sums it up this way: "With every one of these transitions, I have had to ask, 'Who am I?' all over again."

It is particularly important for men and women in mixed-gender teams to share their scripts with each other as they get to know each other. There are so many ways we can misunderstand or just miss each other, given all the ways we are different. Knowing our own scripts is an intentional way we can name ourselves. Sharing our scripts is an intentional way we can come to know each other.

Including a Quest Plot in Our Script

Men have historically had many possible scripts, many possible ways they can live their lives, "if they will but set their feet upon the path." They are permitted to have adventures, to decide what they will do, to take decisive action in their lives with many possible outcomes based on their own action and participation in it. Heilbrun (1988) calls this their "quest plot" (p. 48). We must acknowledge, of course, that many young men today are facing limited scripts that they often attempt to break out of by joining gangs. If we could but understand their actions in this light we would be better able to solve the problems of violence in our culture. The fact remains, however, that men are expected to and encouraged to write their own scripts (Ashe, 1997).

Women traditionally have been allowed only one life script, the conventional marriage or "erotic plot" (Heilbrun, 1988, p. 48). This is the script written for them by the patriarchal culture (Ashe, 1997). I discovered this myself when I traveled in India. At the time a divorced mother of two children, I found it impossible to explain my social position. At first my hosts would call me Mrs. Becker, assuming without question that I was married. When I explained that I was not "Mrs." they were bewildered, especially if I spoke about my children. Somehow it was impossible to explain that I was, by choice at that time, a single mother. I found it curious, in fact, that people always asked about my marital state, as though it were their right to know. After the first few encounters, I gave up and decided that while I was in India my name would have to be Mrs. Becker. Either that or I would have to pretend that I had no children.

Women who have been denied all but one possible script often live lives that are constrained. There is no model for *our* quest plot. "There are no recognizable career stages in such a life, as there would be for a man. Nor do women have a tone of voice with which to speak with authority" (Heilbrun, 1988, p. 25). We women have only the plots of men to follow. But women do not want to be honorary men. We cannot do well by simply adopting the competitive models that men have scripted for themselves. Our own scripts, and indeed our identities, may yet be too grounded in the male whose life script we join. We are too *embedded* in his quest plot to be able to write our own. "For generations, women have lived in embedded roles, roles intimately interwoven into the warp and woof of the social context. By their very embeddedness, women serve as links between other roles, between generations, between institutions, between the private and public domains" (Lipman-Blumen, 1996, p. 288). "Without such relation, women do not feel able to write about themselves; even with it, they do not feel entitled to take credit for their own accomplishments, spiritual or not" (Heilbrun, 1988, p. 24).

The need for a quest plot applies to all women, no matter what our chosen path might be. The women in my interview sampling are no exception. Fredrica, whose story we heard in Chapter Four, provides a good example because she had a twin brother. "I recall always trying to figure out the difference between us," she said in our interview. Later in her life as she approached her own ordination, she said she became "a sort of walking symbol" for other women who wanted to enter ministry. These glimpses into her past are also glimpses into the difficulty one woman had pursuing her own quest plot.

We also heard Erin's story, which included a particularly difficult period in her early life when she could not identify her quest plot. She shares with us vivid examples of the many ways she was denied access to that quest plot. I mentioned in Chapter Eight the woman who was hounded out of her first call in less than a year. She too has been wounded by people who have tried to deny her the quest plot she has chosen for her life. This kind of experience is not unique to clergy life. Just recently I talked to a laywoman who has dedicated her career to service in a church agency. She left a troubled marriage in part because her husband would not accept her desire to return to work. For years she worked for a male boss who was very critical of her work and denied her advancement. Yet she loved her work and did not see the need to change her life script. It took the advocacy of her male peers for her to receive a promotion.

Not all women have such a difficult time writing their own scripts, of course, but we all have to struggle harder than the men to be allowed our quest plot. I talked to countless women who approached mixed-gender team situations with great care, wishing to make sure that they would find a partner who would welcome them as colleagues. They did the things that all women do these days to claim their quest plots. They observed the men and shared their wisdom with each other about those who would partner with them and those who wouldn't or couldn't. They approached teams cautiously. They learned to speak up. They figured out how to work in a man's world. They also gave great attention to their own personal growth, so as to learn how to be strong in their own right. These strategies have helped them claim their own agency in their chosen professions and in relationships with male colleagues. It's hard work for women to claim their quest plots.

The point is that we women, like men, find our authentic voices when we can write own lives. After all, to know ourselves it is necessary that we not be required to keep ourselves a secret. Since the reawakening of the feminist movement in the late 1960s and 1970s, women have felt somewhat freer to write their own life scripts. But the deeply held cultural beliefs that constrain women's role in the public sphere are still in place (Buchanan, 1996). Writing one's life script, considering one's calling, comes more naturally for men, who have been taught how to do it from childhood. It is more difficult for women, who have not been encouraged to try or given a language with which to write it.

Knowing Ourselves and Each Other as Leaders, Followers, and Partners

The third foundational task that prepares us to name each other involves our identity as leaders, followers, and partners. These are different roles that merit much more thoughtful reflection than we usually give them.

The role of leader is one I have already spent significant space exploring. It's a challenge in all situations and doubly so when we consider the demands of a mixed-gender team. Furthermore, I believe that it is legitimate and necessary for us all to think of ourselves as leaders even if we are not the principle leader in our team. This is important because it is through the work of our teams that we are leading the church and its agencies. In this sense, our teams are leadership teams and we are leaders together. This idea fits with our growing awareness that leadership is no longer a solo activity. So the first question for each of us after we know ourselves and our scripts is, how do we know ourselves as leaders?

It is also true, of course, that we are not all leaders—at least, not all of the time. As we have seen in our discussion of teams in Chapter Six, effective teams need followers as much as they need leaders. More specifically, as we can see from the story of the spiritual formation team, each team needs its members to be leaders sometimes and followers at other times. When we know both skills, we can be good partners to each other. This is particularly true in mixed-gender teams where different models of sharing power are advisable in order to help the team work. So we must also ask, how do we know ourselves as followers? Finally, then, we will begin to know specifically what makes each of us a good partner.

Naming Ourselves

Because we have considered at some length what it means to have a name, let us begin there. We can literally put that conversation into a larger context and consider what it means when we call ourselves leaders. We must first think of our ability to guide others. As we consider that, we will of necessity begin to think about our style, our motivation, ourselves as persons, and our ethics. This self-analysis should take us right back to the questions we posed for writing our life scripts. This time we ask the questions from the leadership perspective. What experiences have we had in our growing up that equips us to be leaders? What have our parents or others in our family taught us about leadership? Who else has taught us about leadership? How does our identity as men or women influence our leadership? What cultural forces have contributed to this identity? How do our values, our loyalties, and our religious experience equip us to be leaders? How do we react to others who have very different values, habits, and expectations? Is our primary calling to leadership or to "followership"? What are we good at that we might lead? What vision do we have, that we might instill it in others? Only when we have answered these questions are we prepared to call ourselves leaders.

Every person in this study asks these questions. In relation to leadership, I think especially of Marie, who by reflecting on her own leadership has learned to be more forceful and powerful. I think of Lisa who is the youngest person in a large team in which she as the controller plays the role of "policewoman," keeping track of regulations and finances. Playing this role with older, more established leaders in the agency is not always easy. I think of Ron, a layman who has joined a team that is primarily made up of Catholic priests and women religious. Ron is learning how to be a leader in a context where he, unlike the others, has family responsibilities in a household with small children. I think of Susan, a direct and forceful woman who is now working in an ethnic community where her direct style has sometimes been misinterpreted as aggression. I think of Sheila whose challenge to her team leader was necessary in order for her to establish her own leadership role. I think of Pam, a quiet person who has no need to be in the limelight. Pam, who describes herself as "intense and intimidating," has learned how to speak for herself in ways she can and will be heard as a leader. These people are but a few who illustrate how each of us must examine our leadership based on who we are and the context in which we can work effectively.

We also need to be good followers. To discover how, we can return to the same questions and ask them again as we think about ourselves as followers. What experiences have we had in our growing up that equips us to be followers? What have our parents or others in our family taught us about followership? Who else has taught us about following? How does our identity as men or women influence our ability to follow others? What cultural forces have contributed to this identity? How do our values, our loyalties, and our religious experience equip us to be good followers? When we are not leaders in the group, how well are we equipped to work with others whose values and habits differ from our own? Is our calling to leadership or to followership? What are we good at doing that contributes to following another leader skillfully?

Again, I turn to the people in this study to illustrate the many ways we need to learn about ourselves as followers. I think of Ed who was a senior pastor for many years before he decided to seek a pastoral role in a context where he was not always expected to be the primary authority as leader. Ed decided his style was gentler than that. He wanted to be a follower as well as a leader. I think of Mike, a strong and successful leader who decided to form a team with two women. This decision required that he also learn how to be a follower. I think of Joe, who knows how to be a follower as well as a leader because, he says, "I grew up in a house where I learned that men help just like women." As an adult he worked in India where "all the senior secretaries are men" and this learning was reinforced. I think of Jeff, who has learned to be less dominant in his leadership, both in his marriage and in his work. Jeff grew up with very traditional models of the roles of men and women and has had to reflect a great deal in order to learn how to be a follower as well as a leader. I think of Jane, a gifted woman who is used to being "the brightest person in the room," who has learned how to listen to others and allow them to lead as well. I think of Blair, who says he has "a didactic streak" that he has had to learn to control to be a good follower. All of these people, like all of us, have faced intense questions about their followership.

It has not escaped my notice, as I have reviewed these examples, that most of the people who exemplify the struggle to become leaders are women and most of the people who exemplify the struggle to become followers are men. This, of course, is one of the ways in which gender influences our teams. Culturally, the men are thrust into the leadership roles. Women are still to an extent expected to be the followers. As we consider our individual roles as leaders and followers we are influenced by those cultural expectations.

Once we understand what makes us leaders and followers, we can begin to understand what makes us good partners. Again, the questions can be helpful as a framework for our examination of ourselves. We might ask, what experiences have we had in our growing up that equips us to be partners? What have our parents or others in our family taught us about partnership? Who else has taught us about partnering? How does our identity as men or women influence our ability to partner with others? What cultural forces have contributed to this identity? How do our values, our loyalties, and our religious experience equip us to be good partners? What are we good at doing that contributes to partnering with others, particularly with persons of the opposite sex?

All of the stories in this book are about partnerships and the people in them. Every one illustrates for us how men and women eventually do become partners. In each one, we can see the elements of leadership and followership balanced in ways that, over time and with much effort, create an effective partnership. Overall, the questions that I have suggested to help us think about ourselves as leaders, followers, and partners are more than a list to check off in some superficial way. Rather, they can be an opportunity for us to think deeply about ourselves and how we are equipped to be effective individuals in mixed-gender teams.

Naming Each Other

When we call each other partner, we are essentially naming each other as both leader and follower. Now we move beyond thinking about ourselves in the roles of leader, follower, and partner to consider the other person or people in our teams in these roles as well. Of course, we can use the same questions as a framework. This time they require us to know enough about each other to answer the questions with accuracy and sensitivity.

Here I think of Bruce and Pam, teammates who have each worked hard to know the other as leader, follower, and partner. I briefly introduced Pam earlier in this chapter as a quiet person who has no need to be in the limelight. Bruce, her partner in ministry in a Baptist church in New Jersey, is an extrovert who takes a more public role. Their partnership began shortly after Bruce joined the congregation as senior pastor. Pam was already serving the congregation as associate pastor. After a very few months, Bruce approached Pam about redefining roles to form a copastorate. "I was supposed to supervise her work, but I said I couldn't and wouldn't do it," he recalled. "There was no way in which she was not every bit as qualified to be pastor as I am. In fact, she had been doing pastoral work for over a year before I came. For her to step back to a subordinate position felt wrong." Bruce was in fact naming Pam as his partner and at the same time calling her a leader in the congregation. He was also signaling his willingness to be called a follower as well as leader.

Bruce's suggestion challenged Pam to name herself leader and think about herself as an equal partner rather than only as a follower in their professional relationship. She was also challenged to name Bruce a follower when she was in the leader role. "Bruce has done a lot of the encouraging to make this partnership happen. We could have been a team in a different way, but in terms of sharing things equally, it has really come from him," Pam said. "It's not always comfortable for me. I tend to be a 'leave things alone' type person and I don't like a lot of attention on me. I wasn't sure how people in the congregation would accept the change. Bruce is more willing to test the waters." She agreed to the equal partnership, she said, "first because I like preaching. I want to use it as a gift. Then, in terms of other areas, maybe my confidence is growing as I've been here longer and I start to see that it makes sense for me to do more."

Bruce agreed. "I didn't know if the congregation wanted this or was ready for it, but I knew it was going to be good for the two of us," he said.

The nature of their equal partnership was worked out in written detail in a single job description. It begins with a common statement about their pastoral function as being a peer relationship in which they share roles and responsibilities. It also identifies how they will each assume particular roles and functions "within the generalist responsibilities of pastor." Their specific areas of responsibilities in pastoral care, education, worship, missions, church administration, evangelism, denominational relations, and community work are then outlined in some detail. Their pastoral relations committee approved the job description and they have used it as the basis for their partnership for seven years.

Teammates can with honesty call each other leader, follower, and partner in this way when two criteria are met, Bruce suggested. The first is competence. "The ability and gifts for leadership need to be present in each member of the team," he said. The second is less tangible. "It includes trust, regard, respect, and confidence—all the things that assure me that if I were to die tomorrow, everything would be in good hands, and vice versa."

Bruce and Pam are very different as people and as leaders. That's part of the secret of their ability to call each other leader. In claiming their differences they are better able to see each other as leaders in appropriate contexts. "We know each other's strengths and let each other work to those respective strengths," Pam said. "For instance, I tend to be more visionary and Bruce tends to be better at making things happen. So I tend to come up with a lot of the ideas and I give them to him and he makes them happen."

"I'll speak in a public meeting," Bruce added. "Pam would be much more reluctant to do that. But in terms of influence, we are similar. We both provide leadership." As a way of explaining their differences further, Bruce added, "I do much more that's visible in the congregation and in the community. Pam would not seek that role at all. But when it comes to planning a process for the congregation, that's where she shines. She just has so much vision that she leaves me in the background. I stand in awe at times of how she captures a view of where we should be going. I follow right along then, because then she is the leader."

Pam increasingly has become comfortable in the leader role. "The opportunities that have come up because of it have been good. It has opened the doors to trying some things I haven't done before, to grow and change. As I've done it, it's come across all right and I have more confidence to try something else."

In essence, Bruce and Pam complement each other and so are leaders at different moments when different skills are required. They understand this, and both are comfortable in the role of leader or follower. But the congregation tends not to see these shared roles as clearly as Bruce and Pam do. They are more inclined to identify Bruce as the leader. By virtue of the fact that he is male, a decade older, and came to the congregation as senior pastor, Bruce tends to be called the leader more readily that Pam. It's the classic dilemma for mixed-gender teams, especially when the male partner is also an extrovert. But Bruce and Pam have not been content to settle for the labels others have given them. They have worked hard to know and treat each other as both leader and follower. In doing so, they have demonstrated their unique way of being partners.

"Equal strength among partners is absolutely critical. Pam is strong in terms of intellect, capability, and public leadership, but there are certain aspects of pastoral ministry she doesn't like, and she has a more introverted personality. That tends in some people's minds to cast her in a secondary role, but only for people who don't watch the inner workings of our partnership," Bruce noted. "Extroverted personalities tend to shine and introverts take a back seat. But that's not the way it is here. Pam is a fine, fine worship leader and excellent preacher. Some people consider her preaching superior to mine. But in a business meeting, she's more likely to sit and listen and I'm more likely to speak. This has probably worked to her detriment though it doesn't bother her. She knows that's her nature. She is the reflective one. Yet it does influence people's view of her leadership," he adds.

"A lot of people in the congregation still see Bruce as the boss. We're trying very hard not to use a hierarchical style. It's been hard to get them to see that we are not boss and underling," Pam confirmed.

Bruce and Pam must also work at allowing each other to claim the name of leader in their different ways and in their own time. Pam's pace is slower and this causes Bruce concern, especially because the congregation is so much more ready to label him the leader. "I do feel indebted to Bruce for pushing this equal partnership. He has been incredibly supportive and encouraging, sometimes a little too much," Pam said. "He is a very nurturing person and wants to take care of me. Sometimes he speaks up for me a little too much."

"I get plenty of recognition. It's embarrassing sometimes," Bruce explained. "That's one place where I get uncomfortable in our partnership. Pam just doesn't get the same kind of recognition I do. I have done a lot with her and with the congregation to bring attention to her accomplishments, lest she never take credit for anything. It's just not in her nature to care about recognition. She doesn't have a lot of ambition about going on to bigger and better things. She's happy to do what she does. If anything, she looks for ways to live more simply, without the need to succeed or excel," Bruce said. He admits a level of discomfort about getting more recognition than Pam because of his extroverted nature. "She is every bit the pastor that I am, but she isn't likely to do the things that draw attention to herself."

The problem that Bruce and Pam describe is simply that others are more willing to name him the leader. Pam "wonders how much of this is gender-related, how much of it is related to my call here, and how much of it is personality." To be sure, this problem is not entirely gender-specific. Men who are introverts report the same difficulty having their accomplishments recognized. At the same time, the differences in the way constituents see their leaders are most marked in situations like Bruce's and Pam's. As Pam becomes more and more comfortable as the leader, she faces a dilemma every woman encounters. She feels the frustration of not being claimed as leader by others. "I've bought into this partnership now and I am getting more annoyed that people in the congregation are not getting it. I'm doing a lot of the pastoral work, and still he is the person they perceive as the pastor. The way people use language is part of the issue. They often say, in asking about Bruce, 'Where is the pastor?'"

Ultimately, what saves Bruce and Pam from falling into the trap of stereotypical roles that others try to apply to them is "that we are both flexible and neither one of us wants to steal the limelight or get ahead at the other's expense," Bruce noted. "Advocacy for each other is also important," he added, emphasizing that the strongest advocate for a partnership like theirs has to come from the person in the team who is in the senior position or is perceived to be the senior. Then both partners have "to be conscious enough of the partnership to let it shine." In the final analysis, they will go on seeing and treating each other as leader, follower, and ultimately partner, no matter what others outside the team think. That's the essence of naming and claiming each other.

13

INCLUDING EACH OTHER

WE CAN'T BE A TEAM unless we *include* each other. Of all the criteria that I classify as reflective, this one requires the deepest inner work from each of us. Including each other is the true challenge of diversity. It goes far beyond accepting the fact of gender or any other kind of diversity, even beyond managing diversity. Including each other requires opening ourselves to each other, allowing ourselves to be changed by each other.

If we are diligent in how we *name* each other, we will begin naturally to *include* each other as well. The close relationship between these two criteria is evident in the story of the spiritual formation team. While Jorge, Binh, Rick, Cecilia, and Jack daily name each other in all the ways we discussed in the last chapter, they also continually examine their inner attitudes that prevent or allow them to include each other fully in their shared work.

In this chapter, we shall discover what *including* each other requires. We will define the difference between personal prejudice and institutional racism and sexism. Then we will examine how these failures—both personal and organizational—limit leadership and partnership. After that we will be ready to go on to the more active criteria, which address how we work together.

Understanding Diversity

Our negative prejudices, supported by institutional racism and sexism, are still the number one barrier to the advancement of nontraditional leaders (Morrison, 1992). They prevent us from achieving diversity. Stereotypes still make it acceptable to screen out both white women and minorities when differences are highlighted as flaws. This plus the troubling fact that our prejudices prevent us from working effectively together in mixed-gender teams should be enough to encourage us to change our ways. But even if we can exorcize all our negative prejudices, we still cannot achieve diversity. We also have to work together to eradicate the underlying cultural habits and values—the racism and sexism and other "isms"—that support our prejudices.

To understand how our stereotypes create prejudice, how prejudice is reinforced by racism and sexism in our institutions, and how we might achieve true diversity, we need clear definitions to begin.

Definitions to Guide Our Thinking

Diversity means difference. In our time, it is a term that has become "the new shorthand for the multiracial, multicultural, multiethnic makeup of American society" (Overton-Adkins, 1997, p. 19). It is more than the melting pot we all learned about in school. In fact, how we understand and approach diversity has everything to do with leadership in a connected world. Today, diversity includes both mutuality—a focus on common interests and values—and inclusiveness—the willingness to include even those who are very different from us. This definition is still obscure until we realize that including the other means we agree also to be changed by the other. It goes beyond wishing the other to become more like us. Peter, who shares his story in Chapter Fourteen, has learned this in his own context. His own understanding of "the full participation of women in Judaism," he said, has moved "from the classic position of equal access to the point that women's experiences should be included as well as men's . . . so that they are not honorary men but are really valued as women and as equals." His insight is important for all of us. It reveals to what extent we must all overcome the liberal idea that minorities are to be included or integrated into "our" way of doing things and also the conservative idea that they should be well-behaved and worthy of acceptance by "our" way of life. Both of these narrow attitudes fail to see that the presence and predicament of black (or any minority) people "are neither additions to nor defections from American life but rather *constitute elements of that life*" (West, 1993, p. 3; see also Rhodes, 1987).

We must put aside the assimilation theory, in which we understood diversity through the metaphor of the great American melting pot. We must also put aside any notion that managing diversity as "an unavoidable cost of doing business" is enough. Nor can we benefit much by simply celebrating diversity and hoping that our increased awareness about each other will help us cross the chasm between us (Overton-Adkins, 1997). With our eye on the demands of a connected world, which we discussed in Chapter Five, we can understand diversity in a new way. Overton-Adkins—and others—asserts in fact that "in the future, the first and crucial role for leaders may be to concentrate on understanding difference in order to get to places of connectivity, rather than highlighting similarities so we can bypass difference" (p. 22). Our diversity thus becomes an organizing principle of our leadership for the future. "We are all on the same team *with* our differences—not *despite* them" (Thomas and Ely, 1996, p. 86). This stance prepares us even to overcome the frustrations of including people of other races, cultures, or psychological temperaments who have values and habits very different from our own.

Personal prejudice and racism-sexism both affect our stance toward diversity and thus our ability to use diversity as a leadership principle. Our primary concern as we look at the fifth criterion is personal prejudice, but it will be useful to distinguish between this and racism or sexism (or any other ism) for our discussion here. A prejudice is any unfounded attitude we may have that prevents us from truly knowing the unknown other, whether that person is of the opposite sex, another racial or cultural heritage, or even a different age or different capability. We are best acquainted with negative prejudice in our tendency to view people who are different as somehow deficient. Prejudice is often based on a stereotype, a commonly held and unverified idea about a group of people, such as "Women are too indecisive to make decisions in a crisis," or "People over sixty are too old to put in a good day's work," or "Men are smarter than women." The difference between prejudice and racism or any other ism is critical for us here. Prejudice is in us. Racism and sexism go beyond us as individuals; they are in our institutions. They are the sum of our corporate language, habits, and values that ensure privilege for some at the expense of the others. In order to know each other, it is our personal prejudice that we must overcome. Yet we cannot entirely separate our prejudices from the racism or sexism embedded in our institutions. They are intimately connected with each other.

Although we think of prejudice as a negative, it is not necessarily so. We can have positive prejudices too. White people feel positive prejudice about themselves, living and working as they do in a context that rewards them. Their work and ideas are accepted as the norm, and the rest is subculture. This point is well illustrated by a reflection I heard recently from an American man at the time of his first overseas trip to work with an international organization. When he came back he said, "The experience taught me that there are places in the world where my way of thinking and my way of doing things don't matter at all." I give him great credit for this insight. He was, after all, confronting the racism, sexism, and class-ism that have kept Euro-American white men at the top of the heap for a long time.

In contrast, minorities are often encouraged to carry negative preju-dices about themselves. Over two hundred years of slavery and another century "of institutionalized terrorism in the form of segregation, lynch-ings, and second-class citizenship" have worked together to encourage African Americans to hate their own bodies (West, 1993, p. 85). Centuries of being told they are not capable have caused women to buy into their own intellectual inferiority. It is not just a matter of "us" bearing a prej-udice against "them"; it is also "them" hating something about them-selves or us hating something about ourselves.

For teams in church-related nonprofit organizations, theology, values, and teachings of the faith are of inestimable value in modifying or exor-cising our divisive prejudices. A Christian team, for example, would remember the teachings of Jesus that women, "those Samaritans," and the "lost sheep" are supremely valued and the object of God's concern and grace. They might also remember that the ministry of Paul and Peter demonstrated that women, Jews, *and* non-Jews, different as they may be, are never to be disregarded or put down. We are forever called to acknowledge that "there is neither male nor female," for Christ has bro-ken the dividing wall between us. In the same way, given our various faith traditions, we can go back to the values of that tradition to find the path beyond our own negative prejudice.

Diversity in Church Organizations

The foregoing summary of our individual relationship to prejudice and the underlying racism and sexism that support it should be understood in relation to the stance of our organizations, including our denominations. It is here that our prejudices become aligned with policy and practice to ensure privilege for some at the expense of others.

Though church organizations and denominations do embrace diversity better than many secular institutions, they do so within systems that are patriarchal. They deny the feminine principles that are at the heart of faith, miss the value of experience as an element of theology, and infor-mally debate the value of diversity (that is, *including* people who are dif-ferent from us). This does not happen because the people of the church want it so or because any of us is cavalier about the fundamental values of our faith. It happens because the prevailing worldview in our culture ignores any theology of differences. The result is that men and women working together in the church get caught trying to learn new ways of leadership that will embrace diversity and demonstrate interdependence in systems that actually lack the ability to be truly inclusive (Nuechterlein and Hahn, 1990).

Evidence that our culture has no theology of differences begins with the fact that our institutions are organized to reward one sex, race, and class of people above all others. White men thus live and work in a context that rewards them. Their work and ideas are accepted as the norm, and as I said before, all the rest is subculture. This is racism, sexism, and classism. But do these isms really mean that we lack a theology of differences? The answer is yes, because *we are still largely unaware of the fact that our institutions are this way.* We still think we can overcome the isms simply by addressing our individual prejudices. In fact, what we need is not just a whole new theology to inform our organizational life but also denominations (and other institutions) that will use the new theology to change our culture. Only then will we become truly inclusive.

In this context, the patriarchy of every faith tradition illustrates the flaw of any dominant group. It forgets that others are not like them. The dominant group is thus caught in a dilemma. It ends up trying to build community by eliminating diversity, by excluding the "others," or by welcoming them to become like "us." This is the very problem that Cornell West (1993) warns us about, as mentioned earlier in this chapter. The hierarchy of our church and secular institutions, by virtue of the fact that they are patriarchal, cannot achieve diversity. Hierarchy, or rank order, is not in and of itself a bad thing, of course. Hierarchy in nature is good. But the assertion by one of my male clients that hierarchy in nature justifies the hierarchy of our institutions is a logical leap across a wide space. For the hierarchy of our institutions is more than rank order. It is rank order established for an ulterior motive—either institutionalizing authoritarianism or ensuring privilege and power for a few over the rest. If we are precise, this is the difference between hierarchy and patriarchy. Once we see the difference clearly, we can see that the problem is not hierarchy but patriarchy. The result of *patriarchy* is that women and minorities have been taught "that community means sameness, uniformity, control" (Russell, 1993, p. 160). That's why the church cannot hear minorities—including women—cannot help them succeed in the system better, cannot embrace their images without fear, cannot in the end know the unknown other.

Thus many nontraditional leaders of all kinds have the experience of this clergywoman reflecting on seven years of service in her denomination: "No one is really asking my opinion. I thought when they made this big deal about having a certain percentage of women here, they had some expectation about what that was going to mean—that there would be an intention to include women in decision-making circles. But that has never, never happened." Another put it more bluntly: "I finally figured out that I'm not supposed to change anything here. I'm just supposed to work here." As we have shown earlier, our sociocultural system is "one in which a very few men have power over other men, women, children, slaves, and colonialized people" (Russell, 1993, p. 160). Thus men too can be victims of our too-narrow view of what diversity really means.

Confronting Prejudice

In order to *include* each other fully in our teams, regardless of whether we are male or female, Asian, Caucasian, African American, or anything else, we must move beyond our limited understanding of diversity. What we should strive for is what members of one team said they want from gender equity: "an environment in our teams that embraces diversity as an opportunity for us to learn more, establish wider social relationships, make better decisions, and achieve higher levels of satisfaction from our work."

In order to do this we will have to move beyond our own negative prejudices. We will also have to understand the relationship between our prejudices and the institutional racism and sexism that we alone cannot control.

Where Do We Start?

"Most people start with prejudice, working on the question: 'Why can't people just get along?' And then people start getting along and we become like John and Peter who experienced the transfiguration of Jesus. 'Let's build three booths. Let's stay here,' we say. 'This is such a wonderful thing.' I can feel that I am so much a better person even while I maintain my privilege. Yet nothing in the reality of the woman or the person of color has really changed" (Charles Ruehle, personal interview, 1998).

Reverend Ruehle's comments remind me of a personal experience. For the past ten years I have been occasionally joining my parents in their time-share on Sanibel Island, a resort community in southern Florida. I am writing there today. As in the past, my brother and his wife have joined us. I can remember the first time we came here to vacation with our parents. My brother's wife Robyn was bereft to find that no people of her race could be found on this island. A gifted writer, whose subject is often the identity of the biracial individual in American culture, Robyn is keenly aware of the demands of true diversity. I have come to respect her wisdom and value her friendship over the years. But as I sit here today, I observe that nothing has changed on this island. There are still no African Americans here. My love and respect for Robyn makes no difference in our "resort" experience. She finds none of her own people here—except her own son—and I am not freed from my own white ghetto either. I want to go beyond this story of my own experience.

The men and women in successful mixed-gender teams do break out of the ghetto of their own gender. Repeatedly, they emphasize how much they learn from working with each other. Jorge summarized it well in our interview when he said, "I became more conscious that I am just a human being among many other human beings. The difference of color and language and ancestry are just accidental. They are not substantial. Being a man or a woman is accidental. It does not affect your humanness at the core. You are a human being in the first place and then there is differentiation in many, many ways." When teams get this far, they can experience the "gender magic" the Lutheran relief team talked about in Chapter Nine.

This is a beginning, but it is not enough. A fairly small number of successful mixed-gender teams reaching a point of performing together effectively does not mitigate the fact that many other mixed-gender teams do not succeed. In a sense the teams in this study are in the position of my sister-in-law Robyn. They make it. But they are still surrounded by institutionalized practices that make their success unusual and difficult. The men in mixed-gender teams are particularly aware of this fact. As the culturally privileged members of the team, they know how hard they must advocate for an environment that is more conducive to the formation and success of many more mixed-gender teams. It's difficult because racism and sexism are not in our individual control.

Moving Beyond Prejudice

In searching for deeper understanding of the relationship of personal prejudice to institutional racism and sexism, I interviewed Reverend Charles Ruehle and Reverend Susan Ruehle at greater length. The Ruehles are a mixed-gender team serving as directors at Crossroads Ministry, an interfaith and community-based antiracism training organization in Chicago, New York, and Milwaukee. They emphasize that in addressing our own personal prejudices, we must also take on the isms that support them. The institutional change model used by Crossroads Ministry goes beyond consideration of personal prejudice to consideration of the underlying racism and sexism that support prejudice.

"It requires much more than people changing their minds. You must start broader so that people working on the interpersonal issues do so in context," Susan Ruehle explained. "Racism and sexism make us all victims. It gets to be really nuts if we don't start with this. But this is a deep discussion and people don't want to do this deep work. They want to believe that prejudice is a negative personal feeling, and 'if I have some new information it will go away.' But it doesn't go away. It persists at some level and is fed by the underlying racism and sexism of our culture.

"When we start with racism, sexism, and other isms, they are named and understood first, before we deal with our own prejudices. They are defined as forces that trap all of us. Also, they trap us differently. They say to the African American or the woman: 'You are inferior.' They say to the white man: 'If you just go along with this idea that you are superior, you'll get attention, your kids will test higher in school, we will all speak your language, you will get better jobs, and so forth.' We take these things for granted, yet we say we have equal opportunity."

"We also recognize," Charles Ruehle noted, "that as men and women or white and black we have different work to do. Then I'm not trying to work out my white or male guilt in the group, and forcing my African American colleague or my woman colleague to hear all kinds of things they don't want to know about white men's attitudes toward women or blacks." That's abusive of our relationships, and we do it all the time when we try to solve problems at the level of our own personal prejudice.

He added, "People need to work on their own prejudices in individual ways. But it doesn't work if we start there. If we begin by understanding the collective, corporate, systemic nature of the isms we free ourselves from taking personal responsibility for institutional sin. This is both a freedom from guilt and a challenge. Think about it in steps. First, you recognize that you have a prejudice. Second, because you understand the influence of sexism or racism on your attitudes, you realize that you have been taught to think this way. It is not some intentional evil; it is in the way things are. Now you have the freedom and the challenge. The third step is recognizing that you can change things even if they aren't 'your fault.' Fourth and finally, when you make this commitment, you create a space for your own examination of prejudice without guilt. You also make some inner commitment to working with others to dismantle racism and sexism and all the other isms. You do this because you know that with the end of racism, we all win. We all have the possibility of being better leaders. There is no longer any internal belief that it's a zero-sum game."

We can see from the foregoing that it starts with our recognition that "the way things are" isn't working. We no longer want to walk into a meeting room and find all men or all white people there because *without the others we are not able to do our best work.* Thus for Binh, the Vietnamese priest who is a member of the spiritual formation team, it's not just that the others want him to have the experience of the team. He is there because *without him they cannot do their best work.* Indeed, this is the message from all effective mixed-gender teams in this study.

"In our public life, in our culture, that's exactly where we are right now," Charles Ruehle emphasized. "Either we are going to keep moving forward—but in a new and deeper way—or we will go back. We can't stay where we are. The promises of the civil rights era, the potential that we lifted up and offered, has not yet been realized. We got stuck because we believed that if we changed the law, racism and sexism would disappear. We also believed that if we just talked about prejudice, it would go away. That didn't happen, so now we have a whole lot of dissatisfied people. Those folks want to see some new things happen."

What the Ruehles describe is purely reflective work, and very hard work at that. Yet, paradoxically, it is based on our full knowledge that it's not up to us as individuals. It's much harder than that. It demands much more. And like all reflective tasks, it leads us ultimately to action. On the other side, our very way of working is different.

How Team Members Name and Include Each Other

Now we are ready to put it all together. We are ready to see how effective mixed-gender teams *name* and *include* each other. Recall with me that the prerequisite for *naming* another is knowing oneself. Remember then, that the tasks of naming suggested in Chapter Two include respecting each other as individuals, building trust, understanding our differences as men and women and as leaders with a variety of styles, seeing and acknowledging each other's skills and strengths, recognizing that both men and women have a legitimate calling to leadership in the church environment, and assigning value to each other. *Including* each other requires opening ourselves to each other, and allowing ourselves to be changed by our encounters with each other. Remember also that the most-often-mentioned ways that effective teams name and include each other, discussed in Chapter Two, are these: believing in the strength of every member of the team; building trust, yet recognizing the delicacy of trust in the midst of all the ways we can misunderstand each other; achieving and maintaining parity among all members in the team (everyone in the team counts); and knowing the benefits for each member of the team in being a part of the team.

These overlap. Essentially, the team interviews verify the reflective activities that I have suggested are part of *naming* and *including* one another.

Four Ways of Naming and Including Each Other

For the sake of simplicity, and because my list and the list suggested by interviewees overlap significantly, we're best off sticking with one or the other as we consider how men and women *name* and *include* one other. Let's remain true to the interviews and use the suggestions of the team members themselves.

MEN AND WOMEN IN EFFECTIVE MIXED-GENDER TEAMS BELIEVE IN THE STRENGTH OF EVERY TEAM MEMBER. In general they say, as one woman did, that "good people are the secret of the success of this team." They generally describe the good people in their teams as "people who are strong in themselves." That is, they are strong as individuals and as professionals *before* they come to the team. Many cited "finding the right partner" as a key in forming an effective mixed-gender team. My probing unearthed two criteria for the right partner: someone who is compatible and someone who is strong. The bottom line, as one man said, is that "it pays to hire people for their talents."

This does not mean, however, that the people are all alike. To the contrary, they cite differences among team members in personal style, ways of thinking, and skills as essential to team success. In fact, different strengths are essential in a team. In behooves the team members to understand how important it is to "recognize the different gifts" of each team member, one woman said. Another team leader went so far as to say that the leader "must have a clear perception of his weaknesses" and must effectively "use the strengths of others." This kind of leadership strategy presumes different—and to a certain extent complementary—strengths in different members of the team. Another team member emphasized the radically different styles in his partnership with a woman as a benefit, adding, "We are both strong." Together they provide a wide range of styles for leading their organization.

Although these team members are confident of each other's strengths, they do not necessarily think they do a good job of acknowledging each other publicly or privately. One woman even said, "We too often operate on a philosophy of scarcity in the way we acknowledge each other. We need to add a hermeneutic of generosity toward each other." To be sure, people on these teams do recognize each other's strengths and successes.

They mention what they call the usual things: verbal and written thank-yous, some time out for celebrating a major achievement, and periodic social time. They don't consider these activities unique or even adequate. I would agree with them. In and of themselves, they are not adequate. But there are two things unique about the way effective mixed-gender team members acknowledge each other's strengths that *all the teams* failed to see in themselves.

First, they demonstrate a level of civility toward each other that is largely lacking in our organizations and our culture today. This civility is a palpable mark of respect for each other. It governs all their actions toward each other. So although they do not necessarily go out of their way to praise each other, their deep respect for each other conveys a strong underlying message that supports the team and the people in it.

Second, there is in these teams no cumulative sense of failure. In contrast, there is a healthy sense within the team that they are successful. Over and over again when I asked team members to share projects that had succeeded and projects that had failed, I got the same response. They could readily tell me about the successful projects that they had done. They were stumped when it came to a project that had failed. Their responses were typified by one man's statement: "We have tons of little failures where we have to make corrections, but nothing comes to mind as a failure." These teams are not afraid to make mistakes. They can correct their course and they often do. But they don't fail. What's more, they have very little memory of the small failures or mistakes that require a course correction. It's not that they aren't important or that team members do not learn from them. It's that they are *expected* as part of the routine. In this sense they are not memorable. Team members do not dwell on them. Once experienced, they are forgotten in the normal routine of effective teamwork. Team members have to believe in each other's strengths to behave this way.

MEN AND WOMEN IN EFFECTIVE MIXED-GENDER TEAMS TRUST ONE ANOTHER. That trust does not come without a great deal of reflective time getting to know one another. As one woman put it, "I came with a healthy dose of skepticism. I have as many horror stories as any woman does about team situations. I told my partner I would be skittish and I had some ground rules." Like this woman, they all know that trust can be broken by misunderstanding, missed signals, behaving in ways that other team members (especially team members from other ethnic backgrounds or gender) do not understand. But once trust is created it becomes, as another woman said, "sacred between us." Team members begin to care about the team so much that "we simply do not want to let each other down."

Once team members trust each other at this level, they do not have to make all their decisions together. They can work on trust and delegation as much as consensus, said one male member of a large team. They can also "allow room in our relationship for us to be wounded by each other" and still be a good team, said another. "We don't want the good to be a straitjacket," he added. Another team affirms this approach and even provides a structure for "both appreciations and resentments to be discussed in our team meetings." Operating in this fashion requires strong trust among team members.

MEN AND WOMEN IN EFFECTIVE MIXED-GENDER TEAMS ACHIEVE AND MAINTAIN PARITY AMONG ALL MEMBERS. They make sure that everyone counts for everyone else in the team. One woman recalls how her senior partner "made a place for her" when she became the first associate in the congregation. Some teams go so far as to eliminate titles to ensure that everyone will have parity on the team. Most also provide some informal mentoring to bring the newer or less experienced team members up to speed. Achieving parity may require a confrontation between team members if they do not agree on their relative skill and position in the team.

Parity in the team does not mean that all teams are egalitarian. We shall hear more about the difference between egalitarian teams and hierarchical teams in Chapter Twenty-One. Both types of teams can achieve parity among members. Parity simply means that every team member counts equally for every other member in the team. This condition, of course, presumes that all team members have a common understanding and acceptance of their roles in the team. Essentially, parity means that all team members are *equally valued* in the team no matter their role or position.

Parity allows team members to help each other when necessary. As one team leader described it, "When one team member falls short, the others rally. There is no finger-pointing, no possessiveness." Mentoring becomes a possibility in such teams. Successful projects help boost parity and strengthen the give-and-take among team members.

WOMEN AND MEN IN EFFECTIVE MIXED-GENDER TEAMS KNOW THE BENEFITS FOR EACH MEMBER OF BEING PART OF THE TEAM. These teams have no trouble recounting the benefits of working in a successful mixed-gender team. First of all, men and women learn from each other. Everyone has a chance to grow. Both team members and constituents benefit from different leadership styles. The benefits in this regard can be very specific, as with the team in which the male member said, "I was willing to give her space to do ministry—to try things, to be in the pulpit, to experience a whole range of pastoral work. In return I got someone to talk to." It was surprising, I might say, how often men counted this very thing as a principle benefit of teaming with a woman. The female professional partner, it seems, often provides the male partner with "safe ears."

There is also a greater sense of shared mission in effective mixed-gender teams. Overall, as one person said, "Work is better." Some say that the atmosphere in the office is better. People perform their jobs better. Even people outside the team benefit. "Everyone feels involved in the role and life of the institution," as one team member put it. "The burdens and satisfactions are shared," said another, "and we get a sum greater than the parts."

These four elements of including and naming each other may seem a bit formulaic and contrived. They are useful in giving us a framework for how successful teams address the two reflective criteria of naming and including, to be sure. But beyond the four ways these teams have suggested, how does it all work? Let's look at it a bit more organically, without the formula this time.

Trust and Partnership

It's a miracle we cannot explain. When we acknowledge each other in the ways we've discussed in these two chapters, trust is born in the team. In fact, *being with* each other in the radical way we have discussed here is critical to identification-based trust formation in mixed-gender teams. I mentioned this point in Chapter Six, in summarizing how trust is normally formed in teams. Identification-based trust grows out of empathy and shared values. We cannot get to this level of trust in mixed-gender teams unless we acknowledge each other fully as persons with strengths, differences, and legitimate claim to leadership in the church. Conversely, when we do acknowledge each other fully, we build trust that is the foundation of an effective team.

The trust that develops when men and women deeply acknowledge themselves and each other may not always be apparent. One woman remembers what she calls "the migration to trust" in her relationship with a male colleague in what they talked about in their frequent conversations. First, she said, "it was all about our projects and tasks." As they got to know each other, the content of their conversations shifted to "50 percent about how we worked together and 50 percent about our tasks." Even-

tually, these two teammates began getting to know each other. Their conversation expanded to include information about each other as people. Then
they observed that they talked about all three areas: tasks, how they
worked as a team, and themselves as people. "When we established trust,
we could talk about a wider range of things, including the more personal," she said.

Trust forms when team members understand and accept their differences and don't use those differences to say, "Mine are better than yours"
or "I am better than you." Each member of the team must believe that
every other member of the team is strong and has something to contribute
that is of value. It's as simple and as complicated as the observation from
one woman, who said about her team: "We get along as a group, though
we are very different. We have a lot of respect for the gifts of each person." This perception of strength among all individuals in the team is
absolutely critical, in the words of the team members in this study. Making this simple statement requires each individual in the team to address
all the complexities of *naming* that we discussed in Chapter Twelve as well
as the complexities of *including* one another that are the focus of this
chapter: knowing who I am, understanding the challenges of leadership
and believing that my colleagues and I are leaders, overcoming prejudice
in myself, and understanding the role of prejudice in our racist and sexist
world. Having done all these things we can name each other and come to
the point that we too can make this simple statement about ourselves and
our teammates.

A prerequisite to believing in the strength of others in the team is that
each member has to believe in his or her own strength. Individuals in the
team must be "very self-assured in their own personhood, not threatened
by the skills of the other," as one team member described it. Another said,
"Trust in my own gifts enables me to trust the other person's gifts."

Having done this work of *naming* each other and *including* each other,
we come to the point of feeling honored to be with each other. We claim
each other as partners. Literally, we declare that we want to *be a part* of
the life and work of the other. One man said it simply and yet profoundly
when he shared this about his teammate: "She has a wonderful future in
the church. I am happy to be a partner in that." This comment reveals
how much of our partnership should be about the other, not about ourselves. Remembering what we have said earlier about the challenges of
knowing the unknown other in our culture, we can now reflect on a profound change that happens in effective mixed-gender teams. We not only
get to know the other but we also see our work and ourselves *from the
perspective of our part with the other*. This is *part*-nership.

PART FIVE

COMMUNICATING
AND
WORKING TOGETHER

14

ELEANOR AND PETER

COMMUNICATING WITH EACH OTHER

ELEANOR AND PETER ARE RABBIS at a Reform Jewish synagogue in Chicago. They have been partners for six years. Peter came to the congregation in 1980. Eleanor came as the first associate rabbi in 1993, directly from rabbinical school. Peter and Eleanor's partnership is unusually long. "Normally, a second rabbi would be with you for a fairly brief period of time and then you would change. You would go on to a new person and mentor them in succession, one after another," Peter explains.

Peter and Eleanor have broken that model. Even so, Eleanor is the newest member of the extended team at this synagogue. In addition to Peter and Eleanor, the administrative staff in this synagogue has a male cantor and three women members of the professional team including an executive director, an education director, and an early childhood program director.

In their fifth year working together, Peter took a seven-month sabbatical leave. Eleanor led the congregation as sole rabbi during that time. Concurrently, she received an offer to become the associate dean at the rabbinical school she had attended. When Peter returned from sabbatical, Eleanor discussed the offer with him and eventually decided to turn it down.

Talking to each other is a foundation of the team relationship between Peter and Eleanor. Their talk is energetic, lively, often challenging, and not without its difficult moments. Here is their story.

○

Eleanor Speaks Her Mind

I was honored when I graduated with many opportunities in several cities. This synagogue was special and different in ways that so distinguished it that my husband gave up his job on the hunch that this was a worthwhile journey for us to make. The team has a good cooperative spirit. It is representative of an unbelievable range of issues, personalities, and styles. There are lots of subsets of the whole team. Peter and I are one.

We have a particularly intense and intimate relationship for a lot of reasons—one being that we are the two rabbis. Peter and I share so much work. We share one huge job. There isn't any other kind of duplication like that on staff. We also like each other a lot. We have a repartee. Peter is a very exceptional senior rabbi. There are few like him in the country. For most, there is a deep sense of "this is my place and you are not going to take away my glory." When I came, he asked for advice from another rabbi who had had many assistants. The advice was this: "Don't ever let them call you by your first name. Take them out to lunch once a month so they know what's going on." Luckily, Peter did not take his advice.

I also made it clear in my interview that I was looking for someone who would make me a partner. First of all, I don't think I am genetically capable of anything else. I said, "I'm not interested in sitting at your feet for three to five years until you deem that I have mastered whatever skills I need." From the moment I came, Peter moved over and made a huge, huge place for me. I could say now that except for a very few things . . . it's a total partnership.

One of the big moments for a congregation in the Reform and Conservative movements is sermons on the High Holy Days. There are four such sermons here. The first year, Peter said there would be one for me and three for him. I said I wanted to do two. I said, "I need to know when we will share that forum." He told me, "Next year." Then he said something else that reveals his incredible strength. He said, "This is an ego thing and I am not quite ready to share it with you yet. It's not that you don't have the skills. It's just that I am not ready."

I know Peter and I know myself and I know our relationship. I so respected his honesty that if he had said two more years, I think I could have waited. I was right out there with him and he was right out there with me. We worked it out. The next year when I preached two sermons during the High Holy Days, I started by thanking him and acknowledging and really praising him for how unusual he is—and for his ability to make a place for me.

Our friendship has had an interesting time this last year. Peter went on sabbatical and left me alone with 950 households and no diminution of the work that we do. Normally we both work a six-day week of twelve to fourteen hour days. It was a brutal winter and spring with some tragic deaths in our congregation. My own children were ages two and a half and one at the time. Peter didn't keep in very close touch. To this day, I don't know how we managed. When he came back I had just been offered the job in New York. I was drained and bitter from the experience and he was high and ready to come back. I said to him, "As my friend I have to tell you that you didn't take very good care of me when you were gone. Our leadership didn't think it through very well and neither did you. And that had to come from you."

Peter recalled that in his previous sabbatical, there was no other rabbi here to take over. The congregation just naturally shifted into a different mode. He said, "I had great confidence in your competence."

I told him that I was tired and resentful, that it had been very, very hard. I could see the very moment he got it. His eyes changed and he said, "I am really sorry." I knew that he did get it and he was sorry. It took away a huge part of being mad. I needed him to know. I needed him to hear me. It was the only way to go on with our friendship, which is so much the core of our working together.

What I love about Peter—and he expresses this—is that he learns from me as I do from him. We often acknowledge each other publicly. After his sabbatical, Peter organized a thank-you evening for me to mark my fifth anniversary in the congregation. I resisted. We usually don't do that until the tenth anniversary of a professional tenure. But it turned out to be the most unbelievable evening. It was so special and Peter was so sweet. He and I give each other kudos all the time. I'm sure some people think it's corny sometimes, but it's not phony. It's nice. We also communicate in writing sometimes. He wrote me a beautiful letter about my job offer in New York and my decision to stay. He couldn't have handled it better. I was very grateful.

We still disagree about things, of course. Peter is in charge, but sometimes he allows himself to be overruled. Some things that come up in staff meeting are up for grabs. Sometimes he states his position and it's uncomfortable when there are strongly opposing views. We have one situation now we haven't really resolved. It relates to the number of verses of Torah that we will read in services. The Torah is written in Hebrew script, and it's difficult for lay readers to do properly. It's really an exercise in memorization. When poorly done, it's laborious and hard to listen to. Peter would like to diminish or dispense with this ritual reading, and that makes me crazy. We have different ideas about the tradition. We've had meetings in which we've just had to stop talking about it.

I'm a real advocate for myself and the things I really care about. In relationships I care about, I'm right out there. Early on we had to work some things out. We handled our early conflicts in a way that made us both feel secure that we could trust each other and we could work it out. Moreover, we have a lot of fun together. Peter is not a confrontational person, but he's come to trust the process between us so that on rare occasions he'll bring something up. I think now there's a very great and sort of sacred mutual respect between us. I've been respectful and loyal to him—as the boss in a lot of ways—and he has been respectful and loyal to me as his friend and partner and colleague—and as another rabbi in the congregation.

Peter has really created a culture here where you want to use your energy and resources in the right way. There is not a lot of petty wrangling. It makes for a very healthy extended family. This place has grown by almost 50 percent in the five years I have been here. I'm not necessarily a big team person, but our team can change people's lives. I want to be a part of that. We really come together on ideas and planning and not so much on execution. When I'm working with a family I have the opportunity to do that. But I can also go to my colleagues and say, "What do you think about this?"

○

Peter Leads

When we began looking for a second rabbi, we went to two campuses of our rabbinical college to interview anyone interested. I took a layperson along with me to each. It became crystal clear to us when we met Eleanor that she was the person we were most interested in. She is an extremely well-put-together individual. She is well spoken. She has the ability to be blunt without being offensive. She seemed smart. She was engaging, warm, and mature for her age. She was somebody who would fit well in our congregation, especially to take a position that had never been filled before.

I don't know how we laid the groundwork for Eleanor in any specific way. At least in my own perspective, I have been a deeply committed feminist for many years. My first act as rabbi of the congregation was to add the matriarchs to the liturgy. Furthermore, we do not have a classic women's organization here. It is expected that women who participate in the leadership of the congregation will participate in the leadership of the congregation, not the leadership of a single-gender organization. I have moved from the classic position of access to the notion that women's experience must be included as well so that women are not honorary men. This is also a congregation in a unique community. The people who live here are largely committed to an egalitarian perspective. It was inconceivable that gender would be a question. In fact, the most significant issue was that many people wanted me to promise that I would find a woman.

I am the short bald guy who has been here for twenty years, and if I have a title, it is senior rabbi. On some level there is probably a slightly greater power that resides in me. But we don't use titles here. Eleanor is not the assistant to the rabbi or the assistant rabbi. She was never the assistant no matter what her title is. She is one of the rabbis of the congregation.

I believe you hire very good people. You allow them to do their thing. You support them, and they make you look very good. I don't like the notion that in order to look good you have to have "yes people" around you. So it was very important for me not to get someone who lacked quality so that somehow in comparison I would look good. I wanted somebody who would be a dynamo and would be able to do all the things that need to be done in this job. That was crucial.

One of the things that I think is unusual in our team is that I don't expect other members to agree with me—even in public. Eleanor frequently chooses to take the other side of an issue—and that has been valued as part of our working relationship. So, if I want something and she doesn't think it's a good idea, that subject is not limited to our private conversation. I let her take her view and I take mine. If it differs with hers we will argue vigorously. Rarely do we decide that we won't disagree in public.

It works fine to disagree in public because we don't take it personally. I took it personally once. I behaved inappropriately. Eleanor and I straightened it out and it's never happened again. We talked about it and I apologized publicly. It was the right thing to do. If I expect my laypeople to behave appropriately, I expect myself to behave appropriately.

This has a healthy, energizing influence on the community. I think that's because nobody cares about power around here. Power for what? How did we get here? It's the place. Laypeople don't care about power. Clergy don't care about power. We care about getting stuff done. It's amazing how much you can get done when you don't care who gets credit for it. That's what this place is all about. I don't know how we got there. It may have to do with my personality, though I don't know. I never think it's a mistake to do the right thing. You certainly can't expect something from others if you are not willing to do it yourself.

My sabbatical did affect the team. On one level it had a negative effect because Eleanor felt burdened and undervalued. This was not apparent to me until I came back. We underestimated what would happen with another rabbi here while I was on sabbatical. Last time we had only a cantor here and a lot of things got put on hold. With a rabbi here, they didn't get put on hold. It became a burden to Eleanor and she felt undersupported. So we had some things that we needed to do to repair the relationship. We just talked about them. We laid them on the table. You have to be willing to lay them on the table— to listen not only to what is said but to the feelings. You have to be willing to acknowledge mistakes if in fact you have made them.

I think we have created an ethos that makes the team work. We have that expectation. I have a very strong expectation that people will work together well—and will take care of each other. When we don't do that, we're not very happy. We have tensions. It usually becomes my role to tell a team member that we think that person isn't pulling his or her weight on the team. It is the responsibility of the team leader to make sure it works, to make sure that his or her own ego does not get in the way, and to make sure that no member of the team seeks advantage over another member. One other thing. Whoever is the team leader has to have at least some perception of his or her own weaknesses and allow other members of the team to shine where he or she may be weaker. The success of the team is in the willingness to understand that it's a team. You are working together. These are ultimately not people who work for you but with you.

Then it's easy. It is easy if people are committed to the past. It's easy if people are largely unconcerned about who gets the credit. It's easy if people believe in the mission. I've learned how much fun it can be to work with a person like Eleanor. I've learned to be a better listener because she is a very perceptive listener. I've learned a greater appreciation for the use of beautiful language because she writes and speaks beautifully. I've learned about great honesty when you are feeling hurt or angry or ill-used. I like the fact that we have a really good partnership.

○

15

COMMUNICATING IN MIXED-GENDER TEAMS

THE STORY OF ELEANOR AND PETER teaches us much about how a healthy team uses language. It's clear right away that these partners talk to each other a lot. Both are also very articulate. As Peter said about Eleanor, she is "well spoken, able to be blunt without being offensive." Peter doesn't do so badly at that himself. As a result, their talk is direct, honest, and to the point. They share ideas, experience, and feelings as well as information about the day-to-day. Furthermore, they do not necessarily expect to agree, in private or in public. There is no sense in which one has more of a voice than the other, and they learn from disagreeing with each other. They seem to *enjoy* discourse.

Peter and Eleanor also listen to each other. That's the other side of talking. Sometimes that takes a lot of time. It took a while for Peter to hear Eleanor's experience of serving the congregation while he was on sabbatical. But in the end he did, because he was listening and Eleanor was willing to stick with her message. Eleanor could use her own voice and her own way of speaking, and Peter worked hard to understand her. Eleanor does the same for Peter. Ultimately, they have achieved a unique relationship in their discourse and in their working life. Where men and women have different ways of expressing ideas and recounting experiences, Eleanor and Peter are able to use those expressions with each other because of the quality of listening they provide for each other.

In order to talk as honestly as they do, Eleanor and Peter must also have parity in their team. The sense of equality they share, in spite of the fact that Peter holds a superior title, comes in part from the commitment both have made to gender equality. It may not seem significant to their discourse that Peter has included the matriarchs of the church in the liturgy, but it is. We shall see why as we consider language and communication in more depth in the course of this chapter. What we shall discover is that it's not just a matter of how Eleanor and Peter—or any other team—communicate. It is also a matter of how the team understands the use of the language and the importance of providing a voice for both men and women.

How We Use Language

The imperative to communicate with each other is best understood in the context of how we use language. Therefore, we will start by answering some questions on this subject before we look further at how effective mixed-gender team members communicate with one another. We don't often analyze how we use language because we take it for granted as a tool for describing our experience in the world. To be sure, language does describe our experience and express what we believe, with symbols we call words. It's simple at this level. What we say reflects what we know and what we believe, based on what we have experienced. Yet the converse is also true. Language also shapes our experience. There is "a kind of circular movement by which one's personal language, thought, and experience constantly interact. On a larger screen there is a connection as well between language and social change, and it too is circular" (Ashe, 1997, p. 62). As we have become more and more aware of how language influences as well as describes, we have begun to play the politics of language. Here's where it gets complicated. Gender is a major influence.

We are all familiar with the inclusive language debates of our time. This may be the most obvious way in which we experience the politics of language. But in order to understand the current debate about inclusive language, we have to go back to a time in our history when language belonged almost entirely to men. Let us follow the trail back to that time, and then come forward to our own time once again. We can do so by asking four questions about how we use language: Who speaks? What do we say? How do we speak? How do we name God?

Who Speaks?

There is a Pepsi commercial that is popular right now in which a small girl and her father go into an Italian restaurant and step up to the bar. The girl, a cute, innocent-looking child of about eight with curly black hair, chubby cheeks, and dimples, asks for a Pepsi. The bartender, a big, burly middle-aged man, says, "Sure, honey," and pours her a Coke. She takes one sip and knows right away that she has been tricked. Suddenly she has the voice of Don Corleone from *The Godfather,* and she threatens the bartender with his life if he does not give her a Pepsi. Now when she speaks, everyone in the restaurant takes notice of this little girl. Everyone is scared and snaps to attention. Then there is gunfire. Everyone ducks, and the bartender hands over a Pepsi.

It's a cute commercial, and we all laugh—at first. Then when we think about it we see the truth in it. This commercial is revealing of the fact that, in our culture, men's voices are heard, remembered, and heeded. It's not so cute a phenomenon when we look at it deeper. Many of the men in the mixed-gender teams in this study expressed concern that their female partners are not more vocal in the important meetings. The relative silence of the women, they say, costs them important visibility and power among constituents. Some of the women said they are reticent to speak up in these settings. Others said they chose not to play a major role in administration and governance. The fact is, women have to work much harder to have a voice. It's one of the gender traps we'll hear more about in Chapter Eighteen that illustrates how women—and ultimately the whole mixed-gender team—is negatively affected by the differences in how men and women are heard.

Research shows that men and women alike take men more seriously as speakers and do not hear women as well as they hear men. Men, socialized to be dominant, "often can hear only their own voice" (Nuechterlein and Hahn, 1990, p. 42). One male team member observed this about himself when he said, "I have a didactic streak in me that loves to tell other people how to do things. My partner tolerates that with wonderful grace. I try to recognize that in myself and not be overbearing." This man, like most in this study, is willing to assert his view without apology. In contrast, I noticed that the interviews with women in this study included many more assertions preceded by the qualifier "I think." Women have more difficulty than men in asserting their authority, considering themselves authorities, expressing themselves in public so that others will listen, gaining others' respect for their intellect and ideas, and fully using their capability and training in their work. As a result, they often end up feeling unheard even when they have something important to say (Belenky, Clinchy, Goldberger, and Tarule, 1986; Nuechterlein and Hahn, 1990).

This is not necessarily because women aren't capable, intelligent, or forceful speakers. It may be because a man's way of asserting himself as an authority in conversation is the norm, and therefore the standard by which we judge women as well. Tannen (1990) explains three critical points among the many conversational styles she has researched with empirical observation of male-female conversations. First, she verifies that it is very difficult for women to get the chance to speak. Men, she says, tend to need someone to listen and agree with their point of view or their explanations. Women comply by being the listeners. Second, men interrupt more, without thinking about it as impolite. This happens, Tannen observes, largely because men tend to approach a conversation as a contest whereas women tend to approach it as a connection. More troubling even than this is Tannen's observation that women in conversation get judged more harshly than men, even when they *do* converse in the same way. She cites studies of tag questions—statements with little questions added to the end of sentences ("It's a nice day, isn't it?"). Women, she says, are expected to use more tag questions in conversation than men. Even when men and women use the same number of tag questions in conversation, she adds, the women are judged less knowledgeable and intelligent than men who also use them. Furthermore, "women who do not give supporting evidence for their arguments are judged less intelligent and knowledgeable, but men who advance arguments without support are not" (Tannen, 1990, p. 228). Men and women in successful teams have had to learn to overcome these language habits that favor men and what men have to say. Even when they have overcome them inside the team, they still confront them every time the members of the team talk in other groups.

The generations-old belief that women should not speak is partly responsible for the fact that women are not heard or attended when they do speak today. Here's where history can help us. Women in sixteenth-century England were not even permitted to read the Bible aloud in their own homes to their own families (Tannen, 1998). Over a hundred years later, women in colonial America were held under water, publicly gagged, or fitted into iron frames with metal mouth bits if they spoke too much or too publicly (Ashe, 1997). As recently as the nineteenth century, "the very thought of a woman standing up in public and facing an audience to speak was unthinkable." In the United States, "early suffragists and anti-slavery activist women outraged society not only by the policies they were advocating but by the very fact that they were speaking in public" (Tannen, 1998, p. 201).

With this background to overcome, it is little wonder that women today are still reticent, still learning to speak with our own voices, and still suffering some consequence when we do. It is not only that women are silenced but also that men and women who wish to work together as equal partners are hampered in their ability to do so. If we are going to be successful in communicating in our mixed-gender teams, we surely need an environment in which women as well as men can speak. And we would do well to make sure that women as well as men are heard when they *do* speak.

What Do We Say?

If both men and women *can* speak and *can* be heard, we might then ponder how to use the opportunity. Here again research shows some important gender differences. I can illustrate them best by recounting a recurring dream I had when I began writing on the subject of women in leadership. In the dream, I was in a foreign country, walking the streets of a town, naked. I did not know where I was. I was always silent in this dream because I did not know how to speak the language. I simply walked around cloaked in my own silence, feeling very exposed, unable to connect with anyone around me. I think now that this dream was about how it felt to spend my working days in a man's world. I *was* in a foreign country. I *was* exposed. My dream reflected the inner struggle I was waging to survive and prosper. Once I figured it out, moved beyond trying to be like my male colleagues, and even decided I could speak in my own voice (at least sometimes), the dream went away.

We women long to have the opportunity to speak in our own language, if only for a part of our working day. One of the women I interviewed put it well when she said, "I have always cultivated women friends and I meet with them in spite of my busy schedule—not to talk about what it is like to be a woman leader but to have people with whom I can check out my view of the world. It's a reality check for me." Sometimes men trivialize women's talk as gossip, small talk, or silly chatter (Ashe, 1997). Or they get nervous when we women get together to talk. We women are mystified by men's reaction. If we are up to something it has nothing to do with our male colleagues. We are about creating a time and place to talk in our own language. We use language to establish relationships and connect with one another. We are not so inclined as our male peers to be confrontational with language and may be uncomfortable in situations where we do have to be confrontational (Tannen, 1998). It's just nice to be together in an environment where we don't have to do that for a while.

Men, who often think competitively, assume we are plotting when we women get together to talk. The fact is that men are more comfortable with conflict, and it shows in their use of language as well as their behavior. They are more able (than women are) to argue with each other at work and then proceed with the job as though nothing happened. They use ritual opposition, including teasing, insulting each other, and playing devil's advocate to accomplish a whole range of objectives. They can view verbal opposition as sport and enjoy it as such, whereas women are often uncomfortable with this approach (Tannen, 1998).

But the truth of the matter is that we are all better off if we can talk to each other. Achieving this end requires that both men and women understand how the other uses language and listen carefully to the other. But I have also pointed out previously in this volume how and why the imperative to listen rests more heavily on men. It is simply to even the score a bit, because we women spend so much of our time communicating in ways more comfortable for and familiar to men. We women also enjoy the opportunity to explain our way of talking to men who are interested. All of these opportunities to talk to each other and listen to each other are blessings of a strong mixed-gender partnership, as we can see from the story of Eleanor and Peter and the many others in this book.

How Do We Speak?

With this much background about how we use language, we may come back to the current debates about inclusive language. We women, wishing fervently to be known, call for language that images us and reflects our participation in leadership (Becker, 1996). This is the basis of the call for inclusive language. Women seek inclusivity in the language of human experience as well as language about our religious experience, including our imaging of God. Let us begin with our human experience and then consider how we image the divine.

First, the masculine becomes normative in our speech and is actually written into our rules of grammar. Our habit of using masculine pronouns reminds us constantly that men are active in human history. Women are less visible, sometimes invisible (Becker, 1996). As a Middle and Modern English scholar, I myself used to accept the grammatical conventions that made it so. The pronoun *he* stands for both male and female, but *she* does not. In classical grammar that is the rule because, as Ashe (1997) further points out, "eighteenth-century grammarians decided that number should take precedence over gender" (p. 64). But if I can see beyond the masculine biases that made the rules that way, I can then observe that using *he* to talk about humanity works in favor of men and contributes to the invisibility of women. The effect is that men are more easily able to name and define their experience and present it in our language as human experience (Ashe, 1997). This reality "plays subtly on our subconscious, imaging men for us all the time, women seldom. There are no easy solutions in English grammar, especially with pronouns, but surely there are ways to be linguistically more inclusive of women more of the time. Doing so consistently would not only image women in important ways, but would also help to break down the subconscious but stubbornly masculine bias of our social interaction" (Becker, 1996, p. 88).

When we examine how we talk we can also learn from examining the words and images we use. We are all limited by the fact that the English vocabulary includes many more positive names for men than for women and for whites than for people of color. A majority of descriptors for women, in fact, have negative sexual connotations. There are few words that describe women as strong, sexually healthy beings (Ashe, 1997). The word *black* and 60 of its 120 synonyms have also come to be associated with negative meaning, causing the late Martin Luther King Jr. to observe that "even semantics have conspired to make that which is black seem ugly and degrading" (King, 1967, p. 41). Our metaphors, which create word pictures for us, also speak men's language. Consider, for example, how much we use sports or war terminology to describe our activity at work and play. How often do we notice that our workaday language engages us in *strategies* and *task forces?* How often do people get described as *winners* and *losers?* As a result of this overexposure, some women's organizations will not use any language that images fighting or military metaphors. Sometimes it's exasperating, but it always serves as a reminder that our language habits have to change if we are going to work together with ease and comfort.

Finally, it's worth mentioning a casual and irritating language habit that many mixed-gender teams report. Constituents will often talk about the pastor or the boss as being synonymous with the male member of the team. In teams that strive to be egalitarian, team members find that they are constantly trying to teach an inclusive language habit around naming the leader more generically. It's a small thing that adds up to a big thing when it happens over and over again. Some teams abandon titles altogether in order to overcome this problem and allow people to engage with each other rather than with their positions. Fredrica, whose story appears in Chapter Four, says of her seminary, "This is a first-name school in terms of how we name each other. The language matters. It's one way of respecting difference, and respecting difference is one way of respecting different cultures and individuals within cultures. I don't think most of the folks here would want to live with nineteenth-century constructs of clerical rights and responsibilities and pick up the nineteenth-century titles. I think it's very important how we are naming, how we are honoring one another. The language of it is as symbolic as dress or anything else." This informal naming can work when the whole community agrees to it. It does not work when it is applied to women only. If formal titles are used for men, women in authority need them as well. In this case, a formal title is necessary to confer authority on the woman leader.

In these examples we can see how language works to mask power, to give power, or to establish who has power. The problem we can observe is that our language reflects a hierarchical world in which there are dominants and subordinates. Such language establishes who has power and who does not, in its style, word choices, meaning, and clarity. Subordinates are often assigned descriptors with pejorative meaning, revealing our prejudices as well as how we see the hierarchy arranged. Further, I have observed that the language of our organizations usually masks power relationships. Passive voice in our organizational language "never tells who is doing what, and thereby masks power with a grammatical construction" (Becker, 1996, p. 89). It's weak language as any writer or grammarian knows, but it is the typical style of our organizations. "Passive voice doesn't say who is in charge, who expects what, who is making the decisions. It masks the authority figures," summarizes one clergywoman. And it doesn't work in any collaborative environment.

How Do We Name God?

For those who work in the church or in church-related organizations, an important part of our inclusive language habit should be inclusive language about God, lest we end up as confused as the little girl who asked in a prayer, "Dear God, Are boys better than girls? I know you are [a boy], but try to be fair" (Jewett, 1980, p. 141). Better that we should be like the little boy who, when asked by his clergy mom what God is like, replied: "I think God is more like both of us" (Becker, 1996, p. 89).

Getting to this point requires more than calling God both mother and father. A woman I interviewed put it well when she said, "I don't think that an equal number of feminine images of God would appease me. We need a diversity, a wealth of images for God, and some we can't even imagine that are beyond our comprehension." This comment summarizes the problem we have with our images for God. We debate whether God is man or woman or father or mother when God is the unknowable, beyond our parental images, beyond our gender constructs.

When I was a junior in high school, the young woman who sat behind me in English class was a devout Jew. I noticed that she wrote the word for the divine as *G-d*. I once asked her why, and I have never forgotten the answer she gave me: "Because," she said, "we believe that we cannot name God." God is "not only beyond our gender naming, but beyond our naming *at all*" (Becker, 1996, p. 86). We seem to be bereft of images that help

us see God in anything but masculine or feminine, mother or father terminology. In most cases we cannot even get beyond the masculine to feminine
images of God, and when we do we seem somehow incapable of imagining
the whole of God, assigning instead dimensions of God to the feminine. In
a masculine environment, our language about God persists in reflecting a
man-God. Our human limitations and our tendency to dualistic thinking
also cause us to think about God as male, and even to think of the male as
more like God than the female. This is what women object to.

It is hard to overcome this problem, especially for those theologies that
believe and trust in a personal God. The personal God must have a gender. Biblical revelation and biblical theologies in the Judeo-Christian tradition "rest" the dilemma by regarding God as male. As to the real nature
of God, the only option for human reason is to suspect (since we can
never know) that God is *androgyne* (in the Greek, male-female). There
are echoes of this in biblical theology, echoes that seldom are heeded.

The literature on this debate shows that feminine language for God is
usually understood politically—as God-imaging that merely promotes the
psychological and social emancipation of women. At the same time, the
heavily masculine language of the Bible is *not* seen politically. Instead, it
is understood to provide a connection to the *reality of God* that tran-
scends our images and language. There is a double standard here, which
allows both men and women to hear male language as neutral and female
language as gender-biased. There are many practical ways we experience
this limitation in our language of faith. A high school friend wrote to me
some years ago with a story about an ending in her personal faith journey. She and I had been in catechism class together in the early 1960s. We
had a reputation—well deserved, I am afraid—for challenging our pastor
about evolution, the role of women, the women in the Bible, and a host
of other omissions we felt deeply. But somehow we survived to confirma-
tion. Now, years later, my friend wrote to say that she had finally left the
church because she had heard one too many liturgies couched in the language of male experience. "It was a shame to make it all the way through
Pastor L.'s catechism class only to be felled by language in the end," she
wrote. I laughed at her wry humor, but I grieved too. Hers is the story of
too many women in the church today. Indeed, a mother has said recently
of teaching her daughter the Bible, "While some days teaching in a girl-
friendly way feels like a losing battle, I keep on in the struggle, knowing
that if I do not, she will get only the unfriendly version at church, at
school, and in a society that has God talking to kings and men but rarely
to queens and women—much less queens and women talking back"
(Lapp, 1998, p. 6).

I have been blessed with a different experience of late. Not long ago my son, a music student, invited me to attend a performance of David Maslanka's *Mass* that taught me just how much one creative team can expand our view of God in words and music. Both the feminine and masculine images for God are compelling and passionately beautiful in this work of art, which is based on the Catholic liturgy and incorporates a hymn to holy wisdom written by Richard Beale.

Of this composition, Maslanka has written in program notes, "Almost from the start of my thinking about the *Mass,* I was moved to include the 'female creative' or the 'Holy Mother,' an image which has arisen in many forms in my meditative life. . . . I must say that the awareness of the Holy Mother has become over a number of years the significant catalyst for my creative work, and I acknowledge this presence in my life with a sense of wonder and gratitude." Beale adds, "I already knew that I wanted the poems to be about the feminine side of God to balance the predominantly masculine imagery of the Mass that has come down to us. . . . The creation was not simply an act of masculine godhead, but was feminine as well."

This work of art, incorporating both words and music, is a fine example, created by men, of what we can gain in our vision of God if we can "see" both the feminine and the masculine.

The opportunity for men and women to image God as other than male is a critical factor in women's leadership. Wessinger (1996) has shown that religious traditions that include "a view of God that is not solely masculine" (p. 6) are more likely to include women in leadership. In the patriarchal traditions in the United States, where there is growing social expectation that women *will be* leaders, men and women can effectively introduce feminine images of God into the tradition. This among other things, Wessinger notes, will promote the leadership of women. We can see now that Peter's effort to include the matriarchs in the liturgy is in fact a very important move. It recognizes, at some level, that it is necessary for us to see God as active in the lives of women. This, in turn, prepares us to see the feminine in God. It should not, however, lead us to the conclusion that God is a woman. We have too long been held captive in our thinking by the argument that God is a man *because* men are agents of God. Better that we should revere God as the unknowable be-ing, beyond our understanding.

From Theory to Practice

Our careful review of these four questions—Who speaks? What do we say? How do we speak? How do we name God?—should frame our understanding of how men and women use language in religious organizations. We can see from the foregoing summary that there are both limitations and possibilities. In practice we encounter those limitations and possibilities every day. Effective mixed-gender teams know that they have to make the most of the possibilities and overcome the liabilities in order to communicate successfully in the team and to constituents outside the team. That is the challenge of language. At the same time, we are wise to remember that language not only describes our experience in the world but shapes it as well. With this foundation, we can turn to the more practical aspects of how mixed-gender teams use language.

How Mixed-Gender Teams Communicate

Much of what effective mixed-gender teams do together simply boils down to communicating. This is partly reflective in that it is something teams do together to maintain the health of the team. In effective teams, communication is not limited to sharing information about work projects. Much of it is about the team members and their relationships. Furthermore, people in effective teams spend a great deal of time talking to each other but do not begrudge this time. They do not consider it work, and they seldom name it as a reflective task. A typical response to my question about "what you do to build the team" was, "We don't really do much of anything. We do talk to each other a lot, though." Without naming it as a task, men and women in effective mixed-gender teams know that communicating with each other builds the relationships that they value.

Talk Time

The single most important behavior of successful mixed-gender teams is that they talk to each other. I would have said so before undertaking this study, and the research confirms it. Over and over again, men and women emphasized how important it is to talk to each other. For these teams, talking is not just a practical matter done for the purpose of sharing information. They are not like the rabbi who told Peter, "Take your associates out to lunch once a month so they know what's going on." For these teams, communicating is an imperative activity on which the success or failure of the team rests. These teams know that "if we don't talk to each other, our team will not thrive."

Talking like this takes time. Most teams in this study report that they spend about two hours a day in conversation. Sometimes it is more than that. Some of this talking happens in structured staff meetings, which provide an important environment for the more formal conversations that must take place at regular intervals in an effective team. But meetings do not represent the only way these men and women talk to each other. In fact, meetings are often too structured an environment for their most important conversations. What seems even more critical to them is informal checking in on each other, the back-and-forth from one office to another as a decision is considered, lunch or break talk, conversation on the way to meetings or constituent visits, and end-of-day how-are-you talk. At these informal times, men and women in effective mixed-gender teams talk to each other at many different levels. It adds up throughout the day, as I have said, to hours, not minutes.

The ease of conversation these teams describe is part of the secret of effective communication. People who do not know each other well will not be able to talk this way. Teammates who do not trust each other will not be able to talk to each other this way, either. Anyone who is loath to share information with coworkers will be too guarded to talk this way. It's one thing to describe effective mixed-gender teams as talkers, but it's another thing to understand what that really means. Motivation is the key. The men and women in these teams talk to each other because they want to know each other deeply. Their commitment is to each other, for the sake of an effective working relationship. That's why they talk to each other so often and on so many different levels. They are not talking to each other because they want to be an effective team, though they may have started with that motivation. In the best teams, motivation is derived out of a desire for relationship. An outcome of their relationship is that they become extremely effective teams. This motivation is fundamentally different from that of many other teams who approach talking as a task to be completed. It is also different from many teams who talk to each other in order to be an effective team but who do not desire to know each other as persons on a deeper level.

In teams with a deep commitment to relationship, honest talk is possible. To be sure, the ability one feels to be honest with teammates will determine how effective the team will be at the most difficult tasks. I know this from my own working life. I have many male and female colleagues with whom I work in varying consulting teams depending on the needs of our client organizations. I am well aware that there are some I can talk to very honestly, both about my personal life and about my workplace concerns. These are the people I team with the best. The teams in this study said the same thing.

What Teams Talk About

Effective teams talk about work, about their team, and about themselves. They are able to integrate their talk in these three areas in ways that help team members get their collective work done and get to know one another better. The interconnectedness of getting work done and getting to know one another better and better is vital. It depends on the ability of team members to talk to each other on many different levels simultaneously. We can see this in the story of Eleanor and Peter.

It's easy to understand work talk. This is subject matter talk that includes talking about projects, discussing and making decisions, planning activity, reviewing constituent information, and the like. Eleanor and Peter talk about sermons, how many verses of Torah to read, what to say to a person in the hospital, and a host of other work details. It's what we all know we have to talk about to get the job done. Many teams stay at this level. Teams can be effective at this level, but it's inevitable that they will make mistakes because they do not know each other well enough.

Personal talk is also relatively easy to understand. The openness to share personal information and concerns is based on relationships of deep trust and comes from each individual's self-knowledge and willingness to be self-revealing. Team members who share at this level also demonstrate a willingness to examine their own inner lives and their personal connections to what they do. With this commitment, they are able to share their own life scripts with one another. They recognize this as a shared reflective task that is as legitimate as talking about the team or talking about work projects.

Team talk is a bit more complex. It includes conversation about the team and the people in it. Based on the many ways I have suggested that team members reflect with each other, I can think of five very different ways that teams might talk together about their team. I see all five of these ways of sharing team talk reflected in the conversations of the teams in this study.

First, they tell each other about gifts and strengths observed, being explicit about the benefit to the workplace and to the team of each person's gifts. One team in this study devised a structured way of talking about one another's gifts. They have this conversation periodically. One of the rules of the conversation is that the individual spoken to cannot deny the gift. This team has thus created a way to talk about their individual skills without having those skills denied by the individual who may be uncomfortable hearing compliments. Hearing the positive qualities of team members shared out loud not only helps the individual members but also builds a collective knowledge about the wisdom of the team and helps the team discover the areas in which it may be weak.

Second, the team members reflect with each other on the meaning of calling each other leader, follower, and partner. Whenever team members change roles, this reflection is necessary. It is also helpful as teams grow and mature. Bruce and Pam, whose story appears in Chapter Twelve, did a great deal to reflect on their roles as leader and follower.

Third, as a natural progression from talking about each other as leaders, they talk about their leadership. There are many aspects to this subject, including observing and discussing differences in leadership styles among members of the team, helping each other develop as leaders based on each person's different strengths in leadership, and observing and discussing with each other what it takes to be a leader today and in the future. Ben, Fredrica, and Karen have spent a great deal of time talking about leadership styles as they have worked to change the collective leadership style at the Episcopal seminary.

Fourth, they reflect regularly on what team members learn as they observe each other's participation in the team. Eleanor shared an anecdote that illustrates this point. She and Peter were on a hospital visit together. "Peter read a text. I asked him afterward why he didn't say anything personal to the woman we were visiting, something about her own journey, her own life. He said he'd try it next time, and he did. The next time we went on a hospital visit together he asked the patient how he was and engaged in comfortable small talk. But he didn't pray. So I asked him afterward why not. He said he did not have a prayer with him. I said, 'Make one up!'" In this way, Eleanor shares with Peter her extemporaneous style. For his part, Peter shares with Eleanor his knowledge of how to manage the congregation's finances. "I see what his knowledge means to our lay leadership. It gives him a voice and a vote in a whole other realm of the life of the community," Eleanor observed. This is precisely how members of a team can learn from observing and discussing each other's leadership.

Fifth and finally, these teams observe how individuals and the team as a whole grows and matures. Eleanor and Peter made changes in their team after Peter's sabbatical. This involved talking about how the team functions and how they wanted it to function differently in the future. The Lutheran relief team's Rethinking project is a structured opportunity for them to look at their team and how it functions across service areas. At least two other teams in this study who work with divinity students are of necessity constantly evaluating their own team. They must do so in order to teach others how to team effectively. These are but a sampling of the ways teams talk about the growth of the team.

The story of Eleanor and Peter indicates how this kind of talking at three different levels is often challenging and hard. It's not just fun and games. Eleanor was reflecting on how their team works and talking about her own personal life when she told Peter she had difficulty during his sabbatical. She raised questions about the team's way of assigning work when she asked about sermons on the High Holy Days. She was talking about her own professional life when she talked frankly about what she wanted out of a partnership. Eleanor is able and committed to talking on different levels with her partner. Peter is similarly skilled and committed. He shared his personal as well as his professional need in his response about the sermons. He talks about the effectiveness of the team when he tells Eleanor how much she contributes and when he thanks her. He talks about both himself and the team when he defines the role of the leader. He talks about work when he asks for discussion on the number of verses of Torah to read in services. He talks about the team and about work every time he interprets a difference of opinion to members of the congregation. Because of their ability to be honest and open on many different levels—with work talk, team talk, and personal talk—their relationship and their team is more satisfying for both of them and productive for the community.

The Idea-Action-Feedback Cycle

In the course of my conversations with mixed-gender teams I asked each person in depth about how projects are run and how decisions are made. This gave me more specific information about work talk. I began to see a cycle in team conversations that I call the idea-action-feedback cycle. It goes like this. One member of the team gets an idea about a project or a new program or some other action that can be taken at work. The next step is not to implement it but to take it to the team for conversation. The team talks about the idea. Sometimes the talk is exhaustive. Often the idea changes significantly as a result of team conversation. Once the team is ready to implement the idea, it goes to the appropriate person—often but not always the person who brought the idea up in the first place. During the action phase, talk is mostly about the practical details of putting the idea into practice. But when it's all done, the team comes together again to discuss how it went.

We may take this kind of process for granted, but it's not always practiced in teams. In fact, women report the lack of this kind of cycle as a common problem in mixed-gender teams that do not work well. They report often being left out of idea discussion and even implementation detail talk. They may be assigned work that they do on their own, but there is seldom the energy of discussing and implementing an idea that is apparent in the teams that use the idea-action-feedback cycle.

The theological institute team, whose story appears in the next chapter, used the idea-action-feedback cycle to complete their grant proposal. Their story will illustrate the process in some detail. Ben, Fredrica, and Karen used this approach to reposition their antiracism work in a way that the whole community would accept. Other teams in this study have used the idea-action-feedback cycle to plan a bicentennial celebration, prepare for a certification visit, plan a retreat, relocate a preschool project, and a host of other things. Essentially, what these teams said is that the idea-action-feedback cycle becomes a way of doing business together where projects are concerned.

The freedom to consult one another is an important element of the idea-action-feedback cycle. In fact, without this freedom, the cycle would not get started. Women and men in effective mixed-gender teams do not worry about sharing their ideas with each other because they are not operating out of an ownership model. My idea can be your idea too. We can share it and it will be all that much better.

Jokes Are for Laughs, Not for Ridicule

The jokes are different. It's a small change that gets big notice in effective mixed-gender teams. Most of the men in this study have had the experience of being in an all-male setting, where, as one man put it, "Any number of things might get said because I was a man in the room and there were no women. Everything from the nature of the jokes to specific terms that were used. I mean ordinary sexist terms as opposed to intentionally derogatory sexist terms." The speaker might not mean anything by it, but the men in this study, like the one who shared this feedback, are the kind of men who "could not help noticing" every time such language was used. They are keenly aware that such jokes are out of place now, and in fact were out of place in the past. In their mixed-gender teams, such language, especially the jokes, are absent.

Jokes that denigrate women are often used as loyalty tests, to determine if women (and for that matter their male team members) will play by the rules of the male majority. They include statements that put women down as a category or that lift women up as an exception. They may also be insults or ridicule of women or women's incompetence, kidding, and off-color jokes told specifically because a woman is present. Women in mixed-gender teams can be tested and retested by the dominant male group out-side the team to see if they will be loyal by allowing this inappropriate-ness. At the same time they are tested they are reminded that, ultimately, they are still outsiders (Coger, 1985; Kanter, 1977). Some women find this loyalty testing too difficult to endure and never become part of the dom-inant (male) group. They are thereby left without all-important support from male peers. Others who pass the test are better accepted, but they run the risk of forgetting what it was like to be an outsider and with-drawing their support and mentoring from other women.

The personal relationships that people have with one another in effec-tive mixed-gender teams preclude the kind of joking that ridicules groups or tests individuals. But teams still may have to deal with it from external sources. Women of course will know the jokes are a test. The men may not. But men who are committed to working relationships with women may also be tested with jokes of this kind to see if they will go along with them or object to them. Remember the story of Brain and Martha, and how important it was to Martha that Brian set the standard for how she would be treated in clergy meetings that were largely male. If jokes are used in this and similar environments they should be heard as a test of both the women and the men in the team. The men are targets as much as the women because, as members of mixed-gender teams that have the reputation of being effective, they are a potential threat to the old (male-dominant) way of doing things. The plus where gender is concerned: women are not alone in addressing the jokes that ridicule women as a gen-der or test them as individuals. The minus: the jokes are still around. Men and women in effective mixed-gender teams both hear them.

It's important to know how to deal with these kinds of jokes. Men should realize that the women often can't confront them without being further ridiculed or singled out. The men are in a better position to deal with the affront, either publicly or privately, with the offending party. Some men in this study *prevented* jokes like this in public settings by let-ting it be known among their male peers that they would not tolerate any ridicule of any kind of the female members of their team or of females as a group.

Misunderstandings

Bad jokes are one thing, but honest misunderstanding is quite another. Men and women in effective teams do misunderstand and even hurt each other. They don't necessarily set out to avoid this possibility at all costs. Blair, whose story appears along with his teammate Mary's in Chapter

Twenty-Two, has explained it this way: "I want us to enjoy the relationship we've got and bless it, but I don't want the good in our relationship to become a straitjacket. Life is not that pretty. I want us to leave room in our relationship for us to be wounded, to be angry at each other. . . . I want to make sure we don't calcify our good feelings about each other."

Honest talk requires taking risks. One of the primary risks is that one's partner will be hurt or will somehow misunderstand. At first Eleanor's message to Peter about his sabbatical was not heard clearly. Eleanor had to continue to tell him until he did hear. Why persist? For Eleanor, it was because she needed to be heard. Remember what Eleanor said when she was finally heard: "It took away a huge part of being mad. I needed him to know." This is one legitimate reason to persist with a message, as men and women in effective teams know. It's acceptable to need to be heard. It helps to have a partner who we know wants to hear us. In the end, Peter said that Eleanor taught him something about "great honesty when she was feeling hurt, angry, and ill-used." Discernment comes in deciding how far to go. We don't want to reach the point of venting in ways that may seriously damage our relationships with one another. Yet honesty and a willingness to be vulnerable with each other is for some of these teams the key factor cited in their success.

We can and do also misunderstand each other because we are men and women. From Shakespeare's *Taming of the Shrew* to Gray's *Men Are from Mars, Women Are from Venus,* men and women have documented how we think, process information, and talk differently because we are of different genders. The popular wisdom that I mentioned earlier in the chapter is that men compete and want control whereas women want relationship and connection. Of course, these are stereotypes containing kernels of truth we can use if we are cautious. They are useful to a point and limiting beyond that point. If we want a system that explains how we are different, personality type is another factor that we ought to consider alongside gender. There is simply no one way to understand our partner of the opposite sex.

I've mentioned two possible ways in which men and women in mixed-gender teams could misunderstand each other. There are undoubtedly others as well. I mention these two ways to provide examples. The real point I want to make is that men and women who know each other the best and have the most effective teams are not afraid of the misunderstandings. They do not strive in their communication to eliminate misunderstanding at all costs. They do strive to avoid unnecessarily hurting each other. But they are willing to risk misunderstanding for the sake of the growth of the team. The literature supports this view of the best teams. "One of the myths about effective teams is that they are characterized by chummi-ness," but in fact always being nice is not on the list of essentials for an effective team (Billington, 1997, p. 4). Not all the teams in this study can be classified in the ranks of those who risk this much. Some can. Others are working on it. A few do not have this as a goal for their team.

Affirmation

Affirmation in mixed-gender teams is most often handled verbally as a part of talking to each other. In this sense, we might consider it a part of calling each other leader and partner. It's one of those conversations that many teams say they could do better or at least more often. One male team member admitted, "I could grow in this area. My teammate has told me this." Another man credits the only woman on the team with teach-ing them about affirmation. "She plays a major role here," he said. "Men are lousy about affirmation." A woman who has a similar problem with her male partner on another team said, "Mostly successes here are not noted. I just ask my partner when I want to know what he thinks about how something went." Said another woman of her teammate, who tends to be more controlling than she is, "The times when my partner gives up some control are worth a hundred affirmations!" This kind of affirmation is, for her, better than words, although she hastens to add that her team-mate does give verbal affirmation as well.

Most teams do report some verbal way of affirming a job well done. And not all men are bad at it or forget about it. One male pastor even calls himself "the cheerleader." Another commented about the importance of male team members giving affirmation to the women to help them be more visible. "I am very good at affirmation, and I lavishly praise my teammate's accomplishments. I draw attention to what she has personally been respon-sible for because I want people to know these things just don't happen. She brings so much to the process."

Affirmation is given in staff meetings, at impromptu parties held to mark successes, and in the informal thanks team members give each other. More rarely it happens as it did for Eleanor when the congregation rec-ognized her for her five years of service. Still other teams create their own unique ways of verbal affirmation. In one congregation, "We heard when we came here that nobody ever says thank you in this church," team members recall. "We've responded to that by enlarging the recognition circle to include the congregation." Another team that has taken this ap-proach is careful to pass on their own affirmation of each other as well as affirmation from laypeople.

It's important to hear how well we are doing from each other. "In my former position, I never knew if what I did was good, bad, or indifferent," one woman recalled. "It all comes down to communicating."

How Talk Contributes to an Effective Team

Most teams have the impression—correct, no doubt—that they spend most of their time on work tasks rather than team building. Yet their talk reflects a balance of conversation about the team, the work, and the people involved. Is there a contradiction here?

The answer is no. Effective teams do spend most of their time on work. At the same time, they demonstrate a facility for using their work as a platform for talking in all three areas. With an admirable focus on their work, they talk about the work, the team, and themselves. The outcome is that they get the work done, build the team, and deepen their knowledge of themselves and of each other. This does not happen without challenges, misunderstandings, and some hard conversations. It requires sensitivity to the language issues I outlined in the first part of this chapter. It also requires a commitment to putting aside our own agendas and listening to each other. Successful mixed-gender teams are not afraid of the hard conversations, however, because their talk is based on trust, a commitment to honesty with each other, and a mutual ability to listen as well as talk.

When all is said and done, team members use team talk to create and sustain an effective mixed-gender team because they can talk to each other. Their talk is a firm foundation for the other elements of working together that we shall hear about in the next two chapters.

16

THE THEOLOGICAL
INSTITUTE TEAM

KEEPING THE DAILY COMMITMENT
TO WORKING TOGETHER

WORKING TOGETHER in a mixed-gender team is a way of life for the administrative team at a Dominican theological institute in the Midwest. This administrative team includes six people, evenly split between men and women. Four (Charlie, Diane, Albert, and Sheila) are Dominicans, and two (Ron and Eileen) are laypeople with families. Charlie and Diane, who have known each other for twenty years, form the core partnership in the team. They are the president and academic dean, respectively. They have worked together for the past nine years. Others have joined the team more recently. Sheila has been with the team five years, progressing from administrative assistant to registrar. Albert joined as the finance director five years ago. Eileen has been on staff five years, most recently as director of development. Ron is the newest member. He arrived two years ago to manage admissions and public relations.

Just before my interview with this team, the institute was one of forty seminaries in the United States to receive a $1.5 million grant from the Lilly Endowment. To receive a grant, theological schools had to write proposals for unique projects of their own design. This school will promote theological education and ministry to Generation X. The grant to this institute was a direct result of the proposal written by this administrative team. "It was a perfect opportunity where we came together to work on a project," Eileen recalled. "It was very mission-focused and it was certainly about the future. We really did it in a very synergistic way."

199

Yet as Charlie pointed out, "It wasn't that much different from the way we normally work. It was more intense, maybe, but we didn't change our modus operandi." In order to find out how this team does work, I talked with them about the Generation X project and their commitment to working together. Although their story illustrates the synergy in a successful team, it also reveals how a successful team faces problems and challenges.

○

The Generation X Project

DIANE: It started with conversations . . . talking . . . and in processing our ideas.

CHARLIE: We discussed it, we broke it into parts and had individual people work on it, and then we brought it back together. Of course, that didn't work! So we edited, revised, passed drafts around. In the end it worked. Ultimately, we did have to have someone chairing the team. It was a successful project for all of us, not just my project. I hope that's true. Again, it's related to the mission. Everybody was (and is) on board about wanting this school to be better. It was never an issue of my part or your part, as opposed to the mission.

RON: The grant proposal started as a conversation about an opportunity to be well funded if we could come up with a plan. No one had a foregone conclusion in mind. We even brought the board into the discussion. Collaborative team building requires a sense of suppleness, an openness to what is going to be fashioned, and a willingness to allow that to take shape as we continue our deliberations.

EILEEN: The project forced us to look seriously at our mission, to look seriously at our future, and to work together. We had to name who we are and what we are committed to. We had to figure out who would write and how we could word it. We had to figure out who would take the leadership—who would do what and how the pieces would come together—because not everyone was going to have an equal role.

We did well, but it was stressful because we are all perfectionists. Some of us are perfectionists at the very last moment. Others of us are perfectionists from the beginning. There was a lot of pressure on me to manage the time line and pull it all together. That took a lot of time and I didn't always necessarily get the message that the amount of time I spent on it was valued. The day after it went in the mail, I said to

Charlie, "Let's talk about how this went. I learned some things." And we talked.

These are the realities of human beings coming together on any kind of project. You bring your differences and your styles. There is difference between one person who is a primary coordinator (which was Charlie's role) and one person who dominates. Charlie is the president. He sets the vision. He has to carry that responsibility out. But in a team effort, he has to let go at some point in order to let others do their part and contribute. He did that. To everyone's credit, we've all figured out what we're here for and we're all very committed to it.

SHEILA: The main people who worked on the project were Charlie, Diane, Ron, and Eileen. I contributed the statistics, but I was not as up to speed on it as a whole. It was a very successful project but not without its problems for us. It will mean changes for us because we will grow. At some point in the fall the question of changes in our team came up. I was not at that meeting. The others discussed a model that would affect my position on the team. I was upset. Eventually, I had to raise this with Charlie. But first I spent three weeks wondering if I was overreacting. Charlie was surprised by how I felt, but he was great about it. We talked about it, and Diane has followed up to ask how I feel about the conversation. We haven't resolved it but we are talking about it.

DIANE: That's the value of putting the issue out there. We can go at it again.

○

The Art of Collaborating

ALBERT: We use a collaborative consensus model but still realize who has the expertise in certain areas—and we leave those decisions to that person.

RON: Conversation and communication are at the top of the list in our style as a team. In order for collaboration to work, one of the requisite factors is a high commitment to communication and respect for each person's point of view—not a point of view that is just opinion but one that is based on that person's background, office, competence, and authority. Our team uses a deliberate consultative procedure that allows each person to contribute his or her voice and gifts more fully.

Charlie has such a good institutional history at his command—and his personality and his gifts are such that he can gather these insights and perspectives. There is a sense from Charlie that we all offer a valid point of view. Then there is an honest sifting—not a predetermined outcome that gives us a token voice. There is really a dynamic conversation that yields direction. This is the genius of his leadership as he facilitates the team. What he gathers from us is larger in the summation than any component parts.

SHEILA: Charlie works very hard at collaborating. Diane just does it. She is a natural. They are very good for each other. Albert comes at collaboration in a superorganized fashion. Ron and Eileen are constantly collaborating. Ron especially is always asking, "How is this collaboration?"

CHARLIE: We try to use consensus. We try to be honest too. I don't withhold information from either the administrative team or from the faculty. In my own leadership style I try to stay very focused on the mission. It's very easy to get distracted. Whenever we make a strategic decision we try to ask, "Why does this school exist?" and "What is it supposed to be doing for the church?" We all have to be willing to share honestly—both what we think and how we feel about something. We all have to have the ability to set aside our own agenda in favor of the mission of the organization—as we see it together.

ALBERT: I think that each one of us is dedicated to the mission of the school and it becomes our personal drive. I feel a personal responsibility to doing my job well. I'm basically not a team person. Sometimes it's very stressful for me to work with a team. But I realize these other people, their talent and ideas, are necessary for the work I do. That's the way it is. I know that there are certain things I can't do without their part in it, and I realize that's the way things work. I take it as a given. I can't image another way of doing it.

DIANE: Charlie is a very decisive person but he also allows others their input, and he will back off. He has grown more and more skilled in allowing people their expertise to be part of the process so they can make a contribution and in welcoming their contribution. But it is not just Charlie. Everyone feels a certain active role in making the institution go. All the intersecting circles which are the various areas of institutional life, they all keep them going. People are highly participative in activities generally.

○

The Commitment to Mixed-Gender Leadership

CHARLIE: Our commitment to mixed-gender leadership has to do with the identity of this school and our common Dominican mission. It started in the late 1960s. A very conscious decision was made at that time by the Dominican men in the central province to include women in whatever we were doing. It has evolved from that beginning. Our province, which owns this school, is very committed to collaboration between men and women. In the Roman Catholic Church, we are probably the only order (except possibly the Benedictines) that could do this. Most of the others don't have the commitment to the intellectual life and to theological education in both men's and women's communities, and enough people to pull it off.

DIANE: In the religious orders there is greater potential for men and women to work together than in other places in the Roman Catholic Church. Especially in the Dominican order, we've actualized this value in new ways since the 1960s. I was one of the first women students to graduate from this school and I did my graduate work on the collaboration of men and women and the question, "How do you get men and women working together well?"

RON: When I came here, everyone stressed that collaboration is near and dear to the heart of the Dominican order. Collaboration is truest to who we are. We try to play that strength to the degree that we can. There is seldom the instance of someone declaring, "This is the way things are going to be." The whole notion of sharing the vision and the work together is at the heart of our mission. Day by day we work at it. Maybe we stumble sometimes. But we are committed to working collaboratively.

EILEEN: We are in a church that is hierarchical. As a laywoman I have worked with religious men and women who have been formed in a hierarchical model. And yet here I work with men and women who come from a collaborative environment. There is a collaborative model between men and women, lay and religious that is intrinsic to Dominican life. It's always there to call us, and we always go back to that.

RON: The mission statement says we will be collaborative. This is a progressive stance in the Dominican order. It isn't about "saying the right things." It is a substantive involvement of the order based on a philosophical commitment to collaboration. The pragmatic payoff is that our work is better because of it.

SHEILA: It works because everybody here wants it to work. We are not only collaborative between men and women but also among ordained, men religious, women religious, and lay. Because that's part of the mission, we are committed to modeling that and to be that.

RON: We intentionally model collaborative ministry, which we hope will form our students and shape the future church.

○

Building the Team

CHARLIE: The first two years I was not aware of how important staff meetings are. I even used to make comments about "having to have one." I realized at some point that I should not do this. Then I tried to change the way the team functions. I took it more seriously. I developed advance agendas for our meetings, devoted more time to planning them.

EILEEN: You have to take time to be a team. You have to make time to pay attention to one another. It's very easy to come into the office and start to work instead of taking the time to do those things that build the relationships.

DIANE: We don't bolt in and out of meetings. We take time to greet, to connect with one another. We learn to loiter.

ALBERT: I don't really like all the chitchat. Sometimes the others think I am grumpy because of that. They tease me about it. But they know that I do value the team.

CHARLIE: I also fine-tune with members of the team individually. I work with them one-on-one if there has been a problem at staff meetings or a problem in a relationship. There is a legitimate way that the president can facilitate team functioning by working with individual members of the team.

DIANE: A question I try to ask myself is, "What do I need to do enable Sheila to do her work as well as she can?" Or, "What do I need to do in relationship to Ron and Alison [another member of his team] to enable them to do their work as well as they can?" It's almost like a constant examination of conscience. It has to do with turnaround. It has to do with rate of response. It has to do with a lot of things. What do I need to do? How do I need to alter my patterns or move ahead what I'm doing because their work is very connected with the way I do my work? When you sum that up it's like trying to think in terms of relationship with other people, other roles, and other offices.

RON: This is a growing edge for us. There are always conversations between individuals. But as far as setting aside a staff meeting to take our own temperature as a team, we don't. We tend not to assess ourselves as a collaborative team in any formal way.

DIANE: We tend so often to be dealing with either the immediate or the short-term. Do we need at times to clear the agenda for a more extended conversation on values, issues, or aspects of strategic planning, a more extended conversation in which we wouldn't be just problem solving or planning together but thinking together?

SHEILA: I was thinking even different from that. Just a retreat day. Something we would do together as a team.

ALBERT: We've had days where we took time for off-site planning and reflection on our work as a team.

DIANE: In many places it's an institutional reality that once a year they have at least a retreat day just in order to be a faith community, because the mission is grounded in faith. Just to relax and reflect. It nurtures the foundation of the mission. We don't do that. We call them retreats. Then we go off and do work.

RON: In order to allow space for the team dynamic, I think we need a little space free of the workload itself. Then we could really ask, "How do we manage this cooperatively, collaboratively?" To allow that collaborative style to really come through might require a reduced workload.

ALBERT: I have some concern about how thin we can spread ourselves in serving all the needs of the school.

CHARLIE: I think one of the biggest challenges I see right now, which was not a problem for the first five, six, or seven years I was here, is the fact that we've grown so much in different ways in the past couple years and we're trying to cope with that in terms of constantly redefining job responsibilities and working relationships among us. They've changed in a number of different ways. I haven't done that before as someone leading the team, and we keep coming up against that. It's controlled growth, not just in terms of our programs but in terms of how we continue to work well.

o

Gender Issues?

ALBERT: I don't know if there are gender issues in this team, but I feel there are gender issues in the school. I remember one time we were shocked when we learned the school has a reputation for being feminist. But I know that I often have a fear of saying something lest it offend a woman. I do! And I know that some of the male students feel the same way. I'm not putting any value or judgment on that. I'm just saying it's there.

EILEEN: One of the values of working together in a team is figuring out how to get beyond that point. If you're going to be on a team and work from a relational model you may go through that stage and you may understand what the issues are, but you have to work out of that in terms of how you relate to one another.

DIANE: Working together means being honest, working things through. Sometimes you work to clarity and sometimes you don't achieve it. But you can't just vent whenever you want. You pay a price. It can be hazardous to the long-term relationship if you are foolish. You have to ask, "Is it going to help or hinder?" Just because it's going to make you feel better, it's not necessarily going to improve trust. I call it ongoing growth in the virtue of prudence.

CHARLIE: I know I didn't realize when I became president what I was getting into. We had women on the faculty, but Diane was the first woman dean. It was the right thing to do, and I felt strongly about it, but I didn't see clearly all the implications of it.

I've become more aware. I teach ethics, so I am aware of the literature on how men and women make decisions differently. The more I deal with it, the more I have come to believe that there is a lot of truth in it. Sometimes Diane and I need to sit down and say how we feel about how we are working together. We've tried to learn to do that with each other. There is nothing worse than leaving those things unaddressed. We've had real conflict where there is a difference of perception.

We joke about how I move to resolution more quickly whereas she is always trying to keep the options open. One day she came in and raised an issue and we talked about it and I said, "I think we should do it this way." Diane left. Then she came back a few minutes later and said, "You thought I wanted a decision about that, didn't you?" I said, "Well, yes." She just turned and walked out, and I thought to myself, "Well, I guess she didn't!" It was an awareness for me that I did not always have to resolve things.

EILEEN: I would agree that things are more human issues than they are gender issues. I sometimes think we attribute things to gender. But there are some areas where men and women do differ. I do think, for example, that we bring different styles of talking about things. We have to make adjustments to that in one another in order to communicate and to be a team and do our work. So some things can be attributed to gender. I don't necessarily like that, because it's easy to stereotype. But I think there are real things to talk about—leadership styles, experience, and view of life. Some of these can be particular to our experience. And we don't need to be threatened or worried or say they are bad. But gender certainly is something that makes for a good conversation about how we lead.

DIANE: There is nothing human that is not gendered. So I think gender plays a role in a whole unfolding process in our time and our culture as we discover what it really means. It's a moving horizon in terms of our level of understanding. But we're also living in a blessed time when we've all expanded our understanding of ourselves, what it means to be a woman, what it means to be a man. This allows us to be in new roles and learn new ways. It's a perilous but wonderful time. The jury's out on this one. We're writing the history with our lives. We've got to get beyond some of the absolutes we've had in a lot of this. We're trying to be the best human beings we can be and recognize our differences as well as our commonalities.

CHARLIE: I think we have gender issues but I don't know that we have gender problems. I would have to agree with Albert. I think a lot of it is personality differences, but I also think there are some differences in the way men and women generally look at the world. There was a point for me when I thought that there's a man's way of looking at this and a woman's way. It's got to be one or the other. Now I think I've grown to see that some of the women on this staff and faculty bring a perspective that I simply do not have. I become more comfortable relying on that and realizing that I'm missing some pieces here . . . and to say I don't know how this is all going to work out. As you say, we're in shifting sands and times are changing. This issue is also very highly charged for Catholics because of all the ecclesial issues outside the team.

DIANE: It's not easy to collaborate in a mixed-gender team, but it's the only way to go. We enrich one another. There are gender differences that have nothing to do with inequality. As men and women we often approach things differently. We can have similar strengths and weaknesses. But I think as women and men we bring some ways of doing things that are proper to our gender.

I've also learned that we have to be faithful to ourselves and our way of doing things—not be other than who we are. At the same time, we need to be mindful of the other. The other is not going to perceive as I do, but the other's perception can expand my perceptions. That's a lesson in life.

O

17

WORKING TOGETHER

"I FIND IT a lot more interesting to work in an organization that is not all men. The natural gender interplay helps to maintain a certain level of interest. It makes things not the same all the time." This comment from Joe, a member of the Lutheran relief team, sums up his perspective on the difference between working in an organization run by men and one run by a mixed-gender team. How, exactly, do mixed-gender teams sustain what Joe calls the "level of interest"? To put it a bit more bluntly, how do mixed-gender teams *work* together successfully day after day? To answer this question, we turn our attention to the theological institute team.

The story of the theological institute team provides us with many insights into how a successful mixed-gender team works in the day-to-day. It should also dispel some of the myths about mixed-gender teams. Although there is undoubtedly synergy among the team members, making it work is not necessarily easy. Furthermore, it's not easier or better for the team if all the members are alike in temperament. The theological institute team includes people who are very different in their work styles and personalities. Some are more vocal than others are. Some gain more energy from the team effort than others. We can notice from the team dialogue that Sheila and Ron are less vocal. We can also observe that Albert does not have a strong personal need to team in order to get his work done effectively. Yet each of these team members contributes as much as Diane, Charlie, and Eileen. Each makes a major contribution to how the team works because each one is different from the others.

Commitment is the foundation of the team effort. This particular team has a commitment both to their common mission and to the Dominican value for effective collaboration among men and women. Using this commitment as the foundation, the team works hard every day, both on the team and on the work of the educational institution they serve. Still, they have conflict. They aren't perfect at everything, especially taking the time out to assess their team. The team includes people who are not alike and who have to work hard to understand one another. And as they face change, they too are challenged by the future. We shall look at all of these realities in this chapter as we consider how effective mixed-gender teams work well together.

Living the Daily Commitment

We have seen how being together in the same work setting is best sustained by continual reflective activity together. With this foundational activity always in place to ensure the ongoing strengthening of the team, the members of the team can turn their attention increasingly to working together. This involves careful communication, firm boundaries, clear decision-making paths, accountability among team members, and the freedom to fail as well as succeed. It's all cemented by the will to work together and a healthy sense of humor.

Making Decisions

It's a popular belief in our culture that decisions are best made by an individual leader acting alone. This stems from our belief in the hero-leader model. The corollary to this view is that teams take "forever" to make decisions that, once made, are mediocre or even ineffective. Another stereotype is that women team members more often than men tend to push for consensus, thus slowing down the process of getting the work done. Finally, we all fear what we expect might happen: that conflict over decision making gets ugly as people fight with each other about what to do. Both recent literature on effective teams and the accounts of teams interviewed in this study proved all of these notions incorrect. In Chapter Six, I summarized recent studies that show the greater effectiveness for decision making found in diverse teams, especially in mixed-gender teams. What, then, can we learn further from the teams in this study about the practical ways that effective mixed-gender teams go about making their good decisions?

Consensus decision making is prevalent in these successful mixed-gender teams. That's apparent from all the interviews. "We look at the options together and agree on what we are going to do," explained one man who is the senior member of a team. "I don't think there has ever been a time when I said, 'I don't care what you think, we're going to do it this way.' I just don't do that." One woman described this process as "rolling things around conversationally" until both members of the team have heard the other and a decision is reached. Another woman in another team described it as the give-and-take of considering the decision. A part of this give-and-take is determining who feels most strongly about or who has the highest stake in the decision. The discernment that comes before the actual decision is made "often modifies the decision that would originally have been made," another team member observed. In general, consensus decision making is an effort on the part of the team to be partners within the team, no matter how outsiders view the decision-making process. This is especially important in teams with a senior leader.

Yet consensus decision making is seldom used in its purest form in these teams. These teams do not delay decisions until everyone agrees on everything. Nor do they bring all decisions to the team table. Often these teams will discuss their decisions and turn the actual decision itself over to one individual on the team. "We don't always reach consensus. Most of the time we do because we are both willing to give ground. But we are not trying to be one person . . . so influencing of each other that we lose our individual identity," one man explained. In some teams, the senior leader of the team ultimately makes all decisions. In one such team, a member described the team process as "not consensus, but trust and delegation." Trust is the basis of the team's ability to do this. One clergyman put it this way: "We process some things, but we also realize that sometimes you don't have the luxury of the time to do that. You have to trust each other. If you disagree you work it out." Because the trust level is high in the group, team members feel included even if their role is limited to participating in a discussion about a decision that someone else will ultimately make. In the end, the formula for decision making in these teams is well summarized in the words of a woman who said, "We talk things over and decide as a team. We also trust each other's decisions and we keep communicating."

We can readily see, then, that effective mixed-gender teams do not necessarily make all their decisions together. They do, however, follow two rules that seem to be at the core of their effective decision making. First, they talk about major decisions with each other even if they are not going to make the decision together. It seems important to these team members to share ideas and opinions that will contribute to a good decision. In fact, the team members are well aware that they benefit by hearing each other's views. They enter into the discussion with an open mind about how the information might affect the decision at hand. None of them, least of all the senior team member or members, comes to the discussion seeking token input for decisions that have already been made in their minds.

Second, every decision is weighed against the question, "Am I doing something that others on the team can support?" Whenever the answer to this question is no, the individual responsible for the decision—or the team together—takes time out to reconsider. Rarely if ever do they make decisions that do not pass this test. The basis of their trust relationship where decision making is concerned is a fundamental understanding that they can count on each other to ask this question.

This is not to say that decisions are put off until all difference or controversy is eliminated. That, in fact, is the stereotype I mentioned at the beginning of this discussion. It merits a closer look. When effective mixed-gender teams face decisions they do not agree on they continue their dialogue. Hearing each other's different views takes time and careful listening. These teams are committed to the process of listening and talking to each other. But they are also well aware that they will not always reach consensus. Falling short of that, they strive for acceptance by all members of the team. Finally, there are times when they agree to disagree and support each other's decisions anyway.

That's how decisions are made together in effective mixed-gender teams. But some decisions are never even discussed in these teams. They are made individually by members of the team. Again, trust in the team is the basis for the freedom team members feel to make certain decisions on their own. They can do so with the confidence that their partners will support their actions. "Our team leader delegates well. She doesn't look over my shoulder but she expects results. She likes recommendations to be made to her. It's such a refreshing way to work. I can't tell you how exciting it is to be able to make some of my own decisions," one woman said. A part of the freedom to act alone in making some decisions comes from the team's knowledge that everyone in the group knows which decisions should not be made this way. Knowing which decisions to discuss with others and which can be made independently takes a measure of discretion and caring for others in the team.

Finally, it's important to acknowledge that these mixed-gender teams make mistakes in their decision-making process. The theological institute team created a problem when they discussed potential changes in team structure without Sheila's input. It's an important example to cite because it illustrates that even the best and most careful teams trip up in their shared decision-making process. They make mistakes usually because they get too busy, not because they disregard a person on the team. That's the difference between an effective mixed-gender team and an ineffective one, where errors in decision making are concerned.

Maintaining Accountability

Individual accountability is a non-issue for the effective mixed-gender teams in this study. It's not that they consider accountability to each other unimportant. Much to the contrary, they consider it *fundamental*. It's just that they take it for granted. The relationships and the trust are so solid in these teams that they rely on each other implicitly. Remember what Mike said about the Lutheran relief team: "We are accountable to each other everyday. We don't want to let each other down." Of her work in the theological institute team, Sheila said she has "a personal drive to be accountable to the team and a feeling of responsibility to the other team members."

Yet, again, it's important to say that these teams are not perfect. The individuals in them do not live up to their promises to each other without fail. They do let each other down on occasion. But their failures to live up to small promises do not seem to damage their belief that they can basically count on each other. Most often that's because the failures are small, usually related to being too busy.

When they do let each other down, they feel free to point this out to each other. These reminders to each other are just that. They are not challenges or personal attacks or accusations of incompetence or unconcern. They are simply reminders. "Sometimes it's apparent in meetings that someone hasn't done something and we need to raise the issue. But normally, people go to each other and work it out," Charlie noted about the theological institute team. "People are pretty honest about saying 'I didn't get to it,'" Cecilia remarked about the spiritual formation team. As these comments indicate, reminding each other of promises not kept is a simple process based on long-standing trust and goodwill. Because the relationships among team members are solid, the reminders to each other can be made without the potential for misunderstanding or bad feelings. The relationships are foundational and based on trust. These are the relationships, by the way, that have been created in the early months and years of working together by reflecting together.

In a few interviews I did hear of confidences not kept or critical information and decisions not shared. These are more serious accountability failures that do violate the trust of the team. When these more serious accountability failures occur, team members confront each other about them and work them out. If they did not, trust would be broken and accountability could no longer be taken for granted. Because team members are able to confront one another about these more serious breaches of accountability, they ultimately do not let each other down in ways that signal basic disregard for each other or disregard for the mission they share. That's why they can continue to take accountability for granted.

The reminders to each other are also reminders that accountability is shared. When they think about their work together, accountability takes on a whole new meaning. What I said in Chapter Six bears repeating here. All the teams in this study demonstrate their sense of shared accountability for the mission and ministry of their agency, school, or congregation.

Setting Boundaries, Giving Permission

Members of effective mixed-gender teams give each other permission to do their best, to grow, to learn from each other, to fail, to hurt each other, to take risks, and to have fun. That's a list off the top after listening to many interview tapes. It's probably not complete, but it does illustrate a fundamental fact of effective mixed-gender teams. The people in them give each other permission to be who they are, and at the same time, to grow and change. Such generosity with each other requires courage. They are not afraid of each other. They are not afraid to be challenged and hurt by each other. They are not afraid to be changed by each other, either. Sheila has permission in her team to question the way a decision was made. Albert has permission to be a curmudgeon sometimes about the team activities. Charlie has permission to lead the team in his own unique way. Eileen and Ron have permission to act on their need to get away and be with family sometimes even though others in the team do not have the same need. As each individual exercises permission "to be," the others in the team are influenced and the team grows.

Permission giving like this is built on clear boundaries. We all need psychological and physical boundaries in our lives, yet it is surprising how often in our human interaction we do not allow boundaries. Not only in our workplace but also in our families, our marriages, our friendships, and even our neighborhoods, we often fail to allow each other boundaries. I read recently of a mother who searched her teenager's room, allegedly to make sure he was not using drugs. My parents tell of a neighbor who diverted rainwater runoff into her neighbor's yard and caused a flood in his basement. I know of a wife who will not let her husband take a fishing vacation with his buddies. All of these are ways we deny each other boundaries. Women are particularly victimized in our culture by not being allowed boundaries even around their own physical space. All of these influences make it harder for us to create and honor boundaries in our mixed-gender teams. Yet effective mixed-gender teams have figured out how to create and honor appropriate boundaries. We can learn a lot by observing how the teams in this study have done so.

Boundaries help these teams engage in the intensity of the team and disengage so as to have a private life. This is one way in which these teams are different from clergy couples, who share both work and family life. Boundaries are doubly hard for clergy couples and I hope when some discerning clergy couple writes the book about their partnerships, one chapter will address this subject. But for the teams in this study, boundaries exist first to allow the transition from private to work life and back again.

Boundaries also help these teams to know the terms of their relationship with each other. As an example of this point we might consider communication, because that has already been discussed in some detail in Chapter Fifteen. When we talk to each other, we should not assume that everything has to be said just because we are a close working team. That's what Diane meant when she said, "You can't just vent whenever you want." When we allow our teammate to leave some things unsaid, we allow a boundary. When we cross that boundary, we demand too much. We may in fact damage our relationship rather than nurture it. The same may be said for how we share decision making, the subject of the previous section. We ought not demand that every decision be made together or that every idea we have about every decision be shared. Instead, we agree to share, and we establish a process for making the decision. We may, for example, agree that no decision that costs our organization more than $10,000 will be made without team dialogue. This process defines the boundary. Every team member who agrees to the process agrees to honor a boundary. This is how effective mixed-gender teams work.

The Intimacy Boundary

The big boundary is physical, of course. In our culture, it seems almost to have disappeared. Yet crossing it is destructive to mixed-gender teams in many, many ways. To understand why, we have to look beyond our Puritan heritage, which suggests that sex is a sin and adulterous feelings between members of mixed-gender teams are beyond thinking about.

First, it's important to assert that there *is* sexual energy in effective mixed-gender teams. "The level of energy that goes into a good team is a kind of intimacy. The dynamics in a mixed-gender team that are very creative, very exciting, very high energy can be confused with love or sexual attraction," one clergywoman said. "People are scared to name this. For a lot of teams this does not get named. People are fearful because they think, 'Oh my God, this is sexual—what I am feeling for this person!'"

There is a certain spark present when men and women engage in creative, exciting work together. When that work is founded on a common sense of purpose in life and a common mission to be about work that is bigger than our individual selves, the spark may burn that much brighter. "There is incredible intimacy in our shared work," another clergywoman agreed. "We also have intimacy with other people's lives, but that only compounds the intimacy between us in terms of the things we share and talk about. We're not CPAs, after all." It is not wise, therefore, to deny the existence of sexual energy. In fact, said one team member, "Sexual energy is a part of a good team regardless of the gender of the individuals."

What mixed-gender teams do with this energy is what's important. The main thing is to talk about it and set boundaries. There are three things to talk about: the feelings themselves, the boundaries, and what's at stake if the boundary is crossed. "The overriding thing that makes it possible to live with the sexual tension in a good team," said one man, "is the belief that we have so much—relationships, work, friendship, and our partnership—at stake. We have to recognize where the importance is, and if these things don't give us the motivation to behave, something is really wrong." Clear boundaries are required but there is motivation for them in effective teams, as this man's comments suggest.

The appearance of intimacy is also important, one team pointed out. The team members recalled a time when they met in a restaurant and ate sushi together from the same plate. Other members of the congregation were eating at another table. "It felt fine to the two of us, but we have a principle in Jewish life called 'the way things look to the eye.' We know what the integrity of our friendship is—and the safeness of it. We are both happily married, which I think is a very important piece. But just the appearance of these things is also important," commented the female member of this team, in remembering the incident. Some teams take more care than others to monitor "the appearance of things." One team meets in an office with a glass door when they have to close the door. Most are practical about the realities of needing to be about their work without unduly changing their habits to make others comfortable with their work intimacy. "We aren't going to build in boundaries that are unnatural to the working relationship," a man explained.

Second, it's critical for us to be discerning about intimacy. It is more, much more, than sexual energy. There is an appropriate intimacy that comes from working together as these teams do. Team members talk about this in their interviews all the time, almost without realizing it. One woman emphasized the positive "intellectual intimacy" in her partnership with a man a generation older than she. This intimacy "gave us the opportunity to say things we wouldn't say anywhere else because it would be disastrous," she commented. "When you're under pressure in an administrative environment, you have to have someplace to talk like this," she added. "It's incredibly hard for people to do this with their spouse because of the way marriages work and the way two careers work in the household. Initially in my career, I think I did tell my husband a lot, but after a while I didn't. My teammate knew more about some of the job-related things than my husband knew. It was fine. It was in the right place." If we can get beyond our fear of intimacy and keep the physical boundary clear, we can enjoy the many ways we feel intimate with each other when we work together as these teams do.

Team Projects

All of the teams in this study do projects together as a part of their working life. The theological institute team talked about their grant-writing project as a way of illustrating how they usually work together. Their story is instructive at many levels as we consider how mixed-gender teams successfully undertake projects. The first answer to the question is, "Not that differently than we do anything else." That's what Charlie said about the theological institute team. It's typical not only of this team but of most in this study. When they do projects together, these teams employ many of the same techniques for working together that they use in everyday work life. They communicate, make decisions, give permission, honor boundaries, sustain accountability, and have fun in all the same ways they do every day. They are able to set specific guidelines for the project quite successfully, relying on all the good work habits I have just itemized. Their daily work life, based as it is on sound relationships with each other and structured by good habits practiced a majority of the time, make setting up special projects much easier. If team members are communicating effectively in their everyday work life, they will be able to rely on the same habits to communicate effectively when doing a special project. If they have good decision-making practices in everyday work, they will be able to use those for carrying out a special project as well.

The challenges arise because most projects for these teams are added to their normal workloads. These are busy, committed, self-actualized people. A special project seldom takes the place of something that has to be done in the day-to-day. It's extra. They have to figure out who is going to do what, add a dimension of communication for that, and keep up. They must also establish protocols unique to the project. When they are busy, they often rely on the usual protocols of their work, the strength of their relationships, and the skill of the team members to carry the project when additional protocols are really necessary. If they get into trouble over a special project, this is the place where it usually happens.

Finally, it's worth noting that team members need permission to fail when they take on a project. The permission to fail is a part of their permission giving, but it's not something they take advantage of. In fact, these teams are not afraid to make mistakes. They can correct their course and they often do, especially where special projects are concerned. But they don't think of this as failure and they don't dwell on it. That's the essence of the permission to fail and try again.

The Extras

The bonds that are formed in effective teams allow their members to enjoy a depth of relationship with each other that includes some extras. Among these are an increased spiritual dimension to working together and the ability to have fun together. Jack, a member of the spiritual formation team, mentioned these two elements as the secret of his team's success. First is "just the praying we do together. . . . Sometimes we take a full hour before we launch into what we believe the Spirit is calling us to do. We just take the quiet time and go off." The second is "having fun together, going out and wasting time together. That's helpful too."

THE SPIRITUAL DIMENSION. Even when they are not of the same faith group, these team members share the spiritual dimensions of their lives together. If they are clergy, of course, they not only share a faith tradition but also guide others in the congregation in the practice of the faith. In these cases, team members not only pray together but also worship and study together. Even in agency settings, many of these teams pray for and with each other on a regular basis.

Peter and Eleanor include Torah study as a regular part of their schedule. The spiritual formation team members use prayer and Ignatian discernment as part of their decision-making process. Ben, Karen, and Fredrica have prepared and offered chapel services together for the seminary community. Blair and Mary, whose story appears in Chapter Twenty-Two, include the staff and even the wider community in prayer time just before lunch each day. Pam has recently completed a sabbatical during which she studied life in community. Her partner Bruce will benefit from some sharing of this experience that will be a part of deepening their spiritual lives. This habit adds a dimension to their work lives that deepens their reflection and solidifies their ability to act with each other day in and day out.

HUMOR AND FUN. Humor is important to effective mixed-gender teams. If nothing else, it breaks the tension of always being an example to other individuals and other teams. Every one of these teams is engaged in work that can in some way change lives for the better. It is very serious work that is taken seriously. Yet they all know that it's a dour person who takes life seriously all the time. They are not afraid to use humor to lighten the load, lighten the day, and lighten their time with each other. Effective teams use humor in two ways. First, they joke and have fun with each other, though never at each other's expense. Second, they laugh at themselves.

Most teams do something to socialize. Parties held regularly throughout the year to mark special occasions, honor accomplishments, or just as an occasion to relax and talk to one another are typical. One woman observed the value of humor in commenting about a team in her workplace: "Everybody in our office knows that they have a lot of fun. You walk by their area and they are always laughing. But they get a tremendous amount of work done, so much that their workload has been expanded and they're still getting it all done."

The spiritual formation team comes to mind as one that knows how to have fun in a setting where others are often envious of their capacity to do so. Once a month they go out and enjoy themselves for an afternoon and evening. They readily cite this as a critical strategy to keep them fresh and effective in their work. "We don't feel isolated. We don't feel much pressure. Some people in other departments look at us with jealousy. 'How do those guys have such a good time while we work alone and have many pressures?' they wonder. We enjoy each other," said Binh.

Another team confirmed this reaction among others. "People say that it is clear by the way we work together that we enjoy working together and are in sync with each other. This fluidity carries to other things." Peter and Eleanor commented about this too. Above all, said Peter, "I've learned what fun it can be to work with a person like Eleanor." The point is, he added, "It is just that easy."

These team members are also willing to laugh at themselves. Many cite a sense of humor or the ability to enjoy each other's sense of humor as critical factors in their overall success. Hard work is hard work, but the load can be lightened by a laugh now and then. And in mixed-gender teams, there is often plenty to laugh about in the ways they misunderstand each other, miss signals from each other, and just plain get embarrassed. One clergy team in a particularly difficult situation used humor between them as a way of "preventing the criticism of the congregation from breaking down our team." None of this can happen of course, if partners lack the ability to have the serious conversation about the gender traps that cause serious problems for men and women working together. The ability to be honest with each other when honesty is required comes *before* the ability to laugh at ourselves and each other.

Mentoring Each Other

Although the best mentoring may happen in formal relationships in which there is reflection, accountability, and support for the mentoring relationship, the teams in this study mentor each other in informal more than formal ways. They tend to view their teams as partnerships rather than mentor relationships on the whole. Still, it is apparent that they learn from each other. Some teams, like Blair and Mary, whose story appears later in this book, begin as formal mentoring relationships and evolve into partnerships. This is the exception rather than the rule. "In the first couple of years I looked to Bill for information about how to become a pastor," said one woman about the changing mentoring relationships in her team. "I also mentored Bill in learning how to work with women. He was more sensitive than most men to women's concerns, but he still had a few things to learn. And I was more than willing to teach him. He learned from my positive attitude."

Other teams that include junior members working for senior members have a mentoring quality about them by virtue of the fact that one member is more experienced than the other. "I consider our team leader my mentor," said one laywoman who has recently joined a parish team. "I value his guidance and support, and I try to integrate what he says in my practice." Still others are clearly partnerships in which the members have parity in experience and education. Even in these teams, there is a measure of informal mentoring as team members learn from each other. "It is continually a mentoring process between us," said one man, adding, "I probably learn more from her than she learns from me." Wayne listed many ways he and Erin have mentored each other based on their different gifts. "She drops books on my desk all the time. She is also more attuned to spiritual development than I am, and she's working with me on that. In the business of the presbytery, I work with her. Also, I have some opportunity to help her gain broader experience and build her resume for the future."

Mentoring is possible because of the permission giving we discussed earlier. Team members are willing to learn from each other and so they do, whether their relationship is set up to be mentoring or not. It's as simple as that.

Finally, it's worth observing that a few of the teams in the study mentored other individuals or teams outside their own team. Interns regularly join the Lutheran relief team and have a chance to learn while doing a specific project to promote the mission of the organization. Many of the young staff members who join this growing organization begin as interns there. Blair and Mary supervised divinity school interns, teaching them about working in a mixed-gender team. They recollect on this aspect of their work together in their story. Though this situation was not typical, in those teams where it happened, people inside and outside the team benefited in different ways. Team members clearly benefit in that mentoring causes them to reflect on their own work together. Outsiders benefit in gaining access to the techniques and values that make the team successful.

Menschlichkeit

When it's good, it's very, very good. This is essentially what effective mixed-gender teams have to say about working together. We have seen in this and the previous chapter what it takes to *make it* good. It's not something that just happens. And in spite of what some of the teams say, it's not just the luck of finding the right partner. Even compatible partners have to work at it. If they succeed, they create an atmosphere of *menschlichkeit*. This Yiddish word used by Peter and Eleanor conveys warmth, humaneness, caring. A *menschlich* place is a good place with a good spirit, a space where people feel cared about. "Just a really good place to be with each other."

18

TRAPS FOR WOMEN AND MEN

WHEN WE VIEW successful mixed-gender teams through the lens of the strategies they use to maintain their working relationships, they look very healthy and productive. But it's not all rosy. All is not *menschlichkeit*. Women and men who work together, even those in successful mixed-gender teams, encounter gender traps as part of their daily routine. Gender traps are catch-22 situations created by the differences in the way we understand the leadership roles of men and women in our culture. Knowing the gender traps reveals the difference between what we can and cannot control in the workplace as we strive to work together.

Gender Traps for Women

We have already seen that women are "the resident other" in patriarchy. In the workplace, women are still aliens, strangers, the permanent *ex matriates* (Schaper, 1990). They encounter many gender traps. In Chapter Eight, I described the you're-too-bitchy trap. This is a trap we women commonly experience when we adopt an aggressive style to get things done. We are too bitchy, as the saying goes, because we are not also being feminine. We women encounter many other traps not only because of sexist attitudes in our organizations but also because our leadership departs from the patriarchal models of our culture (Russell, 1993). When a woman in an effective mixed-gender team encounters a gender trap it affects not only her but her partner as well, as the examples from teams in this study show us.

Invisibility Traps

No matter what position we hold, women in leadership cite invisibility traps as the most common and perhaps the most frustrating (Becker,

1996). These are the traps that "catch" us nearly every day of our professional lives. All of these traps have something to do with a woman's lack of visibility (as a real person) and the resulting consequences.

WHAT DOES IT FEEL LIKE? Gender is always an issue for women in leadership. It is the first invisibility trap for us. I call it the "What does it feel like?" trap because when we land in this trap we find we're always having to tell other people what it feels like to be a leader. People often want to know what it feels like "for a woman to work here." This happens most often when the woman is in a prominent leadership position. Furthermore, it is still sometimes difficult for us to overcome the charge that we got our jobs because we are women. This is the trap of affirmative action, and the resulting mythology that women get jobs because organizations have been required to hire women, not because women are competent. A woman caught in this trap becomes a "kind of zoo exhibit"—a representative of a species rather than an individual person with hopes and dreams (Howe, 1982, p. 195). Her performance is often interpreted to mean something about all women's ability to succeed or tendency to fail (Coger, 1985).

This tokenism is stressful for women for three reasons. First, it makes us representative of all women, and not individuals, thus isolating and marginalizing us at the same time that it gives us a certain notoriety. The themes of isolation, marginality, and notoriety "create an image of managerial women as high-wire artists. [We] live in the spotlight, highly visible, very much alone up there" (Sheppard, 1989, p. 145). It can be heady, yet very uncomfortable. With all eyes focused on us, we begin to realize that we have not been told all we need to know to stay up on the high-wire. Second, it puts pressure on women to overachieve and contributes to our burnout. Third, it makes women the visible targets for the pain, confusion, and grief that men and women feel over their changing roles in society at large (Howe, 1982; Coger, 1985).

One of the team leaders I interviewed experiences this trap routinely in her position. She is the first woman in her denomination to head this particular agency and by far the youngest person, male or female. I realized in the course of our interviews that the pressure of notoriety this woman experiences is not even recognized by her team. In follow-up feedback to the team I pointed out that team sensitivity to their leader's notoriety could both help her and help the team function better in the external environment.

THE INCREDIBLE INVISIBLE WOMAN. Another commonly reported invisibility trap for women is simply that we remain invisible no matter what we do. Every professional woman has a story about a situation in which she was not heard, not seen, or perhaps not noticed for weeks or months on end. When this happens, we feel like the "incredible invisible woman." Every woman in every mixed-gender team in this study who has had a constituent ask for her male partner instead of dealing directly with her has experienced this invisibility trap. We women also encounter this trap whenever we share our ideas in a group only to have them ignored, brought up later by a man, and then suddenly heard and valued. As a result of these experiences, we women sometimes feel voiceless.

One of the clergy teams in this study had encountered a striking example of this invisibility trap at the time of our interview. A couple in the team's congregation was leaving because they did not like working with a clergywoman. This couple had made repeated attempts to get the male team partner to change the working relationship with his female colleague. In effect, they pressured the male partner to take over the leadership role himself. He refused, and eventually the couple chose to join another church rather than work with the woman on this clergy team. This example shows how women and the men who are committed to working with them can *both* be caught in the invisibility trap. In cases such as this, women and men in mixed-gender teams must resist the pressures that would make the women invisible.

WHOSE IDEA WAS IT? The impact of invisibility on women can be devastating. We eventually begin to wonder if we are really invisible to the others (both men and women) outside our team. After all, for women as for men, *being* is intimately connected to *being heard*. What we women do about this trap often lands us in yet another invisibility trap that I call "Whose idea was it?" We sometimes give up our ideas to men in order to make sure that our good ideas *are* heard. It's a way of finally getting something done. In the end, we lose out because men get the credit for our ideas or our work.

Remember the story of Bruce and Pam in Chapter Twelve. Bruce expressed concern that Pam does not take more credit for her own ideas. In contrast, Pam is willing to give her ideas to Bruce because he is a trusted partner. In this situation Pam does not have much concern about her lack of visibility, but Bruce does. He is rightly sensitive about getting credit more often than Pam for the accomplishments of the team. In this situation, because he is a trusted partner (to Pam) and a more powerful person in the team (in the eyes of the congregation), Bruce bears a great burden to ensure that Pam does not become invisible.

THE COST OF INVISIBILITY. When a woman is invisible in the workplace, she cannot make a difference. In fact, she cannot be an effective leader *because she isn't*. The overall effect of these traps is that they render women invisible and therefore incapable of doing. Of course, women literally exist. We see them all around us. We who are women see ourselves in the mirror. But we women cannot function as active persons in the paradigm if we are rendered invisible there. When this happens there is loss on both sides. For women, there is deep personal loss on a psychic level. For the church and for our organizations, there is loss of talent and possibility (Becker, 1996).

The Cinderella Syndrome

Bruce and Pam's story takes us right into the next set of traps. Women who want to advance must work very hard. Many men work very hard too, of course. But the result is different. Men who work hard—so the ethic goes—can count on rewards for doing so: praise, advancement, even fame and wealth, all the trappings of success. Women cannot count on the same outcomes from their hard work. We women are all a bit like Cinderella in that no matter how hard we work, it may never be enough.

Bruce and Pam have experienced this difference. Bruce gets "lots of affirmation" for what he does. Pam's contribution is often little noticed. This difference puts both Pam and Bruce in an awkward situation. Let's look at the traps and then come back to how they trip up men and women in effective teams. There are several different situations that we can classify as part of the Cinderella syndrome (Becker, 1996).

MAKE ME COMFORTABLE. First, if we go about our business and forget to help the men around us feel comfortable with our competence, we women can be trapped before we actually do anything. I call this the "Make me comfortable" trap. This is a tricky trap for women because there are so many ways we *might* make men uncomfortable without even knowing it. We women risk making men uncomfortable when we challenge a man's way of doing or thinking, when we engage a leadership style that is unfamiliar to men, or when we state a point of view that threatens the prevailing (white male) worldview. These are examples of how our actions can make men uncomfortable. We also make men uncomfortable by virtue of the fact that we are female and we are present in the workplace *as women*.

The issues in this trap are complex. They involve competition, power, security, and the very nature of femaleness. Deborah Sheppard (1989), Barbara Gutek (1989), Albert Mills (1989), and others have documented, all in separate studies, the effect of being female in management. Sheppard concludes, "For women . . . moving into male-dominated culture, learning how to manage the world of the organization, necessarily implies learning how to redefine and manage 'femaleness.'" Managing this, she continues, "takes place within a male-defined set of norms and expectations." In order to help the men feel comfortable with their presence and therefore survive in an alien (white male) paradigm, women in Sheppard's study viewed their gender as something to be managed. Thus Sheppard (1989) states: "Being a woman in a male-dominated environment demands handling one's gender in particular ways" and is done "with reference to one's interpretation of the prevailing power structure in the organization" (p. 145).

To understand how this trap affects women, we can think in particular of two women who have told their stories in this study. First, remember Erin, who in her early life was active in Intervarsity Christian Fellowship. Erin had to manage her role very carefully so that the male leaders would allow her to participate as a leader. Erin was caught in the make-me-comfortable trap. Second, in Chapter Twenty we will hear about Marie's struggle to be proud of her work and to speak with authority about who she is and what she does. Once she learned how to do so, Marie realized how many other women around her were still reticent to speak with their own voices or even take up physical space in the room. Marie describes for us another example of the make-me-comfortable trap that she and so many women experience.

WORK TWICE AS HARD. Women also have to work twice has hard as men to get anything done. "Work twice as hard" is the second Cinderella trap. It goes like this. We women often must outperform men in order to get jobs at equal (or even lower) levels in an organizational hierarchy. This trap adds to the pressure women feel to overachieve, and it contributes to women's burnout.

In many seminaries and graduate schools we can document that women who do better than men as students do not necessarily have more promising careers to look forward to once they graduate. In fact, one group of female seminary students who reviewed this manuscript emphasized that opportunities for women to advance are still quite limited in the church, in spite of the hard work that women to do prove themselves.

The experiences of mixed-gender teams in this study seem to verify this view. Many teams I interviewed sought to rewrite the job description of a woman team member. Their aim was to position the woman at a higher level in the hierarchy of the congregation or organization and therefore closer in rank to her male partner. Often the team was unsuccessful in getting the woman's title changed. Thus in terms of the hierarchy, the male team member retained higher rank even when the team didn't want it that way. This is a perfect illustration of the work-twice-as-hard trap. In spite of our hard work and competence, women have a hard time gaining status because we are not viewed as *"full* organizational members" (Mills, 1989, p. 38).

Women have to work the hardest in professions that are largely viewed to be men's because of some notion of skill, "a complex of rules about the nature and value of a person's work." Furthermore, "a number of factors combine to ensure that skill is rarely attached to the work of females" (Mills, 1989, p. 38). Thus "in any formal organization there is a 'job to be done,' often in a culturally prescribed way, sometimes expressed as 'the way we do things around here.' The various tasks and mode of accomplishing them . . . incorporate assumptions about the nature of men and women; assumptions that are drawn upon that exclude or undervalue the work of women" (p. 36).

THE BETTER WE DO, THE WORSE IT GETS. Sometimes, we women say, the better we do the worse it gets. This is a perfect description of a third Cinderella trap. We women are often punished for being better at something than a dominant man in our peer group. Coger (1985) cites one male manager who comments, "It's OK for women to have these jobs as long as they don't go zooming by me" (p. 21). For some men, the single most significant indicator of their masculinity has been their role as providers for women (Faludi, 1991). If women are "doing better" than men, or are at the very least able to take care of themselves, their success is not only their success. It is also a threat to men who will no longer feel like men when they are not in charge of taking care of women. We women (and some men too) don't necessarily understand this, because for us gender identity and success are not related in the same way.

Success may also earn female leaders the wrath of other women who accept the idea of male dominance in the workplace. These women believe that it's "right and proper" for men to have more opportunity and higher status than women. Unconsciously, they view their limited roles and their lack of experience as their own fault. They direct a lot of anger against themselves for their "failure" when they do not advance. When they see other women succeed, they only feel worse about themselves. I counsel many successful women who are confused by this response from female colleagues. In fact, not too long ago I spent some time with a friend who had decided to apply for a major promotion. She received great support from the men in her office, but the women were devastatingly critical. She could not figure out why until we discussed how some women view the success of their sisters as a personal affront. I helped my friend understand that women do this when they are not themselves willing or able to assert their own capability.

FINDING FAIRY GODMOTHER. These traps make working women into Cinderella, the poor sister who must work hard for little or no reward, and whose work is fundamentally devalued. Like Cinderella, a working woman can't get out of the trap by working harder or better, by making her male peers and superiors feel comfortable, or by doing a superlative job. What she needs is the fairy godmother to come and whisk away the old paradigm for one short evening so that everyone around her can see the world in a new way. In this new world, the woman's ways of working are valued differently and she really does become a "new person" in the eyes of everyone around her. Of course, she is the same. It's the paradigm that has changed.

Ironically, in the mixed-gender teams in this study, the men play the role of fairy godmother. By virtue of forming a partnership with women in which they value the women as peers with equal and sometimes superior professional skills, *the men change the working paradigm for their female colleagues and for themselves.* They form a buffer with the external constituency, which often encourages them, as men, to take over. They allow their women colleagues to shine in their own right and to be known as real leaders. They do so by advocating for their women partners, helping them survive and grow in a male work world, and ultimately by moving over and making room for the women in the limelight they themselves have always expected as their due. Men do this for a lot of reasons. Some are prepared for it by the influence of their early lives and their own careers. They cite mothers, wives, and women colleagues as influential in preparing them to work effectively alongside women. Others do it because it is right. They recognize the inequity that women have encountered as they enter the work world, and they consider it a moral wrong.

Harassment and Other Hazards

A woman's gender is most painfully a liability when her sexuality comes into play. Because we are regarded and expected to behave primarily as sexual beings just because we are women, we are easily trapped in situations that violate our privacy, our physical boundaries, or our sense of self as whole. Women often report feeling unsafe, ashamed, or exposed because these traps are a part of our regular experience. In an ironic and perverse way, men also become victims of the harassment traps (Becker, 1996).

HARASSMENT. Harassment is the most widely discussed (though still poorly understood) trap women face. We all know about harassment. We all know that sexual harassment in the workplace is forbidden. Nevertheless, it still happens routinely, and many forms of harassment are not well recognized. The men in one team in this study told me that sexually explicit jokes about women were prevalent in the organization until a woman became executive director. These men were glad to have finally eliminated one aspect of harassment from their workplace, as they had long felt uncomfortable with it.

Sexual harassment is "any sexually related behavior that is unwelcome, offensive, or fails to respect the rights of others" (Inskeep and Mroczek, 1993, p. 1). Thus unwelcome comments, touching, gestures, jokes, and the like are all included in the catalogue of harassment. I would include in this definition at least two behaviors that are not always identified as harassment. First, ridicule about a woman's size or body type, even if it not sexually explicit, is harassment. Second, those situations in which a woman finds that her job opportunity, advancement, or leadership role is questioned or curtailed because she is considered to be primarily "domestic" constitute harassment.

Men often commiserate with each other about the fact that, in a highly sensitive environment, "We can't even compliment a woman anymore." This is exactly the bind. Even if women are spared the experience of harassment we are still held responsible for the fact that "we all have to be so careful." In a similar way, women are blamed for sexuality in the workplace at the same time that we are expected to be sex objects. In fact, the problem is not women; it is a sexualized workplace that we think is neutral. Sex-role stereotypes, which are a part of the prevailing worldview, present women as sexual beings but continue to reinforce the view of men as organizational beings no matter what they do. This fact, verified by research, leads Gutek and others to characterize the workplace as "an outgrowth of the male psyche" (Gutek, 1989, p. 64; see also Shep-pard, 1989). So long as we miss this point and continue to view the work-place as neutral, we will continue to hold women responsible for any manifestation of sexuality we experience there.

The way women look, the fact that we are "tempting to men," that we have babies and take time off as a result, and in the end the very fact that we are present in the workplace *as female*—all these realities are held against women when we operate out of the white male worldview with-out the awareness that another worldview is possible. This is the essence of harassment. Erin's story (in Chapter Seven) illustrates a number of the subtler aspects of harassment as I have described them here.

Because organizations are largely viewed as neutral even though they are in fact structured to reinforce notions of sexuality pleasing to men, women are in a real bind. "Although their attempts to manage their sex-uality are a response to organizational structure, policies, or norms, they frequently have to deal with them on a personal level or treat them as exclusively interpersonal encounters" (Gutek, 1989, p. 65) even though they know they are not. Gutek's studies further show that the workplace is sexualized even though most people don't think it is and don't consider any sexual expression in the workplace appropriate. This leads her to wonder: Is it possible to create a social setting in which sex is clearly inap-propriate? She thinks not. On this point, I have said something previously:

> The church, however, tries, and thus becomes a victim to the most per-verse of all forms of sexual harassment: clergy sexual misconduct— the use of a relationship of trust between pastor and parishioner for sex. The instances of clergy misconduct are frighteningly high, and we wonder why. But it shouldn't be such a mystery. The church actually denies the sexuality of its male clergy in an effort to create a radically asexual environment. That which is denied emerges then in its darker forms, as 'conduct unbecoming clergy.' Should we be so surprised that so many men are victims? No, but we should be clear that in this tragedy for the church, men are most often the victims of the church's views of sexuality and women are victims of the inappropriate behav-ior of men [Becker, 1996, p. 120].

HOW DO I LOOK? Women know that appearance counts. Anyone—male or female—in senior management knows this. But for those of us who are women, it counts in ways that it should not. Appearance is never a neutral factor. This too is a trap for women. I call it the "How do I look?" trap.

We women remind men of sex in one way or another, depending on what we look like. Whether appearance helps or hurts a woman depends on standards set by men. The carryover of sex-role stereotypes into the workplace is responsible for the view of women as sexual beings and men as organizational beings. Unfortunately for women, it seems we cannot be both "because femaleness is viewed as not-maleness" (Gutek, 1989, p. 62). Thus a woman's perceived sexuality could blot out all other characteristics of her as a worker. What is doubly troubling about a woman's inability to be both sexual and organizational at the same time is that women are not the ones choosing.

Unlike women, men have little experience of being sexualized in the workplace. Gutek's studies uncovered startling examples of men's overtly sexual behavior that coworkers did not view as sexual at all. Instead, men's sexual behavior "was subsumed under the stereotype of the organizational man" (1989, p. 62). It was explained as part of being competitive, assertive, goal-oriented, even rational. For this reason, men may reject outright the experience of women as sexual beings in the workplace. By contrast, other men, including all the men in this study, are to be commended for working very hard to break out of the prevailing paradigm, as did the one who said, "Women are my colleagues. I see them doing good jobs and doing them well. They have become my friends, not my sex objects."

WHERE ARE WE SAFE? Safety is the ultimate issue for women where these traps are concerned. Women are physically threatened by harassment. It renders us uncertain about our physical well-being. Because harassment can happen anytime, even in the places that should be safest, women feel vulnerable most of the time. Women are also physically threatened by the constant focus on our appearance. Appearance shows; it's available for men to comment about all the time. Living with a body that is routinely violated by talk and by inappropriate action is a source of vulnerability that men cannot understand unless they *feel* it. One woman pulls no punches in saying: "Only men who have been in prison can appreciate what it is like to be in constant fear of bodily invasion." Women live with it, and indeed, have little or no experience of being physically safe.

As I have already emphasized, the men in this study are not guilty of the harassment I have described as elements of these gender traps. However, in a certain respect they have to take responsibility for them. The plain fact of the matter is that most women have experienced these traps in one way or another. Thus they approach working with men as partners with a great deal of caution. Many of the women in this study told of feeling very uncertain as they considered becoming a part of a mixed-gender team. Many had also had bad experiences in their immediate past. The men they work with now have all had to work very hard to help their female colleagues feel safe and comfortable in the partnership. This requires deep commitment and includes taking on responsibility for the harassment traps in a unique and personal way.

Traps for Men

Men have plenty to say about the traps women negotiate on a daily basis. The basic message is clear: "We are trapped, too."

Sometimes the traps are the same for men; more often they are different. Always they are related in some way to men's presumed dominant position in the prevailing paradigm. Because men are dominant, they are hindered by stereotypes of women and by the very behaviors for which they might be rewarded in an all-male workplace—principally their tendency to be action-oriented. At the same time, much like women they are trapped by the patriarchy and by stereotypes *of them* and what *they* are supposed to be like. Finally, as dominants, men must always come to terms with losing their position and power on the top (Becker, 1996).

Attitudes That Trap Men

"We have to start with the stereotypes we carry around," said one man. "In the male-dominated workplace, they get shared and discussed, but in the end we each have our own that we must confront and deal with." Negative stereotypes of women are the first gender trap for men. They are reinforced by patriarchy, the second gender trap for men, and by attitudes about sexuality, the third gender trap for men.

STEREOTYPES OF WOMEN. Men's negative stereotypes "may include the belief that women are (1) not as skilled as men, (2) not as capable of critical thinking, (3) too emotional, (4) too willing to make decisions on the basis of personal experience rather than objective analysis, (5) less dedicated to their careers, (6) indecisive, unable, or unwilling to make tough decisions, and (7) not as good at the financial aspects of leadership" (Becker, 1996, p. 128).

Many men have grown up with the idea that, by and large, they are superior to women as thinkers and leaders. Men—especially men who are forty-five and older—are less likely to have learned *from their own experience* that women are capable leaders. Younger men, whose mothers have worked and who themselves have never been in a workplace that did not include women, have an advantage over their older male colleagues. They are more likely to have personal experience that shows them how capable women are. But all men, no matter what their age, have the challenge of *believing* what is increasingly self-evident: women leaders are as capable as men.

Yet it's still too easy for men to reject this belief and hold onto their stereotypes of women. Lack of experience of women in leadership is only one reason. Another is the influence of our culture—and indeed every culture in the world—which tells men that they are superior to women.

To get out of this trap, men have to overcome their assumption of superiority and get to know women from a neutral stance. This may sound easy, but in fact this trap is tricky and tempting for men. It's one that the men in this study have only partially escaped. They may have completely overcome their own stereotypes about women. But they are regularly tempted back into them by constituents who encourage them to "take over" on the assumption that men are "the real leaders." A man who decides to form a true partnership with a woman is always fighting the cultural expectation that he should be decisive, in charge, aloof, analytical, even domineering. When he is not, others around him may wonder, "What's the matter with him?" or they may say, "He doesn't know how to be a leader."

THE PATRIARCHY. Men who overcome their stereotypes of women and want to work with women aren't home free yet. Patriarchy—which I have defined elsewhere as rank order established to ensure the privilege and power of men over women—traps them next.

The patriarchy is a trap for men who want to affirm women as leaders because patriarchy by definition elevates the interests of men over those of women. The patriarchy is especially a trap for men who work in faith traditions that limit the leadership roles for women. Said one such man: "The most serious threat in the limiting environment of patriarchy is that we won't hire the right person for each job—woman or man" (Becker, 1996, p. 129). His point: when we aren't free to hire women without questions, we aren't really free to hire men either. I have said this previously:

> Everyone gets caught in the employment trap because we still have limitations about hiring women. These limitations may be masked as opportunities, as in the directive to "hire a woman for this job." Neither men nor women like this. It's demeaning to everyone's professionalism. On the other hand, men and women agree that it is

important to be intentional about placing women in leadership positions. It's a real dilemma. Men tend to get caught in this trap frequently, because they are still more likely (than women) to be in the
position of doing the hiring [Becker, 1996, p. 129].

The men in this study have faced this gender trap head-on. They are
committed to partnership with women. Many would agree with the man
who said, "A strong mixed-gender partnership provides the best environment for a woman to emerge as a leader in the church" because it provides
her with a safe place to be herself and showcase her skills.

SEXUALITY. Men are also trapped by the ways we all ignore the sexuality of the workplace. Men are set up to be aggressors and encouraged by
many complex cultural influences to see women as sex objects (Gutek,
1989). Thus behaviors and attitudes toward sexuality in the workplace
are the third gender trap for men.

When women become their work partners, men are required to make
a radical shift in behavior, if not also in their thinking. They must treat
women as coworkers at the same time that they receive many subliminal
messages that encourage them to keep on seeing women primarily as sexual beings. It requires a daily struggle that, for the men in this study, is
founded on deeper knowing of their female colleagues. The hard reflective work that women and men do together helps men to a point here, as
long as the boundaries we talked about in Chapter Seventeen are in place.

Harassment is an outcome of the sexuality of the workplace. We have
discussed how harassment affects women, but what about men? It traps
them too. Men are both victims and unwitting perpetrators of harassment.
First, of course, is the recognized fact that men can also encounter unwelcome comments, touching, gestures, jokes, teasing about their size or body
type, and situations in which their job opportunity, advancement, or leadership role is questioned or curtailed because they refuse the sexual
advances of women. Men do not report feeling the same kind of physical
vulnerability that women feel when they are harassed. But they do find
harassment an uncomfortable and difficult situation to deal with. In contrast, men are often befuddled by charges that they have been harassers.
Often when they intended to compliment a woman colleague, they are
accused of harassment. This happens because men learn to think about
and comment about women as sexual beings. The men often can't see the
difference between an honest compliment and a remark that is harassing.
When they are corrected or reprimanded, they feel trapped themselves.

The only real way out of this trap, for men as for women, is for our work-place to become less sexualized.

There is yet another way in which men are trapped by the covert sexu-ality of the church that is much less obvious but potentially much more damaging. This is a special trap reserved primarily for *clergymen*. I men-tioned it earlier in this chapter in relation to the effect of harassment on women. Men in church leadership are powerful, visible figures in an envi-ronment that is intensely uncomfortable with any sexuality. As such, they are encouraged to deny that sexuality is any part of their identity at all. When they are successful in denying that energy in its positive form, it can become negative and emerge in unhealthy ways. Men do crazy (sexual) things and women or children become their victims. Nowhere do I see evi-dence that the men who do these things are understood to be victims of the church's fear of sexuality. To be sure, I am not suggesting that male sexual misconduct is excusable. It is, however, predictable when we see it as a gen-der trap. Male sexual misconduct provides us with the most compelling case for clear boundaries and a renewed church in which both female and male sexuality among its leaders is understood to be a gift (Becker, 1996).

ATTITUDE TRAPS LIMIT PARTNERSHIP. Men who are caught in the atti-tude traps may not even know that they are limited in their ability to work with women. It's akin to being in a black hole. You can't see any-thing but the blackness, and you have no idea that there is anything out-side the black hole you are in. Men who hold negative stereotypes of women, who accept patriarchy as the norm, or who have not learned to relate to women in nonsexual ways may in fact not know their own lim-itations. They are limited by their worldview, which is for them a black hole. They need literally to get out of the black hole to escape these traps.

Many men who think of themselves as supportive of the leadership of women get caught in these traps. The men in the successful mixed-gender teams in this study know how difficult these traps are to overcome. The best way, they say, is to commit to the reflective tasks. Once on the re-flective path with teammates, it's hard for a man to remain trapped by attitudes.

Fear of Loss

Fear of loss is another trap for men. It may be the biggest trap for them. Men fear losing power, position, and jobs. They fear opening up and shar-ing themselves as well as their ideas. They wonder if a different way will really be better. They don't know what women are really "up to," and they fear the change of accountability that nonhierarchical leadership implies. They fear that women will really be better than they are at the job. And in the final analysis, they are so used to power games that they suspect women are trying to "put one over on them"—pretending to be collaborative while they secretly steal the power. To understand this trap better I have talked to many different men over the years and have written about their comments (Becker, 1996). The feedback I have received from these men contrasts with the wisdom of the men in the mixed-gender teams in this study.

Let's start with jobs, and the power and positioning that come with them. All of the assumptions men have about jobs and their right to have position are shaken when women enter the workplace as peers. Women are suddenly competing with men for the jobs that men have always assumed were theirs. For men, the ground rules change and they may not know what the new ground rules are. Men can't count on the workplace to be "a place where we can do our guy bonding," as one pastor put it. More threatening still, the men don't get the jobs they could once count on.

Men generally recognize, as one said, "that women have experienced this for centuries, so how can we complain?" Still, the loss is difficult to deal with when it is personal. Men have had to learn the hard way that no one job is all that important. They report being angry and grieving. The discipline for them: "Finally being able to see that the woman who was hired brings something to the job that I could not, and saying to myself, 'That's OK. I'll go do my thing somewhere else.'" This point of reconciliation with the loss of a job is hard to achieve for men who feel that the woman hired was not as qualified as they themselves are. However, those who were able to reconcile the loss went on to work successfully with women, in some cases the very women who got the jobs they sought.

But even where jobs are not lost, men fear that power is lost. This fear comes from viewing power as a limited commodity. It also mixes like a volatile chemical with men's other power losses, observed one pastor in my 1994 study, who pointed out candidly, "Many men in middle age notice a diminishing of power and vitality. It is all part of the loss of male potency. Power is lost not only to women who challenge. It is lost politically, financially, and in a number of ways. So there is a kind of built-in fear of the loss of power for men. I suppose that any new challenge, particularly if it is based on new rules, is even more threatening." Still, the fear of loss of power is based on the assumption that power is limited. This may be true for men biologically, but it is not necessarily true in the workplace.

Men also fear opening up. Listen to this story recounted by a man who is not used to reflective activity but found that it was expected of him in staff meetings. "In our staff meetings, the women want to have a time of sharing where you lay yourself on the table. The men just want to do business. They get turned off by the women who almost insist that we talk about our feelings and our hurts and so on. The men go away grumbling, saying it's a waste of time. The women carry it too far even though it is a strength they bring to the workplace." Men recoil because they are uncomfortable. They fear that "revealing too much means that I might be giving up some information or something that would infringe on my power or demonstrate my weakness," my interviewee admitted.

It's also about unfamiliar territory for men. "We know intellectually that people are emotional beings," another man explained to me, "but we have learned to keep our emotions down. We don't often deal with other people (or ourselves) as emotional beings. We expect logic." Said another man: "We don't talk about relationships and personal things because we are uncomfortable with touchy-feely topics." When a woman asks a man to do this, she pushes his panic button.

She may also be pushing his patience. Men report frustration and impatience with the process orientation many women bring to the workplace. For many women, personal sharing is an important part of the process. But when women ask for relational sharing, men often believe that they are wasting time. Furthermore, they fear that a lengthy process will leave them wondering where the accountability lies. They simply don't know how "getting to know you" contributes to getting the work done. Unlike the men in this study, men who are afraid to open up do not know the value of the reflective work that the best mixed-gender teams do. In the final analysis, men often wonder "where these women are going" and are not so sure they want to go that route to complete a project, build a budget, or do any of the other tasks of parish or organizational life.

A part of men's wondering about where the women are going is a real suspicion that women are being manipulative. "Men are not so much gatherers," one man explained to me. "When women get together in groups we tend not to understand. We think it's a strategy or a conspiracy. We wonder: 'Why are those women getting together? Are they trying to figure out how to bash us?' When our women's executive group gets together they are rightly asking, 'What are some ways we can penetrate this all-maleness?' What women are doing over there is nothing more than being a support to each other. Men don't need to do this because we're already together by the very nature of the denominational structure. Still, when the women do it, we're suspicious."

The men in this study have in different ways and at different times in their lives overcome this fear. If they had not, they would not be able to engage in the reflective work so important to mixed-gender team formation. But even the men who are not afraid to be reflective with women encounter fear in their male colleagues all the time. They are wise if they address it in some way, if only for the sake of interpreting their own successful partnerships with women. Unless they do, we will continue to have many mixed-gender partnerships that don't work and a few that do.

Action Traps for Men

Men can be trapped by their actions as much as their attitudes. They routinely encounter at least two action traps. The first is their own tendency to take over. The second is the mysterious reaction they often get from women when they take action. Men have described this trap for me as "walking on eggshells."

TAKING OVER. Men learn to take charge in their lives and at work, get things done, go where they want to go, make decisions. This is a good way to be and to work, they say. They do have a point. But it's a trap whenever it limits a man's ability to work with a woman colleague. That's why I call this the "taking over" trap. If a man takes action too quickly, he limits a woman's ability to think through and resolve her own issues. Women don't need to be helped. They need to learn how to help themselves. Thus when men act too quickly, women say the men are taking over, not taking charge.

This is the trap Diane and Charlie encountered when Diane wanted to talk about a particular situation. Charlie offered a solution because he thought that was what Diane wanted. That's the trap. Diane only wanted to talk so that she would be better equipped to solve the problem herself.

Taking action is also a trap for men when it contributes to their view that they are always right, limits their ability to learn the value of process that so many women bring to the workplace, and hinders their listening skills. It can be very confusing for men to get blamed for taking action when all of their experience has taught them it's good to be action-oriented problem solvers. Thus they are often unwittingly caught in this trap. Charlie was. But he was able to hear Diane's critique and learn from it in the context of a committed working relationship. Given the trust between them, Charlie and Diane could even laugh about it.

WALKING ON EGGSHELLS. Men say they are walking on eggshells when they relate to women. Another image they use is walking in a minefield. They never know when they will step in the wrong place, and *boom!* A man knows he's been caught in this trap whenever he is accused of not caring, or when he gets a tantrum or the silent treatment. It usually happens because of some action he took, action that he considered appropriate but his female partner found offensive. That's why I call "walking on eggshells" the second—and mysterious—action trap.

It works like this, as one man describes it. "Suddenly I'm trapped. I know something is wrong. I did something. I am in trouble for doing it. I am also in trouble for not knowing what it is. And I can't ask because I am supposed to know." When this happens, he knows he has acted in a way that the woman working or living with him judges inappropriate or insensitive.

Men admit that in many important ways, they do not know how women feel. They often act in ways that women find offensive, and this surprises them. It's not as though they meant to offend. It's probable then that they do react with insensitivity. Nevertheless, men caught in this trap still wish for honest confrontation rather than the silent treatment or the tantrum or the political diatribe, which they view as negative confrontation. Many men in this study characterized their female colleagues as strong, willing to speak their minds, focused on the relationship rather than making the political point. This means that they can be confrontational without tripping men up in the emotion trap. It is an important skill for women who are committed to working with men. It will help the men to understand and avoid walking on eggshells.

MEN'S GIFT. Men are good at taking action. It's a skill they learn well when they are young. It's too bad that it traps them when they work with women, but it often does. Men need women to work with them to avoid these traps. Women can help by valuing men's ability to take action in the workplace. Then they can honor men by agreeing to honest confrontation about the actions that offend. Men, for their part, can listen to the women without judgment, with the intent of becoming more sensitive about their actions.

Helping Each Other

When men in effective mixed-gender teams encounter a gender trap, they need interpretation and help from their female partners. Women need the same. When we can help each other by interpreting the traps and helping each other out of them, we will avoid the misunderstandings that destroy our relationships. We will also overcome the divisions between us and begin to build organizations that are friendly to the shared leadership of women and men.

In order to help each other out of the gender traps, we have to be working together. For the most part, women want to work with men because it allows us in on the action. Men may not have the same motivation. They may question why should they bother to work with women. The answer is this: it's the only way out of the dominant position that traps *them* and limits *their* leadership.

PART SIX

INFLUENCING

19

NEELY AND BARBARA, BARBARA AND BILL

TWO POWER STRUCTURES IN TWO TEAMS

NEELY AND BARBARA worked together as president and academic dean of a seminary in California for nearly ten years beginning in 1980. It was a fairly traditional team, with a fifty-something male president and a female dean many years younger. In this team there was an age gap, a gender gap, and an experience gap. When Barbara left to become the president of another seminary on the opposite coast, Bill was a key partner exercising academic leadership. Barbara and Bill were of an age. Their experience was also fairly well matched. They worked together for nearly six years before Bill moved to take a presidency himself.

Each of these three people learned about working together from the subordinate position of dean, as their stories show. "One of the hardest roles around is the dean in any academic institution," Barbara recalls. "The dean can be anything from a gofer for the president to a union leader for the faculty—and everything in between. The dean walks a fine line, flipping back and forth from being an advocate-spokesperson for a constituency of colleagues to being an authoritative agent for the administration. When you add in gender as an issue it gets even more complicated."

The two teams on which Barbara served, first with Neely and later with Bill, were challenging and very different in their power dynamic. "When you have a male president and a female dean, everyone knows the buck stops with the president. The team perpetuates some of the patterns of male-female relationships in our culture," Barbara says. "When it's the other way around, there is a dissonance. Sometimes that's creative and sometimes it's a real block." Both these teams worked well. They illus-trate how power can be harnessed effectively in different ways in mixed-gender teams.

○

Neely Builds a Mixed-Gender Team

I wanted a professional dean, someone who wanted to be dean and was happy in the position, rather than a faculty member who was tak-ing on the post for a limited time. I wanted a colleague in administra-tion, someone who could transcend the job to think about the good of the whole school. I thought I ought to have a dean so good she could become president at the drop of a hat. It's a way of saying to yourself that you want the best people even if they overshadow you. And actu-ally they don't. They make you look better. I wanted that kind of strong team.

I was willing to take the risk on a woman because I was convinced that our school was uniquely ready. The student body was by that time over 50 percent women. Many of our faculty were growing older and all but one were male. They talked a good line, but when it came to calling people they never called a woman. I felt like this was a serious matter. Our school was not like other schools. We were on the front line of affirmative action. So my first commitment was to find a woman dean. I had heard that Barbara was excellent, clear of mind, precise, could make decisions, could follow through. I was looking for somebody like that, even though she was not a full professor. It took me a year to find her and I had to wait six months after that before she could come. The risk paid off.

When she came, Barbara wanted to know if I was through "dean-ing." I think she was concerned that I would keep my hand in it since I had been a dean for so many years myself. I told her the presidency was more than I could say grace over. She needed to be the dean. Since I had done curriculum work, she and I would talk about that fre-quently. But it was Barbara who designed the curriculum and all the things that went with it. We worked well. As time went on Barbara became more and more famous and I didn't have a lot of loose space to say, "Let's sit down and talk about this (whatever it was)." Some-times I think better with people, and I need to talk to folks I can trust. I trusted Barbara implicitly. We had a good, good time working together.

Basically, I think when you talk about power in an academic insti-tution, you are talking about influence. I don't usually use the word *power.* I use *influence* because I think that's more accurate. Ultimately the president is in a position to have more influence than anybody else in the institution. Presidents frequently deny that. I denied it. But I was the only one who had constant contact with trustees. I was the one ultimately who has a say-so over faculty jobs. I was in touch with the faculty too. I had less contact with the students. The point is, the president is in a position to have more influence over all these groups than almost anyone in the institution. In that sense they have power. On the other hand, presidents who don't share power are for sure getting ready to lose what they've got.

I used to say to the faculty, "You are influencing my view on this subject." I wanted them to know they had power and could use power. If you let people know when they have influence, it flows back and forth in a way that people discover is serious and they know what it means when you say that you are listening. It's not that you will act on everything they say, but you really listen and take it seriously. And I did learn from the faculty. Oooh, we had great disagreements sometimes. The same was true with the trustees. But I learned a lot from them. If you're not willing to be influenced, you're going to have a very hard life. People who write about the position of president saying you should be aloof—be absent a lot of time so your presence will have power when you come in—I think that's a carload of garbage. Anyone who acts this way is just waiting for a big downfall.

The president I worked for when I was a dean was not like this. He was not a lone ranger. In fact, I used to push him a bit because he was so careful to hear all sides of an issue. I hadn't thought about it before, but I suspect I learned a lot from him about collaborative leadership. I think most men have a different model.

I never intervened in decisions of my administrative team. Once or twice I had to go to someone and say, "I disagree with your decision. I am going to back you totally. I won't say a thing. But the second time this happens I will come here again and add that you might want to think about working with someone else. I'm not going to run you off. But I am ultimately responsible for what happens in this institution. If you and I can't agree, if you can't talk to me and persuade me that what you want to do is appropriate, you just won't be a part of the team."

I really did trust Barbara to influence the faculty to shape the curriculum and to influence the academic affairs committee of the board. I didn't even go to those committee meetings. She kept me informed of what she was doing and I kept her informed of what I was doing. I trusted her with a big umbrella of influence. I never lived to regret it.

My trustees would say that I had the most power, but then they would say that Barbara had almost as much. They were conscious that I shared influence but they also expected me to be responsible for everything. But I allowed the circle of influence. In our administrative team our rule was, "Never surprise the rest of us." If it was a decision related to Barbara's area, we would hand it off to her. She would take care of it. But she knew all of us were backing her. She had already heard our words of criticism because we had already shared them with her. But basically she knew she had our support. I don't think I ever made a serious decision without talking to that group. When it was a major decision affecting the shape of the school, I had a group of trustees I talked to quite regularly too. There was just a lot of discussion behind our decisions.

○

Barbara Claims Her Power

In some measure, Neely was my mentor. I was learning as I went—what it meant to be an administrator in a theological school. For him, I became very much an ear, a person with whom he could vent and articulate what he was thinking. We would have many conversations in which I would not say a lot. It helped him figure out what he thought and where he was in the decision-making process. If I didn't like what he was doing, or if I questioned it, he didn't get uptight about it. We'd just argue it out. I think a couple times I changed his mind when he was headed down what I thought was the wrong path.

Neely was a strong leader. He gave me a lot of freedom to develop my own corner of the world with faculty. As I look back on those years, I grew. I was nurtured. I was given a lot of freedom. I thrived. I don't think it was a terribly egalitarian relationship. There was the age gap, the experience gap, and there was a gender gap. All of these left me in a subordinate position and Neely in a dominant one, but not in a destructive way. I never felt like I was being manipulated or used. It was just a natural "this is the way the world works with men and women" kind of relationship. I don't begrudge it at all. It was an important learning, growing experience for me. We got so we could almost instinctively anticipate each other. It was very symbiotic. At the same time, we had areas of separate activity and power. We worked well together.

When I came here as president, Bill had already been here five years. He was the inside candidate for president and I was the outside candidate who got the position. I told him if he wanted to leave, I would help him find a presidency. There was no sense in having tension between us. "Let's be up front about it," I said. He said he was not ready to go, so, "Let's see how this works." At first Bill was what we called the director of educational programs and we did not have a dean, although Bill was doing many of the things associated with the dean's role. With a small team of faculty on five-year contracts, however, everyone was involved in curricular planning and leadership. After two or three years as programs grew and the school got more complex, and when it was clear that Bill and I were working well together, I made Bill the dean.

This created some tension with the faculty, who were not sure whether it was good for us to have a dean. Although Bill and I were clear about responsibilities between us, it was sometimes confusing to others. During our accreditation visit several years after Bill became dean, the team told us that the faculty needed greater interpretation of roles—and how the lines of power and authority functioned. Bill and I just looked at each other and said, "We don't want to start a hierarchy. We are doing fine." We were working in an egalitarian team model. We would flip around responsibilities based on who we thought could do the best with the situation or the individual or the calendar. That felt pretty good. We resisted the pressure to make it more hierarchical.

Most major decisions were made in our administrative team. I don't like decisions made unilaterally by anybody, unless they are very small decisions. I thought we ought to be collectively sharing, if only to run decisions by each other before they became public. Bill used to chafe at some of the things that came before our administrative team that he thought were trivial. I figured if it was important to others in the team and if it didn't take too much time, it did no harm to talk about some of these things.

My leadership style sometimes includes a tendency to bring closure on things too fast. The team discipline forced me not to make decisions too precipitously. If I made myself wait and talk to other people, I made better decisions. It's time consuming at the beginning. I was looking for signs and feedback and I'm sure that was frustrating for Bill at first. Now I'm making more decisions more efficiently. I'm more confident. I have more experience. There is a dynamic about women leaders, when we are good, that is not hung up on everything being structured. (This is *not* the same thing as touchy-feely, all process and no results.) Some men can deal with this. Some men get very nervous.

Neely and Bill were able to deal with it without getting nervous. A man has to be secure in himself to do this. He has to like himself.

Bill and Neely were similar in having the human willingness to "hang loose" and an openness to talk things through. As new opportunities and crises arose, we handled each uniquely. When I came here I leaned on Bill. I had to find out the institution's history, patterns, customs, and traps. He was very helpful with this. At the same time, Bill was clear that I was the president. However, in our relationship, power was held mutually. When there was conflict, there was the understanding that I was the president but this did not surface much. I rarely had the feeling that I was pulling rank. It felt like we were in dialogue everywhere. It felt to me like we exercised our power in relational patterns, not in authoritative dictums. Often we were face-to-face, trying to be responsive to people's needs. With Neely, there was an age and experience difference. He still is a sort of mentor-father I can turn to for advice. But I know he was very dependent on me too. I enabled his power by being an ear and a constructive critic. He enabled my power by giving me confidence and wisdom out of his experience. Our relationship was not egalitarian in the same way as mine was with Bill. But there was balance.

Now I'm feeling old and wise. I have been in seminary administration twenty-plus years. I have learned a lot about how institutions, organizations, and structures work. I have learned a lot about myself and how I thrive. I am more confident about claiming myself, not trying to fit into things. I was socialized to please my mother, my father, my boyfriend, my teacher, my colleagues. I was quite bright but complacent for a long time. But sometime about twenty years ago I began to taste some of the excitement of making a difference. I can remember thinking "I can do that better," but not really thinking it was appropriate for me to actually *do* it. One of the issues about becoming dean and then president was admitting I can do this as well as any man. It was important for me to realize that it's not bad, not unfeminine, to say that. However, I believe that it is harder to do this when you're younger. So I think just living longer and getting more comfortable with your own exercise of power helps. It was good to discover that actually doing it my way and finding it worked had some pluses that people appreciated. I've been a pretty compliant person with some credentials in the right place at the right time when they need a token. But in the process of being the token, I've discovered some of my own power.

○

Bill Signs On with Barbara

Some people predicted that our partnership would not work. Barbara and I talked it through. I was comfortable with the board's choice of her as president and I wanted to make it work. She felt the same way. I don't think there was a moment when Barbara or I felt her decision to come or my decision to stay was the wrong one. In a lot of ways, we modeled an effective transition. We both bent over backwards to affirm the other. I used every opportunity to affirm her and be very clear that she was my president. I was also giving myself some standing in the community. In the language of family systems, it was role differentiation. I don't think I went overboard to be second fiddle, but I think it was very clear in informal conversations and in public presentations that I recognized the fact that I was not the president and she was, and I was happy with that.

Power is an awkward term to describe it, but I think we worked hard at the division of responsibility. There are certain pieces that by definition go with the job. Some things only a president can do, and vice versa. Other things somebody has to do. And in a third category are things that one or the other of us loved to do. We did a good job of dividing those up and talking things through with these criteria in mind. I ended up doing some things I'm good at or that I really enjoy that the president would normally do. She ended up doing some things she is good at or that she enjoyed that the dean would normally do. For example, I did more fundraising and foundation work than a dean normally does. Barbara did more curriculum work than most other presidents did. We were able to say, "Let's get beyond the tight role definitions and power relationships and figure out what's the most effective and the most satisfying." One of the best things about the relationship was our ability to look at our work this way.

Our leadership styles felt very congruent. I had been around for a while and I like to think that I was helpful to Barbara in sensitizing her to the culture she inherited. We learned from each other. I certainly learned from her as well. In our decision making, there was a lot of yielding to one another. When one person felt particularly strongly about something, we tried to say, "If it's really important to you, let's try to run with it." A few times Barbara pulled rank. But as I look back I wish there had been more times. There was a lot of spinning of wheels, when a decision would have been helpful.

The whole time I worked with Barbara, I was the only man on the administrative team. There were moments when it was very hard, yes. We used to joke about this in our meetings, but the people on the team knew that I found our meetings very frustrating. It was partly because we often focused on things that seemed to me to be trivial. The others did often acknowledge my frustration in the meetings, saying, "We know Bill can't stand this discussion." I must say, I found myself at war with myself on this point, in one sense enjoying it, wanting to be a one of the gang, and on the other realizing that there are more important things to do. There is a part of me that says, "Gee, it's really great to be one of you . . . that you feel free to talk about these things despite the fact that I'm here." I was one of the girls in that sense. They felt comfortable doing any of the things that a very comfortable and close human community does together when I was there. That's probably the clearest point at which I felt some gender identification—where it was pertinent. But it was not a big issue. It didn't matter that much.

In other ways I was the promoter of open time to be together without focusing on tasks. For twenty minutes every Monday morning after chapel the seminary community would gather for coffee. It wasn't something Barbara had done before. I said, "Trust me on this one. This is the heart of this community." It was a time when we would share information about the week that had just gone by. As dean I knew what was going on and I would encourage people to tell us about various things. For twenty minutes or so the community would be self-consciously a community. It's when we noted birthdays and talked about family. That would be the time when we would have incorporated celebration of things that went well. That continues now. I have been gone for three years, and it's still going on. For some people it's the point at which they feel most a part of the seminary community. I kind of defined my role in pastoral terms. One of my very conscious goals was to make human contact with every employee every week. If I didn't see somebody Monday morning I'd make it a point to get into his or her office during the week, just to say hi. I think that Barbara is more cerebral than that. She is more likely to write a memo than drop into someone's office. I think that was a helpful thing for her . . . for people to see her and for her to see the folk.

The secret of our success as a team was that we worked for a great institution that was successful and also continues to have great potential. It helps when both people are doing important things and have values that are compatible, which I think we did. We liked each other as people, and that also made a difference. In mixed-gender teams, I think everything is gender-related in some way even though it may not be a gender problem. But the women I have worked with who have come into real power have not had a problem with that. I suspect they've had to come to grips with it, or they would not have real power.

○

20

POWER AND INFLUENCE

NEELY IS RIGHT. Having influence is all about having power. To be effective partners, we need to know how to use our power positively and well so that we will be able to influence others toward positive, constructive action. Because the ability to influence is the outcome of using power, I call the eighth criterion *influence*.

The stories from Neely, Barbara, and Bill are rich in wisdom about power. They show us how three different people understand power in their professional lives and how they set out to use it wisely. It should also be obvious to us that these three people have different views about power. Gender is but one influence on their individual power perspectives. Coming together in teams, Neely, Barbara, and Bill had to reconcile their perspectives with each other in order to create two different but equally effective mixed-gender partnerships.

An additional point may seem obvious, but it's worth noting. Neely, Barbara, and Bill all accepted power as a legitimate resource for their leadership. Too often power is rejected wholesale as a negative force that divides people. In the teams that Barbara formed with Neely and later with Bill we see that men and women, who often have radically different attitudes about power, can engage power effectively for good. They can even do so working with each other.

To understand how these partners engaged power effectively, we begin where they left off. What does Bill mean by "having" real power? What does Barbara mean when she says she engaged "some of my own" power? And what does Neely achieve by calling power by the name of influence? In this and the next chapter, we will consider these three questions. As we think about power in mixed-gender teams, we will consider both the team and the individuals in the team. How the team understands and manages the power in the team is one issue. How the team handles its power in relation to the external environment is another. Also, it is important to acknowledge the relative power of different people on the team and to understand how each team member can use power to help the team succeed. We shall look at all of these factors from the point of view of what effective teams do in practice.

Understanding Power

Power is misunderstood and misused even by well-meaning leaders. It is largely interpreted through the lens of the hero-leader model discussed in Chapter Five. Traditionally we have thought of it as a commodity when we would be better off thinking of it as a force active in our leadership. It was power that Obe Wan Kenobi spoke of when he blessed Luke Skywalker with those famous words about "the Force." We who strive to be leaders in the Star Wars generation would do well to remember this.

Our personal attitude about power affects our ability to use power effectively in mixed-gender teams. Men and women are usually very different in this regard. Many women reject power altogether, whereas men are at least comfortable with the idea of it. For the current generation of women leaders, coming to terms with power is a critical factor in our leadership. It is also germane to the success of mixed-gender teams and therefore an issue for men in different ways than for women. Men tend to view power as a competitive commodity, missing its potential as a binding energy in a group. Women's task, then, is to come to terms with their own power. As for men, they must learn that there is more than one way to play the power game.

Power Is as Power Does

Power is the ability to decide what to do, *and do it*. It has been more eloquently defined as "the ability to make and actualize choices for oneself and for others" (Hunt, 1998, p. 2). Put another way, it is "the ability to take one's place in whatever discourse is essential to action *and the right to have one's part matter*" (Heilbrun, 1988, p. 18; italics added). I would add that in the information age power is the ability to name what and who matters. This sounds simple, but it is not. The problem with these definitions is that they do not reveal the real nature of power in human interactions (Stortz, 1997). There are many ways to experience power, depending on situations, relationships, individuals, and structures. What's significant is how we make and actualize choices, take part in the discourse, or name what is important. The *how*, not the *what*, reveals power to us.

The real challenge of power is that we experience it in so many ways. It may be *applied* as authority over people or ideas. It may be *realized* by influencing other people or their ideas (as Neely suggested). It may also be *engaged* as we work with other people. I call these three expressions of power *authoritative power* (power over others), *charismatic power* (power within the person), and *coactive power* (power with other people), much in line with the categories defined by theologian Martha Stortz (1993, 1997). All of these types of power are legitimate in their proper place, and all are based on relationships among people. Power always assumes a relationship (Stortz, 1997). It is inherent in any group. Foucault (1980) first suggested that power is not a *thing to be gotten* but a *force active in relationships*. At the same time, philosopher Hannah Arendt presented power as a "uniquely relational phenomenon" (Stortz, 1997, p. 72). Clearly, power emerges from the chemistry of people working together. *What the relationship is* determines whether power is used well or badly, and here I would depart from others and their definitions of power.

So much that I have read about power is negative. It seems fashionable today to write about power specifically for the purpose of maligning it. I believe the problem is that we tend too often to think of it as an object external to us rather than a force between and among us. As soon as we do this, we also assign attributes to power, usually good or bad. We say, for example, that competitive power is bad or that integrative power is good or that manipulative power is destructive. This erroneous thinking about power leads us to believe that *some kinds of power are always bad and other kinds are always good.* The problem with this kind of thinking is that the attributes we use (competitive, integrative, or manipulative, or any other, for that matter) do not really describe a category of *thing* called power. They describe the way that power is applied. Power in itself is neutral. But we miss this if we think of it as an object that is good or bad.

I prefer a neutral presentation of power to start, as with the three categories I have already suggested. All three of these categories—authoritative power, charismatic power, and coactive power—are, in and of themselves, neutral. They can be abused, and they *are* badly used. They can also be used wisely and well.

A Few Examples

Let's consider a few examples to illustrate. What we often call exploitative power is an abuse of authoritative power. Competitive power is also an application of authoritative power that some view as always negative because of its tendency to exclude the loser. In many situations, of course, competitive power is an abusive application of authoritative power. But I do not think this is always the case. I have seen healthy competition, too. Manipulative power is what we in denominational settings know as passive-aggressive power. This is an abuse of coactive power when the relationship between people is manipulated. It is an abuse of charismatic power when the dynamic leader uses his or her personal charisma to manipulate other people. Women, by stereotype, are said to have refined manipulative power to a fine art. Whether or not this is true, we should all understand the abusive qualities of manipulative power. It is no less abusive of relationships by virtue of the fact that it may be the only application of power available to some groups of people.

We should have the opposite problem with nurturing and connective power. Although we may assume they are always good—the only kinds of power acceptable in our time—we should be cautious. To be sure, these are usually positive applications of coactive power. But coactive power can also be ineffective and even abusive. Organizations or teams can actually exclude those who are not a part of the group in the name of including those who belong. However, we can also work so hard to include every idea that our organizations fail to stand for anything at all.

In my consulting I sometimes encounter groups that drain the energy of everyone in them by their insistence on endless process with little regard for the need finally to get something done. This is yet another abuse of coactive power. It is evident in those situations where connecting for the sake of connecting finally begins to take advantage of people's energy and time and ultimately drains their spirit. My work with these groups begins with teaching them how to engage other forms of power without fear.

What we can see from these examples is that the *application* of power is good or bad, not power itself. The secret to viewing power as neutral is that we understand it as a force between or among people rather than an object possessed by people. Remember what we said earlier: the *how,* not the *what,* reveals the essential nature of power to us.

How Power Moves Among Us

If power is a force rather than a thing, we need to know how it moves among us. Here, we consider the positive factors that affect the flow of power, including both our authority and our identity. As we begin this discussion it will be helpful to remember that our authority is our personal capacity to attract respect from others. It is derived from a combination of external and internal sources. Our identity is who we are, the sum of our defining characteristics as individuals.

Power and Personal Authority

Authority is an element of our power in that it affects how power flows to or away from us. It is given to us by many different external sources to help us claim our power. I believe it is also derived from within us.

Let us first consider the external sources of our authority. These might include our role, our gender, our social position, our education and training, and our competence for the task at hand. It's easiest to think of the authority we have because of our role. Election and installation to public office is one example. Appointment to a civic role as a judge, a member of the police force, or some other public service role is another. In many denominations, ordination is another such source of authority. The authority that we have because of our role is usually formal in the sense that everyone recognizes and acknowledges it. Authority may also be granted informally, by virtue of any of the other factors mentioned earlier: social position, gender, education, competence, and the like. Parents are recognized by the community and the law as having authority over (and responsibility for) their children. Teachers have authority based on social position and education. Wealthy citizens have yet another kind of informal authority that is granted by the community as a result of social prominence. There are many examples of authority externally conferred. Thinking about these shows how obviously authority places our power in the context of community (Stortz, 1993).

Although we may believe that authority is always externally granted, publicly recognized, or institutionally conferred (Stortz, 1993), I believe this is shortsighted. In an age when leadership is changing and our public trust of leaders is schizophrenic at best, we must also have an inner authority that comes from *legitimizing ourselves as leaders*. Certainly we women need this to make our leadership increasingly acceptable in the culture (Becker, 1996). Men need it as well, simply because men too are changing their leadership styles and departing from the hero-leader model. To retain power as we demonstrate new ways of leading, we all need our inner authority to sustain us. This authority will help us interpret our actions as leaders to increasingly skeptical followers.

Formulating our inner authority requires courage. For those of us who are committed to more connective styles, which are essential to the future, our unique authority comes from many things, most of which are absent from the list of most desired traits in the patriarchy. We would do well to give our uniqueness value not only by using it but also by interpreting it for others. That's how we legitimize our own authority. One element of our authority as connective leaders is our ability to join with others. This requires joining our vision to the dreams of others, striving to overcome mutual problems, creating a sense of community, coming together with other leaders, encouraging participation from constituents, collaborating with other leaders rather than competing with them, nurturing new leaders, renewing and building democratic institutions, demonstrating authenticity, and demanding sacrifice (Lipman-Blumen, 1996). We must not only claim these abilities for ourselves but also interpret why they are good for all leaders in a connected world. By generalizing in this way, we claim community and *establish a common knowledge about what it will take to be a leader* in the future. This gives us the inner authority that is a critical factor in our power.

A second way we gain inner authority is through our own commitment to a mission. We release power when we are creative and engaged in our mission. The teams in this study demonstrate for us that the most potent power we know is the power of team energy on a mission. We can see this most clearly in the story of the Lutheran relief team. The sense of common purpose and the sense of urgency in this team combine to give each of the team members as well as the team itself a source of authority that comes from within.

Power and Identity

Up to this point, our analysis of power has assumed that power flows to us because of our authority over others, our internal capacity to attract followers, or even our ability to engage other people. But younger professionals don't necessarily see it this way. A very different point of view came up when I interviewed one of the younger team members in this survey, a thirty-something woman at the beginning of her career. She pointed out that younger professionals view power in a completely different way. "Identity is the issue for us," she said, "not power." Here's why.

Literature since 1980, including feminist writing, developing theories about diversity, and an increasing analysis from Third World writers, has shifted our discourse to identity as the source of power. Questions of how our identity is formed and what role we have in influencing our identity have been critical to understanding power in this discourse. In previous generations, women and people of color of both genders have said that they are powerless because white men constructed their identity for them. They lamented their inability to change the stereotypes that define who they are. In Chapter Twelve, I showed how this social reality has contributed to or detracted from our ability to write our own life scripts. I have also shown that we are beginning to enter yet another phase in our discourse about power as we realize more fully what it means to be an antiracist, antisexist multicultural society.

The early focus on identity as a factor in how power flows to us has assumed that we have a fixed identity that is an accurate representation of who we are. Furthermore, if we could just claim this identity, if other people just knew us, we would have our power. For Generation X, the question of identity is more complex and hopeful. To a point, we are "constructed"; that is, we are who we are known to be. "But we can step into that construction and influence how we are known," explains one Gen X team member. In this view, people contribute to their own identity and that identity changes. "There are many different constructs for who I am. And I can change the way I am known by my performance. The way to fragment fixed-gender (or racial or any other constructed) role is through performance," she adds. Thus she and her age cohorts are more likely to believe that "we can realize power through our performance." This view of power is intriguing and very important for baby boomer leaders to consider. If, as the Generation X-ers believe, we can engage our power through performance, then the ability of our mixed-gender teams to provide a safe place for us to work together is that much more important.

Gender and Power

In discussing the nature of power, I have hinted at some of the differences in the ways women and men understand and engage power. Though men and women in the highest leadership positions use power with relish (Lipman-Blumen, 1996), we as men and women are for the most part very different in our attitudes and approaches to power. Our differences are largely a result of our different experiences as leaders. Remember the stories from Neely, Barbara, and Bill. Neely and Bill did not question access to power. Yet Barbara talked at length about finally learning how to engage her own power. Why? And what does Barbara mean when she says she engaged "some of her own" power?

Men, especially white men, have so much more access to power! This is true no matter our definition of power or our understanding about how we use power. I find myself wondering what it would be like to be a man for a month—or even just a week. I wonder how it would be different to work in a world in which power flows my way all the time. Nevertheless, I know my male colleagues struggle too. There is much about women's experience of the abuse of power that men cannot understand. On the positive side, they would love to know how to use coactive power. We women have a lot of intuitive wisdom about this that we cannot explain any better than the men can explain what it's like to have access to power. It comes from our lifetime experience of accessing power covertly, or at least indirectly. Most women leaders today know all about that. If we are to take Neely's word for it, few men do.

Doing what comes naturally for us as we engage power is different along gender lines. It's different enough to merit taking a closer look in order to understand the challenge to mixed-gender teams.

Women and Power

Women's response to power is complex. "We misinterpret it, fear it, covet it, need it, and at the same time reject it, or at best hold it at a safe distance" (Becker, 1996, p. 162). "Women are often afraid of power," one woman says candidly. "I think in a sense there is a certain amount of dishonesty about this. It's not as though we don't understand it, but we don't use it very directly, and that is not helpful." Why?

First, we women have been oppressed and abused by power so much and for so long that we subconsciously reject it as a bad thing. The abuse I am talking about is both physical and psychological (Chittister, 1990). As a result, we lose our capacity to discern the difference between power and the abuse of power. The safe response to this problem is to avoid power. It's the only way we can make sure that we do not, in turn, abuse someone else. One woman frames the dilemma bluntly: "I am concerned that I might hurt someone or leave someone out in the process, and I don't like that." The result of this fear is that she and other women "have trouble claiming power." Men are often impatient with us for what seems to them like faintheartedness in regard to our own power. What they fail to realize is the devastating psychological effect of abuse on the psychic ability to be powerful. Every woman who has been raped knows what this is about. Even women who have not been raped know, for we all live in constant fear for our physical safety. We have no space we can take up without apology. This, above all, is the reason we have trouble with power.

There are other reasons as well. Sometimes we don't claim our own power because it's easier not to. Instead, we blame men for our struggle while we ignore the power that we already have to be effective partners in mixed-gender teams. Can we imagine what it would be like if no one questioned our right to partnership—maybe even leadership—of a mixed-gender team? We must question whether we need sexism as much as men do, in our case, to protect us from our fear or unfamiliarity of being in charge.

We women also fear claiming and using power because it might be selfish, destructive, or result in our abandonment (Miller, 1986). These fears give us away. We are unrelenting caretakers, so that we cannot put aside the needs of others long enough to claim our own power (which, after all, is part of taking care of ourselves). Furthermore, "we know subconsciously that we have a great deal of power that we have been sitting on like a hand grenade in the nest for a long time. Otherwise, we would not believe that our own power will be destructive when (and if) it is finally released" (Becker, 1996, p. 162). Finally, we are complicit in sexism here as well, giving in to being taken care of by men. Otherwise, we would not fear abandonment (which is different than being alone) so much. These fears are all part of the relationship-care-inadequacy cycle that is such a familiar part of women's lives and that leads to "surplus powerlessness" (Chinnici, 1992, p. 34). This is a commitment on the part of some women to failure, isolation, and weakness—a commitment, by the way, that is so strong in some women that they *redefine their successes as failure* (Chinnici, 1992; Lerner, 1986).

I recall a woman I worked with some years ago, a gifted leader who had been the first in the field of substance abuse treatment to recognize and document that women alcoholics need a different kind of treatment than men. In spite of her pioneering work, she was not yet well known. She was, however, on the brink of receiving national recognition for her work, and she decided to write a book. Her book was much needed at the time. I helped her outline her subject and we found a publisher easily. I thought she was ready to go. Instead, after several months of inactivity she called to say that she had decided not to write the book after all. She wasn't good enough, she said. She didn't know what writing this book would mean for her life, she added. I was shocked and disappointed, for I sensed that she was afraid to step out with her own voice. Rather than address this fear, she redefined her own success as failure so that she would not have to proceed.

Because of our fear of power, we women tend to gravitate toward coactive power. We readily observe that the abuse of authoritative power (authoritarianism as opposed to authoritativeness) is common in our society. This is only exacerbated by the growing violence of our culture. But we err when we assume that *the abuse of* authoritative power is all there is to it (Becker, 1996). The most obvious legitimate application of authorita-tive power is one that women (and men) experience every day in their role as parent or caretaker of children. This, like any other application of power, is not evil, inappropriate, or destructive *unless it is abused*. Because we miss this distinction, we often refuse to see the legitimacy of authoritative power in any application (Rhodes, 1987) or at worst, consider all power abusive, no matter what kind it is (Schaper, 1990). Contributing to this tendency is some discomfort with using charismatic power to get things done. This is the power of our inner authority. We tend not to grant ourselves much inner authority because we are not used to having a voice. We also know that charisma, which is the source of charismatic power, can be abusive when it is used to dominate rather than empower others. For these reasons, we may reject it in the same way that we reject authoritative power.

Women tend to be more comfortable with coactive power. In a sense, it's our only remaining option once we have ruled out authoritative power and charismatic power. It may also seem to us to be the best way to be connective leaders. Whatever our reason for choosing it, we know that it is challenging to use effectively in a hierarchy, poorly understood in tra-ditional leadership circles, and less easily identifiable by outsiders. Fur-thermore, coactive power, like any other form of power, can be abused, as I have noted earlier in this chapter. Suffice it to say that we women limit ourselves when we limit the ways in which we will access power.

The bottom line, says one woman, is this: "We women are fooling our-selves. We really do have power, and we do exercise that power over other people, including other women. We have to come to terms with the kinds of power we do have and the fact that we can abuse power as much as men. Then we have to decide how we are going to use the power we have."

Men and Power

This is precisely what men say to women about their power. It merits some unpacking. Men, who have not been so often abused by power, are less afraid of it. They know that power can be accessed without abuse. If they are truthful, they also know how seductive is the temptation to abuse power. And they know that they run the risk of being the power abuser almost on a daily basis. But many men are thoughtful, wise, and experi-enced in the use of power. With this knowledge and experience, they are comfortable with power. Their advice to women? Get acquainted with your power and use it.

One woman got this advice from a male colleague: "'Ann, I know that you are more forceful than you allow yourself to be. I think it would be helpful if you were more honest and allowed that forceful part of your-self to come forward.' I thought about that and watched him work and I realized it's true. Men are not afraid of power. They are not afraid to use it" (Becker, 1996, p. 161).

Another laywoman reported similar feedback from a male colleague. "A man that I worked with for seventeen years said to me, 'I have never met anyone in all my management years who uses power and authority as judiciously as you do. But you will make a mistake if you don't under-stand that you have that kind of power.' I thought about that a lot . . . and one of the things I learned from it is to take risks. I will accomplish a lot more" (Becker, 1996, p. 161).

These comments come from women I interviewed in 1994. I have been hearing the same thing from women ever since. Men continue to advise us to come to terms with and use our power. Men in mixed-gender teams say that women must do this so that the team can function as effectively as it might. Women also recognize the need to be assertive and powerful in this way. "One of the very positive things about being in a solo ministry was that it enabled me to exercise the power of asserting myself freely," says one woman. "In this new situation I am conscious of wanting to do that. So far, Gil, because he was raised male, can just without blinking an eye assert whatever. My other female colleague and I might assert some-thing, but in a very cautious stepping-back sort of way, which isn't bad in itself unless we give more credence to the assertion that was made more boldly. I'm checking myself. I'm very conscious of wanting to be more as-sertive, especially in meetings."

If men are going to assist women in coming to terms with their own power, they must make a solemn promise not to engage in power games. It goes almost without saying that power games have no place in effective mixed-gender teams. Men have a particular challenge here, because they are both the architects and champions of power gaming. Men have learned to play power games in many ways. They play a power game when they withhold information to "hoard" power under the mistaken impression that power so guarded can be to their benefit. They play another power game when, fearing failure, they fail to take risks when risk is called for. They play yet another power game when they use authoritarian methods rather than the more effective authoritative approaches. Increasingly, men are learning that these power games are not constructive to their own lead-ership or to the partnership they share with women.

Women, of course, are not exempt. We are increasingly at risk for tak-ing on the power game philosophy of traditional leadership models. If we believe in the hero-leader model, we are all at risk of being tricked into thinking that using our power means the same thing as playing power games with each other.

We can see from the stories of Neely, Barbara, and Bill that power gaming is simply not present in effective teams. In the examples from other teams in Chapter Twenty-One, we shall discover more about how effective teams resist the pressure to play power games. Often the external environment exerts this pressure, especially if that environment is patriarchal. Men have a special responsibility here. It goes beyond giving up the games that they have learned to play so well with each other to examining their attitudes about power and women. For it is not just women who contribute to women's avoidance of power. Men too malign or misinterpret women who want or achieve power. Here's what happens: "First, we get to be embarrassed for even wanting it. Then we get to be attacked in public if we show our interest. Then, after we get it, we get to feel guilty for having it" (Anand, 1990, p. 25). This happens because, in seeking power, women defy the gender stereotype, which is as familiar to us as a mantra: women are trained for private virtue, men for public power. Men, by contrast, always have power: "just enough to trick [them] into thinking it is [their] right" (Schaper, 1990, p. 6).

Women Who Have Claimed Their Power

To illustrate the relationship between men and women that supports the power of both and helps women make friends with their own power, we may look at the leadership of one woman in the interview sampling. She spoke candidly in her interview about her own growing awareness of herself as a powerful leader. She has had three male colleagues in her professional career as a clergywoman, two with whom she has partnered to form effective mixed-gender teams. A victim of a violent crime some years ago, she has come to terms with her own power at the same time she has recovered from the physical abuse of an assault. Today, she is in the role of senior pastor getting ready to form another team.

"I struggle mightily with wanting to be liked. It's hard for me to do things that might make people upset with me," Marie began. Like most women of the baby boom generation, Marie also has what she calls "internal conversations" with herself about whether she is capable enough. "It's a constant," she says. "I just have to turn it off." Remember Barbara's comments about the same issue. Women do have inner voices that question their capabilities. Men may question their ability, but they do not routinely report the same kind of constant inner voice questioning themselves.

"Trusting myself has been reinforced by my husband's trust. It also came from Alan, my first partner. I learned more about my own ministry in eight months from Alan than in the previous six years, because I had validation from a male," Marie emphasized. As a result, she began to validate herself and began hearing validation from other women. "It all started with the internal assent to my gifts," she recalled. "I began to feel my authority in a new way. I had never felt it before. Alan's mentoring helped engender the confidence and the leadership quality people see in me now. Whether I needed a man to say it or whether I just needed somebody, it helped me build confidence. It played a key role."

What has happened since then? "I get asked to do a lot. I think it's because *I look good*. It's that self-confidence. It feels so good to have that struggle resolved." Remember Barbara's similar transition. A leader who is now well known in Protestant circles, Barbara had similar questions and reported similar tendencies to want to please other people. Now both these women are feeling their own power and are comfortable with it.

What her partners did to help her was simply to tell Marie repeatedly what she was good at, especially when she was better at something than they were. They also challenged her to think about her own leadership in a way that encouraged her to be ambitious. Now she hears feedback like this: "There is something about your presence that is different than almost any other woman pastor I've ever seen."

Although this makes Marie feel good about her own growth, it concerns her at the same time. "There is a pulling back I see in women, a pulling their shoulders in and keeping their arms close to their bodies. Women are afraid to take up space. We don't want to get too far out there or somebody might hurt us. We keep those boundaries pretty close. I now have a willingness to take up space with my presence. I got that from men convincing me that I won't look bad," Marie said.

Our ability to come to terms with our own power and authority as women is critical to our partnership with men. The stereotype about ourselves that we have to overcome is framed in a question men often pose silently to themselves: When the going gets tough, can I count on this woman? "Women feed this bias with their physical tentativeness," Marie says. "On the other hand, we have to learn a quality of being confident and present that isn't always a challenge to men. It's a subtle relationship."

Marie also asserts the importance of claiming the authority that is externally granted by hierarchy. This is another thing that women often have difficulty doing. I have said before that "too often we expect women leaders to be familiar friends, close to the rest of us who are the followers. We thus deny them the distance that authority requires. The result is that we hurt their chances to be effective leaders for men as well as women" (Becker, 1996, p. 172). Marie's experience supports this view. "If you want me to be an effective colleague to men who have power, I have to be seen as a peer," she said. At the same time, she is "very comfortable sharing power because it comes right back. My colleagues have never kept it. They threw it back and the energy increased."

How energy increases when power is shared in effective mixed-gender teams is the subject of the next chapter.

POWER AND INFLUENCE IN MIXED-GENDER TEAMS

WE NOW TURN from the question of individual power to the many power dynamics in teams. For this discussion we also return to the stories of Neely, Barbara, and Bill. There is so much information about power in their stories that we would do well to note the assumptions they made about power and the ways they used power to the benefit of their teams' success. Their experiences illustrate how mixed-gender teams in this study understand and use power to *influence*.

First of all, there was no one way they used power. Their stories alone illustrate different views of power and different ways of using power effectively in a mixed-gender team relationship. Furthermore, they had similar ways of engaging each other as equals regardless of power structures outside the team. Second, none of them used power to show who was boss. In fact, all three shared their private soul-searching about how well they used power wisely to the benefit of the seminary and the team. Third, their stories illustrate in various ways the importance of the role of the individual with the most power, particularly in relation to external structures. Fourth, they resisted external pressure to define clearly who was in charge when that was detrimental to the team. Fifth, they did many things to manage their personal power dynamics. This, as I noted in the previous chapter, is most critical to mixed-gender teams. Finally, because their teams were successful, they had some influence on other power relationships in the seminary.

Let's take a closer look at these aspects of power in mixed-gender teams. We turn now to Neely. What does he gain by calling power by the name of influence?

Power Inside the Teams

When I asked him about power in his relationship with Barbara, Neely said, "I don't usually use the word power." Neely's comment was typical of a surprisingly frequent response to the question of power. Several team members expressed discomfort with using the word to describe how relationships are managed in their team. One woman said, "We don't think in terms of power. We let each member work to his or her strengths." Another commented, "I don't like the word" but admitted there is power in her team. A male team leader responded by saying, "We rarely use that kind of language here." But the comment most revealing of a negative bias about power itself was from a team member who said of her team leader, "He has the authority, but he does not wield power." This comment *assumes that wielding power is the same thing as abusing power over others.* I would assert that there are many ways to engage power, some destructive and many constructive. The teams in this study shared many creative and constructive ways of engaging power. Nevertheless, many individuals revealed this kind of bias in their interview comments about power.

Others acknowledged the presence of power and commented about how they use it to build the team and the people in it. One male team leader defined power as "the ability to lead and shape rather than dictate." With this definition, he added, "It hasn't been an issue for me. I want a permission-giving atmosphere." Another male pastor said, "I'm not a control leader. I spread the authority around. I give responsibility away." One team member made the point by saying, "Everybody knows who the boss is. Power is fairly well concentrated in a few people. It's the way power is used, not how it's held that counts." Another commented, "Power is often most powerful when given up." A woman commented that in her team, "power held by any one person is held for the good of the whole team." Another man summed up his philosophy about power in the team by saying, "None of us is as smart as all of us."

Whether or not team members named power as energy active in their teams, it always is. For those team members who do not like to talk about power, my probing revealed that power is operative in the team even when the team members do not use the word. They may, like Neely, prefer another, more neutral word that describes the way they handle power. Neely used the word influence. He thinks of power as influence, and he encourages everyone on his team to use his or her influence. This is a neutral way of saying, "Use your power," because the word influence is not loaded. When we hear the admonition, "Use your power," we tend to think of force, authority, or even violence.

These observations amplify a point I made in the previous chapter, which is that women are reluctant to come to terms with power, often failing to distinguish it from the abuse of authoritative power. In these mixed-gender teams there is great sensitivity about power. Certainly these teams understand that power is a loaded word. But whether or not they use the word, power is active in their mixed-gender teams. Refusing to name it does not make it go away. I would suggest that men and women in mixed-gender teams look very closely at their understanding of and use of power. What they are doing to harness power is instructive for all of us. They have much to teach us about how to use power wisely as we expand our ways of working together. But they will not do so by denying that power is at work in their midst.

There are two power structures in the teams in this study. We get a glimpse of these in the foregoing comments about the word power. In one model, the team is structured as a hierarchy, with a clearly defined senior leader. In the other, the team is structured to be egalitarian, sometimes even taking apart an old hierarchical model and building a new equal-partner model for team members to follow and interpret to their constituents. Between these two extremes, all the teams in this study fall somewhere on an egalitarian-hierarchy continuum. Most have some external hierarchy to answer to and are therefore not free to adopt a fully egalitarian style. Many push the limits of their ability to be egalitarian as far as they can inside the team, treating each other as equal partners but dealing in traditional ways with the hierarchies outside the team with which they connect. Others live comfortably with a hierarchical model inside and outside the team.

We should not assume that the "ideal" mixed-gender team consists of men and women who are equal partners in every sense of the word. Many are like the one this woman describes: "Adam is the senior and I am the associate member. He has given me roles I can take and run with. I inform him of my work but do not have to ask his permission. We decide our roles together based on our gifts and interests." Two examples will illustrate this point. For the purpose of this comparison, I've selected two teams in the same environment. Both are clergy teams serving a single congregation.

A Hierarchical Team

Team A is clearly hierarchical. It includes four team members—three clergy and one lay—under the direction of a senior pastor. In this team, "David is the senior. Our congregation wants it that way," comments one team member, adding, "David would prefer more equality in the team." The lay member of the team says, "David has the official power. I see myself as newer on the team and don't feel I have a lot of power. But I think that what I say is listened to and valued. David is interested in knowing what we have to say." The third team member described David as "open about asking opinions before he makes decisions." David's role is typical of the leader in a strictly hierarchical team. The senior makes the decisions and announces them. In less hierarchical teams, the senior is clearly superior in position and authority to others in the team but would not make a decision without consensus of the team members. The range is wide. Each team is somewhat different in this regard, depending on where it is on the egalitarian-hierarchy continuum.

David agrees with his team's assessment. "I hold all the power. That's what is granted to me by the congregation. How that's exercised is often different than the congregation thinks," he commented. "When the senior pastor sets the tone and gives the direction, it's pretty hard for another member of the team to rise above that or to be seen in any role but subordinate. Because that's also an expectation on me, it's an easy role for me to fulfill. I don't mind stepping up to the plate, and I know that makes it harder for the others on the team," he added. In many cases, though not particularly in this case, it's more difficult for the female members of the team to emerge as leaders in this model.

We can readily see how much responsibility his team model places on David. It's up to him to make sure that each member of the team is heard. The team itself contributes to the challenge for David. "All three of the team members look to me to be the sounding board and to make sure that I am okay with something, because then they know they will have a better shot at it. The only thing I've asked of them is to be self-directed and go for it. But no surprises for me," he commented. "My responsibility is having an overall picture of the parish, to know how things fit together. So I want to know what the pieces are. Some team members are very comfortable with this. They know they have the freedom to challenge me. At least one of them gives me too much deference. He is careful about saying only those things that are supportive of me. I've told him, 'You need to speak up.' Others on the team do that freely."

An Egalitarian Team

Team B is now radically egalitarian. It consists of three part-time clergy sharing the equivalent of one and one-quarter positions in a small-town parish. Before this team changed its membership and leadership style, it consisted of a full-time senior pastor and a quarter-time volunteer associate. In forming the new team, the senior pastor's spouse, also clergy, took over half of her husband's full-time job. The quarter-time associate became a professional member of the team. All three team members now share equal responsibility for the ministry. In their faith tradition, plural ministry such as this is part of their heritage and closer to the presumed New Testament model. Volunteer ministry is also common in this denomination and in fact was the only model for ministry in the last century. "Power belongs to the community in our denomination. It is shared. We have a certain watchfulness about persons being raised above others. That's part of our heritage. In this congregation that is embraced," said the male member of this team, in explaining the theology behind the shift. The historical denominational context states that "every believer is a priest with a ministry. Because we are all equal, decisions are made by the community, not by a hierarchy."

This team created its new leadership model out of the historical theological context the denomination provides. The model replaces one in which the male pastor was primary and the female associate was a volunteer. For this reason, it has required careful interpretation. "It took quite a few months to educate the congregation to the idea," the former associate team member reports. In fact, the team "talked and prayed about this change . . . trying to discern what to do . . . for a year," recalls the male team member. "We tried to move slowly and process it with everybody. There was open but very healthy debate. One of the challenges for us was the fact that people were happy with the way things were. They were nervous about any change. Yet they were familiar with all three of us and with the concept of a team ministry." The pastors have answered very specific questions about the pastoral team, the benefits to the congregation of a team, how responsibilities will be divided, time commitments from each member of the team, and budget implications of the team model. They have also preempted questions about how the team will work by telling the congregation how they will build the team and how they will maintain a healthy relationship with the congregation. Finally, they have been specific in telling members what to do when they need a pastor.

This kind of specific interpretation is usually required of egalitarian teams. Constituents outside the team want to know who is in charge. If constituents perceive that no one is in charge, they may assume that nothing is getting done and jump to the conclusion that someone needs to be put in charge. To avoid misperceptions that can crop up around egalitarian team models, successful teams find that detailed interpretation of the team and its work helps a lot.

We too might ask this team why they did it (really) and how they will make it work. The answer to the first question is partly that it is congruent with their heritage and fits the congregation. It also fits the team's approach to ministry. At this time in their lives and their work, the members of this team "are very much more interested in being leaders who draw out the visions of the people and empower them in coming up with their own sets of goals . . . and yet still push people. But maybe with not as much of our own agenda as before," commented one of the women on this team.

The change in team style also fits the team's need to grow. "It seemed clear to me that to be in ministry with each other, we needed a whole new definition of things. Our shift in style was an attempt to change the balance of power and allow the three of us to live out the call," said the male team member. For the women, it may have even more significance. "In order to be perceived as full pastors, we all have to do certain things, like preaching. Beyond these there are certain areas we want to approach creatively as individuals, with support from the others," explained one of the women. "The more I know my job the more I am personally able to assert my power," she added. This woman is typical of a younger generation who understand power as derived from identity and role definition rather than something external, a thing to be achieved. In a team in which roles are clearly defined but responsibility is shared equally, this woman says she will be able to claim her power as a leader. That, she adds, "will be to the team's advantage" as well as to her own advantage.

Keeping things defined will require openness, truthfulness, and a commitment to a lot of talk time. That's typical of open, egalitarian teams. Interpretation of what the team is doing, how it functions, and where the power lies has to be continual *to the team* as well as to the constituency the team serves.

Power Principles for Teams

We can observe from these examples that it does not matter whether the team is hierarchical or egalitarian, so long as (1) the team members agree to the model, (2) the people in the team follow the model agreed on, and (3) the people in the team are always engaged as equal contributors in ways appropriate to the team model. These three power principles are important for every effective team. When followed, they will help the team use power effectively regardless of the structure of the team.

The third principle is particularly important. All teams stressed the amount of time and energy they put into learning from each other regardless of the power structure of the team. Hierarchical teams in a real sense ignore their hierarchy to do this. They behave in the team like a group of colleagues. In such teams, it is the role of the senior person to direct the team in this activity, to take responsibility for the way in which the team engages everyone as an equal partner. Once decisions are made, the senior leader is charged with representing the team to the constituency. In more egalitarian teams, the members of the team are in constant dialogue about ideas, decisions, results, and next steps. They take turns representing the decisions of the team to the outside world.

We can also observe that both these teams have gender issues. Being in an egalitarian team does not nullify the power differential in the team unless people work at it. Conversely, the power issues in a hierarchical team may not be as we expect. In particular, I noted that most hierarchical teams with strong male leaders did not have power issues between the men and the women in the team as long as the team followed the three power principles. The most troublesome gender issues for mixed-gender teams that do follow these principles are with people external to the team, as we shall see. It is clear that mixed-gender teams must be aware of and address power issues in the team for the two reasons mentioned in Chapter Two. First, they must deal with the way power works between men and women. Second, they must be equipped to resist pressure from outside the team that attempts to break down the team.

Power Outside the Teams

"It's easy to talk a good line about being a team, but the expectations of the congregation are otherwise." Men throughout this study echoed this comment by a male leader of a team in a very traditional environment. Congregations are not the only problem environments. As we've already begun to see through the stories of teams in this study, meeting the expectations of people outside the team can be one of the most difficult challenges for the team and the team leader. Where power is concerned, the team faces a particular challenge. People outside the team want to know who is in charge.

If *team* sounds to constituents like *no one is in charge,* they may try to break down the team or at least establish who is the senior member of the team. This happens, of course, because in our culture we still elevate the hero-leader as the ideal. Too often, then, we assume that if we have a strong (often male) leader, our congregations, agencies, and institutions will have good leadership. Men who work in effective mixed-gender teams are on the front line in fighting this bias.

"I did not meet the expectations of some people in the congregation because they still wanted a senior pastor in the old sense of the word," one male senior minister recalled of his team. "In some cases I ignored this. In others I tried to explain that this is not my style." I heard this response from a surprising number of male team leaders, especially from male clergy.

"We've struggled with this congregation trying to develop a shared understanding of collegial leadership," said another pastor who works in an egalitarian team that he and his colleagues have named a *collegium*. "The struggle has been very positive but we have many members who really want and expect to have . . . if not a CEO, then at least an organizing center. One personnel committee member said, 'The collegium can be a gathering of equals but one has to be more equal than the others. There has to be someplace where the buck stops.'"

Sometimes it's not just the leader who gets this pressure. Members of one team commented, "There were pressures on specific team members to make decisions or to follow a certain course of action that ran counter to what the team was trying to do, or that represented one person's opinion—a person in a position of power."

Some male leaders succeed in communicating that their teams are sacrosanct. They stop the pressure from outside. Remember the story of Wayne and Erin who work as equals as much as possible in a denominational hierarchy. Wayne is Erin's supervisor and both admitted that "we struggle with that" difference in power. They sought to minimize this difference as much as possible by making Erin the associate executive presbyter. The Presbyterian hierarchy said no. Still, within the team they practice mutuality. Wayne no longer gets comments or encouragement to make it otherwise, "because people know I would not respond." Wayne increasingly gives up duties to Erin that church practice considers appropriate only for the executive presbyter. This further equalizes their roles outside as well as inside the team.

Other male leaders make symbolic gestures that help communicate to constituents that the team will operate on an equal-partnership basis. Blair and Mary, whose story is in Chapter Twenty-Two, decided that Mary should move into the office that had always been reserved in the past for the senior member. Blair had a new office space created for himself. In another situation, the team is careful to meet in neutral space or take turns meeting in each other's offices. Particularly in parish settings, it's often helpful for team members to mix up their committee assignments, making sure the women and men do not take on roles traditionally expected of their gender. In one instance, a pastoral team decided that the female member should work with the endowment committee of the congregation. This move surprised the committee members, a group of men who had always worked with a male senior pastor.

All these measures communicate the team members' intention to be equal partners and thereby help to diminish the suggestions from constituents that the male member ought to assert his authority as the sole leader. Note that these men are not all in egalitarian teams. I repeat: men who work in effective mixed-gender teams are on the front lines in fighting this bias *regardless of whether their teams are hierarchical or egalitarian.*

The external environment challenges effective mixed-gender teams in a second way when it is hierarchical. Most bureaucracies use hierarchical structures so that power flows to those with higher rank. But the power secret of effective mixed-gender teams is that, at the relational level, they are inclusive of all persons equally. This is true regardless of whether their structure is hierarchical or egalitarian. Thus the team members who work in a hierarchy must strive to sustain inclusive personal relations with each other at the same time that they respond to the external environment as part of the hierarchy.

We saw this in the story of David and his team. Although David wants to and strives to have equal sharing and open conversation in the team, he and his team members work in a hierarchical denomination. In this structure, it is quite natural that the congregation would expect to know who is in charge. David knows, however, that the congregation's point of view does not make the presence or the ministry of any member of the team any less of an achievement. They "just see us in certain kinds of roles," he said. "I have not tried to retrain the congregation. I hope that my style is such that I direct people to the team member who is in charge in any given area. And so long as staff are on track in their areas of responsibilities, I see my role as supporting them. I get out of the way." But it's a challenge to shift back and forth from the hierarchical expectations of the organization to the relational equality of the team. It's a challenge to keep all the team members believing that it's OK to speak up, share openly, and take risks. Some team members are never sure it's safe to take risks in the group. Some team leaders end up saying it's not possible, particularly when the external hierarchy is oppressive.

Responsibilities of the Most Powerful Team Member

Peter, who is team leader in a clearly hierarchical mixed-gender team, refers to himself as "the short bald guy who . . . is the senior rabbi." The joke here, of course, reveals a deeper understanding of the leader as the "least of these." Peter knows that he is essentially the servant of the whole team. That's the responsibility of the team leader—one, I might add, that is well understood by every team leader who clearly holds power in an effective mixed-gender team.

Most often, if a mixed-gender team has a member with more power than others, it is a male leader who is recognized as the head of the team. In an increasing number of cases, such as Barbara and Bill's team, the most powerful team member is a woman. The person with the most authority is usually the "most powerful team member." We saw in the last chapter that authority can come from many sources, both external and internal. Authority may come from status or role in the organization, education, special skill, or even an inner drive for visionary leadership, to name a few. In all cases, the powerful leader carries tremendous responsibility for the success of the team. For the purposes of this discussion, we will call this individual the team leader, though this is not always the case.

Creating an Inclusive Team

"It's the responsibility of the team leader to make sure the team works," said one team leader bluntly. It's as simple and complex as that. For this succinct statement refers to a world of ways in which the leader nurtures the team.

First, the team leader must make sure that power operates in the team to engage all members. This requires creating an environment of listening and open conversation among team members. It means constantly taking the lead in keeping the team engaged in discourse on an even playing field, where all team members feel free to speak. It is based on the leader's wisdom in knowing that effective mixed-gender teams create an environment of inclusion for all team members, regardless of what the external environment expects of them.

Some team leaders also work with individuals on the team to encourage their participation or moderate their dominance. In one respect this task is gender-related. Male team leaders often encourage women team members to be more forthcoming with their ideas and opinions. Blair and Mary talk about this in their team story in Chapter Twenty-Two. "I try to be the monitor of the power stuff because I am aware that a lot of things are unexamined," said Blair. "I tried to name those things and encourage Mary to stick up for herself. I had to develop a kind of sixth sense about how she was reacting to things. Her response was always 'yes' when I asked her if she wanted to do a certain thing. I had to learn when she meant 'yes' and when she really meant 'no.' I remember one conversation in which I said, 'I don't want to do that anymore. I would much rather you be responsible for protecting yourself rather than me be responsible for protecting both of us.' And she has done that." These two team members believe that power and responsibility are shared. Like many mixed-gender teams, the male member must work hard not to take power and responsibility away from his female colleague by deciding and even speaking for her. The female team member must claim her own power by knowing what she means and speaking her own mind.

Another woman team member recounts how difficult it was for her to emerge as a leader in relation to her male partner: "Toward the end of our team ministry, I became his pastor, not because I wanted to but because he chose me. Especially when he was going through some difficulty in his relationship with the congregation, he spent a lot of time in my office sharing his pain and calling me his pastor. I thought to myself, 'You're supposed to be the leader!' It moved our relationship to a new level. I wasn't sure I wanted to be the leader."

We might contrast this challenge to the one Barbara faced in her partnership with Bill. Recall that Bill was frustrated by the all-female (plus Bill) team in which the women often discussed issues he felt were trivial. Bill's challenge, as he pointed out, was to continue participating within boundaries that felt right for him. Barbara's challenge was to keep the team moving and keep all the members participating on a relatively equal footing. The issues are different for men and women but the problem is often the same.

Transforming External Pressure

Second, the team leader is responsible for transforming external pressure to take over. This requires knowing both the external environment and the team very well. Political savvy about the organization and the denomination help. A willingness to stand firm on behalf of the team is often necessary. At other times, leaders who hold the power of the team find that it's judicious to be cautious about pushing the organization beyond its ability to understand how the team functions if that is very different from what the organization demands.

Remember the story of the three clergy who formed a new-style egalitarian team. They spent over a year planning the change and interpreting it to their members and their denomination. By the time they actually began to work together as a threesome, they knew their plan well and were ready to move ahead. But they were also cautious about how ready their congregation was, realizing that their constituents had not yet gone through a period of orientation to their new way of working. Thus they embarked on another period of careful transition, this time not with one another but with the people they serve. This kind of change process is often required of effective mixed-gender teams. We've seen how important it is for mixed-gender teams to create a level playing field for all team members on the team. Much of what this book is about is just how to do that with one another. But once that is done, the team as a whole must go through a similar process with constituents. How difficult this process will be depends on the difference between the internal team environment and the external organizational environment. Obviously, the greatest difficulty occurs when the team is very egalitarian and the environment is very hierarchical. If the team is led by an individual who is perceived by the constituency as holding the power of the group, it is this individual's responsibility to lead and carefully monitor the process as the team interprets itself to its constituency.

I have seen many mixed-gender teams run aground at this very point in their development, for several reasons. The first reason is that the team leader is unclear about the role. The leader may not understand the power of the position or may not realize the responsibility that comes with that power. Or the leader may fail to use that power because he or she doesn't want the role, doesn't think the team needs a leader, or doesn't know what to do as leader. Team leaders who deny their leadership role in this way are forgetting that the constituency externally grants their status as team leader. The only way to give up the role—short of giving it to someone else—is to help the constituency understand the team and embrace its egalitarian style. This move is very challenging in any hierarchy.

Second, team leaders fail to help constituents understand the team because they miss how important this work is to the team's success. Their focus is on the team, and they fail to see how important it is not only to nurture the team but also to guide the team in interpreting itself to the constituency. Pretty soon, someone on the team feels that he or she has been undermined with a constituent, and there's trouble in the team. Or the opposite happens. A constituent or group of constituents misinterprets an action of the team as a whole or an individual team member. Then there's discontent among the membership about how the team is behaving. Either incident can be the beginning of the end for an effective mixed-gender team, especially if the mishaps are not recognized and corrected with careful communication. I see so much of this happen between teams and their constituents that I could literally spend all of my consulting time helping teams in this delicate process.

The third reason team leaders fail to monitor how well the team interprets itself to constituents is that they are kidnapped by the opposition. They literally forget how important it is to be a servant leader to the team. Remember what David said earlier in this chapter: the expectation is for him to be the senior member of the team. That's a temptation, he admitted. "It's an easy role for me to fulfill. I don't mind stepping up to the plate, and I know that makes it harder for the others on the team." Every team leader faces this temptation when there is external pressure to take over as the sole leader to the detriment of the team. Ego gets involved and that seductive voice inside tells us that it would just be easier if we did it ourselves. We all know team leaders who succumb to this temptation. They are the ones who become controlling and maybe even preemptive. They lack understanding of the expansive nature of team energy, so they are always looking for someone's power move. They use power to "show who's boss." They may go so far as to use their power to make their own position (relative to the constituency) stronger and the position of their teammates weaker. This is the most destructive temptation to which team leaders can succumb. Team members really have to know "how the wind is blowing" with team leaders like this. In contrast, team leaders who resist the temptation are like those we read about in this volume. They are like the woman team leader who is described by a team member as "clear in resisting upward delegation. She allows us to learn from our mistakes. She consults frequently and in depth with us." They are also like the male team leader who is described by a team member as "a first among equals" in our team, who "makes more than the sum of the parts out of all that we do."

How Effective Teams Share Power

How mixed-gender teams manage their own power dynamics, both inside and outside their teams, is the critical factor in their effectiveness. So we may ask, how do these teams manage power? Their answers provide us with a good recipe for any successful team:

- *They share it.* We have seen in this analysis how important it is for every team member to be an equal inside the team, regardless of the environment outside the team. This point is fundamental to mixed-gender team success.
- *They appreciate the team leader's difficult role.* We have seen how complex this role is and how many opportunities the team leader has to

make a mistake. Team leaders and team members alike are keenly aware of the huge responsibility that rests on the shoulders of the team leader. They recognize that the role of team leader is a challenge and a burden, not a prize. They pray for the wisdom of their leader, who must guide the team through the delicate process of building effective partnership whether or not the constituency understands or supports the effort.

- *They are not afraid of power.* They know that power is realized in many different ways. They are quite well able to discern that one kind of power is appropriate in one situation and another kind is appropriate in another. They are comfortable with the idea that, as one male team member said, "If the boss has something difficult to do, she has to wear steel-toed boots." They also know that power is not the same as the abuse of power. This discernment is the basis of their lack of fear of power.

- *They use different kinds of power.* It follows from the preceding point that they would be able to use different kinds of power effectively. They are as comfortable with the need to process with each other to reach consensus as with the idea that the boss may use steel-toed boots to get the job done.

- *They talk honestly with each other about power.* They know that differences in the way men and women engage power are at least partially conditioned by experience. When they see their colleague of the opposite gender engage power in an ineffective way based on lack of experience or knowledge, they speak up. The trust that provides a foundation for their work together also provides a foundation for their effective ways of confronting each other about power. Thus in the normal round of their daily discourse, they learn about power from each other.

- *They define their own power.* This they do largely by assertively seeking definition about their own roles in the team and in the organization. Once this is done, they work as a team and further define their power in relation to each other in healthy ways. They do not define their power by trying to limit the power of others.

- *They consider power an ally.* For these teams, power is best described as a unique energy that contributes to the work of the team. Furthermore, because these teams are dedicated to mission-based work, power is an ally in the service of others.

- *They view power as abundant.* They recognize that the more power they share the more they can generate. They feel enriched by this process.

- *They are humble about having power.* They know power can be abused. The still small voice of temptation is in each one of us. They are cautious about using power, but they do use it. The best test of their ability to

PART SEVEN

MODELING

22

BLAIR AND MARY

KEEPING THE TEAM TOGETHER

BLAIR AND MARY are copastors at a seven-hundred-member Presbyterian church in Stamford, Connecticut. They have worked together for over seventeen years in two different settings. After working for fifteen years in a much smaller New Haven congregation, they decided to see if they could move as a team. They were successful in doing so, and in 1996 they became copastors at their present congregation. The Stamford congregation was not looking for a team when they decided to call Blair and Mary. However, the decision of the congregation was to extend a full-time call to both of them. The Stamford staff includes two other men, an associate pastor and a minister of music. The associate pastor served the Stamford congregation for seventeen years before Blair and Mary came, and has worked with the minister of music for all of those seventeen years. Thus, says Blair, "We were really two teams coming together."

Blair and Mary have succeeded in making a transition to a new setting as an intact team. They have also made a transition to full partnership. Looking at their first work setting, we can readily see several factors, any one of which might have prevented this unusual transition. In their New Haven congregation, which had about 150 members, Mary started out as a volunteer assistant pastor. Eventually she came on staff to work part time. Throughout their partnership in that congregation, Mary was clearly the associate member of the team. As the female and younger member, she was also more likely to be viewed by others as the junior member. In spite of these conditions and the fact that mixed-gender teams who are not clergy couples almost never move together, Mary and Blair succeeded in moving from one congregation to another and from a hierarchical mentor-apprentice relationship to a partnership of equals as the pastoral team serving as head of staff.

Although their own team has developed successfully, Blair and Mary have discovered that their leadership has to change in a new setting. The way they worked together in New Haven doesn't necessarily translate to working together in Stamford. Blair and Mary are currently rethinking how to be in partnership ministry in a very different setting. That too is part of the challenge of moving together.

○

Mary Suggests the Team

Twenty years ago I moved to New Haven with my husband and small child. We worshiped at the Presbyterian church there, where I eventually served with Blair. I was at that time doing consulting in Christian education with Hartford Seminary, but I did not have an official call. I had had one previous eighteen-month parish experience that I would describe as not too wonderful, and prior to that served as chaplain at a mental health facility for five years. Blair came to be the pastor of our congregation and I watched him. I liked what I saw. I went to him and said, "I would like to learn about parish ministry."

The first option we explored for our partnership was a parish associate position. In the Presbyterian church, this position creates a relationship (often without pay) between a parish and a clergy in a nonparish call. Our presbytery turned down this idea because my consulting work was not considered a validated call. We ended up changing the title of the job description of parish associate to assistant pastor. At that time, this was a position in our denomination that a session could fill without going through a full search. The presbytery approved this. I became the assistant pastor working ten hours per week donating my time. That's how it started. I was eventually called to an associate staff position, but continued to work part time.

In the beginning I came into this relationship with a healthy dose of skepticism. One of the things I've learned is that we pastors do not realize how much we reveal of ourselves in worship. That's where I saw Blair functioning. That's where most of our people see us functioning. What I saw in Blair was integrity. The words he preached matched what he was doing. They also encouraged me in my faith. Seeing these qualities in him encouraged me to the possibility of partnership. I also went to him fairly early on and told him that my experiences with other male clergy had not been wonderful. I told him I needed honesty in the relationship. "I'm not asking you to prove yourself, but I may be skittish," I said. Blair heard what I was saying and promised we would work on it. He has always been appreciative and encouraged me to speak my mind about my needs and concerns.

I figured this was a no-lose situation for all of us. It was part time for me and I was not being paid. I could always get out of it without involving too many other people if it didn't work. It was not like being called and uprooting my family and moving two hundred miles. My husband had a job and my family was not dependent on me for income. I had a lot of freedom. Also, in order to do my consulting work with congregations knowledgeably, I needed to know more about how the church functions. It always concerns me when pastors go into specialized ministry without experience of the parish because the parish is the foundation of the church and its mission. The parish is what supports all other specialized ministry. I just felt I needed some learning.

Our relationship has changed over the years and become more equal. It was interesting when we left the New Haven congregation to realize how much we were seen there as a team, as their pastors, not head of staff and associate. I felt they were reflecting back to us what we were doing, what our relationship was. When we said we wanted to move together, there was no resistance or questioning from the presbytery. The word had gotten around that we were a good team.

We have succeeded in becoming full partners for several reasons. First of all, we spent a lot of time intentionally looking at what we were doing and how we were functioning as a team. We were forced to do this in a sense because we were supervising students from Yale Divinity School. In the eyes of the students we were people who could share information with them. This forced us to articulate to each other what our understanding of ministry was. Second, Blair's style is to ask those kinds of questions. All along he encouraged us to do that kind of thinking. Finally, I've learned to see the other person and appreciate the gifts and not the title. That has helped too.

We've had colleagues to bring along in both settings, too. In the New Haven congregation, we had a student who eventually came on staff with us. Here we have an associate pastor and a minister of music. Many people have expressed how glad they are that they are a part of the team too. So while I think the two of us have worked on partnership very intentionally, it is not limited to us. Whatever power is held by any person on the team, it is held for the good of the rest. It is not exercised as power over the others. I can't think of any example of competition among us and I suppose we are all doing pretty much what we want to do. There is a real freedom of bringing other people into what we are doing. We have a shared commitment to the people in the congregation. We spend a lot of time talking about things to each other. It takes the right people. It takes people who can communicate, who feel the freedom and have the trust relationship to say, if necessary, "This isn't working for me." It takes people who will not immediately jump to the defensive, people who are willing to be vulnerable with each other. And it takes clear boundaries.

Before Blair and I came to Stamford we talked about some of the things we wanted to have happen. One of those is a regular staff meeting time that includes all staff. Once a week everybody gathers. We also talked with staff when we first arrived about the ground rules for how we function. If someone has a problem with another, go to that person first. We have been intentional about trying to avoid triangulating. We also decided right away that there would be a regular time every day for prayer. And we have regular social time. It's intentional that staff relations are on a variety of levels—spiritual, professional, and social. This has facilitated communication and has given us a good foundation on which to speak to each other. In our first staff retreat we had a pastoral counselor work with us. He said he had never seen a group of people as free with information as we are. He told us, "You had everything out on the table almost from the beginning." That's how we do it.

We had been told that previously the staff here worked more independently of each other. They each did their work and did it well, but there wasn't much conversation about it or sharing of it. We came in with a radically different style. All these people on the staff were here when we got here. It has been interesting for me to see the changes in staff relationships over two and a half years. Our associate has started to drop in on Blair and me to say, "I'm working on this. What do you think?" This kind of informal connecting happens because of what we have tried to do in the intentional structure.

Just as we spend a lot of time listening to each other, we started in this new congregation by listening to people. We have heard wonderful stories. This allowed us to get to know the congregation as they got to know us. We both came here with a commitment to encouraging and empowering people in the congregation in the ministry to which they are called. We are both coming to the realization that in this church there also needs to be more of a sense of the leader and a clearer sense of the direction and vision for the congregation. We continue to value shared ministry, and we are all learning new ways to encourage it that are appropriate and effective in this setting.

○

Blair Gains a Professional Partner

Mary and I developed a real partnership over fifteen years. When the time came to test the waters elsewhere we both agreed that the worst of it would be breaking up a good partnership. One day Mary said to me, "What would you think if we put our dossiers out together to see if anyone is interested in us as a team?" I said, "Surely you jest!" My first reaction was, "There's no way it's going to fly." My second reaction was, "Don't you want to work with someone else? You've worked with me for a long time. Don't you want a break?" She said no, she had worked with other people and would be happy to continue working with me. So we put our dossiers out separately and together. Where we thought there was an opportunity, we put out some additional material explaining our sense of teamwork. The Stamford church bought it. Since it was in the same presbytery, people here had some knowledge of us. They were not looking for a team. It was a bit of a shock to the congregation. But here we are.

We did not designate ourselves in terms of titles. We said we would come as a team and we were prepared to do that as copastors or as pastor-associate. We did that not for any preference of ours but because we didn't want to put anybody off by calling our team by a certain name when it really didn't matter much to us. We had functioned as partners and would continue to do work that way no matter what the congregation called it. It was the congregation's choice to call us and present us as copastors. Since we had not operated with those titles before, it added a challenge to us with the parish, but it all went off without a hitch.

For a while, people here were testing us to see if there was some hidden hierarchy—to find out who was in charge, really. There are some problems on the surface. I'm male. I'm bigger. I have a doctorate. I also have more experience. There are so many things that suggest I'm the real pastor and she is the junior. But it didn't take the congregation long to figure out that we are a team. In fact, our sense of team ministry has reached out to the professional staff and into the congregation.

This transition has been a miracle all the way along, but there are some interesting, providential kinds of things. First, Mary and I came into this job with fifteen years of history, but so did our colleagues. They have a partnership that balanced off our partnership. Second, we all four knew each other since we are in the same presbytery. There was a sense of comfort in coming into this team. Third, they welcomed us with uncommon hospitality and graciousness. We were the ones invading their turf. They moved over and let us do it with great hospitality. They gave us space to do our thing. We for our part helped that to happen by coming in with our eyes and ears open—and put our initial effort into making sure we lived with what was here instead of molding it in our own image. It was a mutual effort. They let us come in and we let them be. The result is a wonderful four-way team that just works great.

When we started working together in New Haven, we spent a lot of time talking about ministry. We divided up tasks and we shared worship from the get-go. Our working relationship evolved for several years. We had the kind of relationship where she was responsible for a few things and I was responsible for everything else. By default it was my job except for those things that were by design her job. From my point of view, one of the things I did was give her space to do ministry. I'm just not a possessive person. I was happy to give her access to the pulpit, recognition, and the chance to try things. I tried intentionally to give her access to the whole range of pastoral stuff, and in return the benefit I got from this was having somebody to talk to. I am an extrovert. I think best with my mouth open. Having a colleague to sit and gab with about what was going on was a great boon to me.

We also had students, so it was never just a twosome. We were just two blocks from Yale Divinity School, and we represented a working partnership between a man and a woman. In addition to anything direct that we did with the students, we represented a role model for them. Whether they were male or female, we gave them a same-gender and opposite-gender experience of leadership in the congregation.

There was an imbalance in our relationship in those early years in that I was the pastor and she was—to start with—almost an apprentice. Several things helped move us to equality. First, I'm secure enough in who I am that I don't need to beat on other people in order to meet my needs. That allowed us space. In fact the one thing that I think is fatal to copastoring is ego needs that are based on fundamental insecurity. Second, I try to be the monitor of the power stuff because I am aware that a lot of things are unexamined. I tried to name those things and encourage Mary to stick up for herself. I had to develop a kind of sixth sense about how she was reacting to things. Her response was always yes when I asked her if she wanted to do a certain thing. I had to learn when she meant yes and when she really meant no. I remember one conversation in which I said, "I don't want to do that anymore. I would much rather you be responsible for protecting yourself rather than me be responsible for protecting both of us." And she has done that.

People have asked me what advice I have for other copastors, and I can only say, "Pick the right person." But I don't know how to do that. Mary and I are an odd couple in our preferred styles. We should drive each other crazy, and we probably would if we were married to each other. She is a detail person. Her desk is clean, her files in order; she never forgets anything. She can be counted on to have whatever we need. I'm the more creative, messy, idea person who tends to react. I love the spontaneous problem solving. She gets nervous when I come up with a new idea. We have very different gifts. At the same time, maybe because we have a fundamental core on which we agree, and also because we've worked together so long, we know each other so well that the communication between us is very hard to put your finger on. It's spooky sometimes how much in sync we are. Yet part of it isn't spooky at all. It comes from having a lot of conversations. We've just gotten into each other's heads so much over the last seventeen or eighteen years. Another thing is that we both value mutuality, partnership, and teamwork. And most basic of all, we share a commitment to "one Lord, one faith, one baptism."

○

23

MODELING PARTNERSHIP

BLAIR AND MARY, like all the other successful teams in this study, are a mixed-gender team that works. They model partnership that makes the team successful. Thus I call the final criterion for effective mixed-gender teams *modeling*. We all need to see effective teams like these in action to know what they require. Then more of us can adopt the strategies of the pioneers that best fit our situations, and we too can succeed. That's what modeling is. But that's not *all* it is. Modeling also changes our systems so that the environment becomes more conducive to effective mixed-gender teams.

Blair and Mary provide us with an interesting example. As a team, they have worked together successfully for almost twenty years—longer than any other team in this study. They have not only worked well but also have stayed together as a team. Their willingness to seek a new position in which they could continue working together represented a kind of advocacy for their team, an unwillingness to see it dissolve just because it was time to find a new job. This too is unusual. Both because of their long tenure as a team and their successful bid to move together, Blair and Mary's team was an obvious choice for this book. I contacted them in the way I contacted each of the teams selected for in-depth coverage, intending to use their story as an example of how systems are changing to allow for more effective mixed-gender teams. I assumed that this team's move was in some way supported and even encouraged by their denomination. Blair called me back to grant permission but also to say, "We don't think we're a good example of what you are looking for. We don't think we have had much influence on our denomination at all."

I was surprised by his response. It caused me to think deeply about the relationships between teams and the systems in which they function. Ultimately, I went back to the literature on organizational change. I thought about the other teams. I began to see the real purpose of *modeling*. In this chapter we shall examine that purpose from three perspectives: that of the team, that of the individuals in the team, and that of the system in which the team exists. We begin with the teams and the individuals in them as models. Then we will return to the question of Blair and Mary and the relationship between the team and the system in which that team exists.

How Teams and Individuals Model Change

Teams model change by their behavior in two ways. First, they take action together that shows what is required for an effective team. Second, the men and women in the teams take action as individuals that promotes effective teaming. This is the practical side of modeling. Let's take a look at how it works in the teams in this study.

What Teams Do

I can go through the list of every team in this study and see some way in which the team models effectively to other teams around it. It is in this collective behavior that the team models *as a team*.

REFLECT. As teams, they model the other eight criteria I have written about in this book. Beginning with the first, which is *reflecting*, I think about the ways in which these teams evaluate how they are doing, both in their relationship and in their work. It is partly a matter of how we reflect in our own lives, as Ned's story shows, and partly a matter of how we reflect together, as Brian and Martha's story shows. Teams report that they reflect together primarily in their informal talk time. Remember also the structured ways in which they reflect with each other, like the Lutheran relief team's Rethinking project or the spiritual formation team's days of reflection. Reflecting together is one behavior that teams model for all of us.

LEARN. The second criterion is *learning*. We have much to learn about if we are to participate in successful mixed-gender teams. I have put the emphasis on learning about leadership and teamwork. As I review the teams in this study, I think that emphasis is valid because mixed-gender teams need to adopt new ways of leading together in order to succeed.

Ben, Fredrica, and Karen are learning, with each other and with their wider community, about being leaders in a new way. Remember what they said about why they have chosen to change the leadership style of the seminary: because they had been peers before and continuing in the same way made sense for them. In order for them to continue to lead together,

Exhibit 23.1. Nine-Criteria Checklist for Teams.

Criterion	Elements of the Criterion
Reflect	Allow quiet time in your personal life. Listen to each other. Talk about the team and the people as well as the work you do. Pray, study, or meditate together. Structure specific reflective work together.
Learn	Learn about the demands of leadership now and in the future. Learn about teams, how they form, and how they work.
Believe	Know the value and importance of having both men and women on your team. Know and commit to your mission and the mission of your team. Develop and sustain a sense of urgency about what you do together.
Name	Know your own script and the script of others in your team. Know how you are a leader, follower, and partner. Know how each member of your team is a leader, follower, and partner. Respect each other. Believe in the strength of every member of your team. Work to develop trust among members of the team.
Include	Examine your prejudices about working in a mixed-gender team. Articulate why it is necessary to team with others who are different from you. Agree to be changed by others in your team who are different from you. Know the benefit of each member of the team to the team.
Communicate	Talk to each other a lot, both formally and informally. Talk about work, the team, and each other. Observe who speaks, how you speak, and what you say to each other. Resolve disagreements by talking honestly together. Discuss the gender traps you experience so they become known in the team.

Work	Establish clear boundaries and honor them.
	Maintain accountability with each other.
	Talk over the big decisions; trust each other to make the small ones.
	Establish an idea-action-feedback cycle in your team.
	Have fun together.
	Develop a spiritual life in your team.
	Mentor each other formally and informally, as appropriate.
Influence	Identify all the sources of your authority.
	Use your personal power wisely and for good.
	Identify how you use power and how you might use it better.
	Agree on a power structure in your team and live by it.
Model	List and observe all the things you can do to strengthen your team and the members of your team.
	As a team, test yourself against this checklist once a month.
	Challenge your organization to be more supportive of mixed-gender teams.

they had to adopt a more collegial style and teach that style to others in the community. This process will also teach them things about their team. I also think here of the team that is adopting a new leadership model in their congregation. They too are giving up the senior-associate model in favor of a threesome copastorate. This decision will cause them to learn a great deal about leadership and about how their team can use a new leadership style. They too are modeling a learning process for other teams.

BELIEVE. Teams model the third criterion, *believing*, in at least two different ways. First, they demonstrate their commitment to women in leadership so that mixed-gender teams might be possible. Wayne and Erin as well as many other teams in this study put their professional reputations on the line to model a partnership between men and women. They often do so in environments that are not very understanding of what they are really about. It's not just a matter of Erin standing up for what she wants to be and do. It's a matter of Erin and Wayne, as partners, modeling a shared commitment to her leadership and showing through their work how much value added there can be in men and women working together. Erin and Wayne are living that process. When teams write gender equity statements as the Lutheran relief team did, they are explicitly modeling their belief in shared leadership for others to see.

Teams also model the criterion *believing* in their passion for what they do. Believing for effective teams means assuming the value of what the team does and having a passion for the mission the team serves. Most teams in this study talked about that passion. Many consider it a secret of their success. Often these teams say they have no gender issues. That's because they don't have time for gender issues. They are so committed to a mission that they can overlook many minor differences and disagreements to be about a mission together. Believing together carries them over many small hurdles. Remember Jeff, a member of the Lutheran relief team, who said, "There is a tremendous amount of commitment to the underlying principles and to what this organization is and does. You absorb it."

NAME. A number of different reflective activities are involved in *naming* each other. Teams model these best in the commitment they make to know themselves and one another. I was most moved by the many ways teams do this with each other. I think here especially of Kris and Jesse, who worked together in a difficult setting. They came to know each other and do for each other in ways that neither of them expected at the outset of their teaming, just because their setting was so difficult. They even learned to laugh together at some of the difficulties. Kris and Jesse were able to do this because, in the process of working together, they made the commitment to truly acknowledge each other. They were modeling the fourth criterion, *naming*.

INCLUDE. Naming leads naturally to *including* each other. There is no better way to model including each other than to work in a diverse team in which the work done reflects the wisdom of the whole team. I think naturally here of the spiritual formation team, which includes people from three different parts of the world and serves students from nine different countries. Also, I think of the many two-person teams consisting of one man and one woman who are partners in a parish or other work setting. They too are diverse and they too take on the challenge of integrating their different perspectives and styles into the work of the team. That's *including*, the fifth criterion. To include each other, these teams have learned what diversity really means.

COMMUNICATE. These teams all communicate well, both in formal and informal settings. In fact, talking to each other seems to be the glue that holds teams together and helps teams work together, reflect on their work, and reflect on their team. The difference between an effective mixed-gender team and an ineffective one is often captured first in how the team talks together. I recall what one clergywoman told me of a former team she had been in, in which her colleague would give her critical information (including decisions he had made on his own) just before they processed on Sunday morning. Think of the difference between this and the deep talking, the checking in with each other, the debate over decisions, and all the other kinds of talking that characterize effective mixed-gender teams! If we but think of these things, we can see how effective teams model *communicating,* the sixth criterion.

WORK. Working together includes many different activities necessary to the mission of the organization. In the day-to-day of being about these activities, teams model the seventh criterion, *working.* The theological institute team provided us with a good example of a specific project and how a good team completes it together. It's not all about doing everything together. Ultimately, it's about working together almost in the way an orchestra plays a symphony. Sometimes everyone is working together. At other times it's appropriate for a small group or even one or another person to work alone. As the project nears completion, the team comes together for the finale.

In the process of working together, effective teams do many different kinds of tasks with skill. So many of the teams in this study seemed to be able to complete the tasks of the workday easily and flexibly with each other. Modeling *work* can be done by individuals alone, of course, but here we are referring specifically to teamwork. This can only be modeled by the team together.

INFLUENCE. Influencing each other or the other individuals and teams around us requires using power. This is the eighth criterion. I think here of the ways men and women in effective teams have taught each other about power. Bruce has encouraged Pam to claim more personal power and thus change her position in the team relative to how others view her. Blair has stopped talking "for" Mary. Barbara has worked with two different power relationships in her teams with Neely and then with Bill. Marie has learned what her own personal power is and how it relates to what she can do in her team.

We do have some ways of seeing power differently, depending on our gender and our experiences. These are culturally reinforced in the ways boys and girls are raised. Because of these differences, men and women who are in effective teams have to talk about power with each other. Then they have to determine how they will, as a team, exert their influence. In so doing, they model effective use of power for other teams.

MODEL. Finally we come to *modeling,* the last criterion. From the preceding summary we can see that in everything they do together effective teams model the critical behaviors for other teams. In addition to modeling together, men and women each model critical individual behaviors that contribute to their ability to be effective partners in a mixed-gender team.

What Men Can Do

The most important task for men is listening. Both the men and women in this study would say so. The men agree that it's challenging to learn to listen. Like Blair, many have a didactic streak they have to overcome. After men begin to listen, they can do many other things to prepare for participation in mixed-gender teams. All require that men open their hearts and minds to partnering with women or advocating for the leadership of women. Here is a selection of things that men can do (Becker, 1996).

CREATE A PLACE FOR WOMEN. Men cannot listen to women if women will not speak frankly. Women will not speak unless "the coast is clear." Men help to create a safe environment for women to speak when they are aware of and challenge the rules of the male-dominated systems in the church. The men in this study do so not only by directly inviting women to enter the dialogue but also by giving women visibility. This they do in many ways: by placing women partners in the bigger office, expecting their male peers to treat the women as equals, sharing the most visible roles of the team, and on and on. Most of these are small things that add up to one big thing. As Eleanor said, it adds up to "creating a huge, huge place for us."

SHARE POWER. Men in effective mixed-gender teams view power as abundant rather than limited. They are, therefore, willing to share power with their female partners (and with other men and women too, for that matter). One man said, "The closer one gets to our team, the more one realizes that the power is evenly distributed." Men like this embrace an empowerment model, "which means that if we share the power, we all have more," one laywoman explains.

Collaborative decision making, a technique used by most teams in this study, gives men a chance to share power with women and other men on the team. In commenting about his team, one man in this study said that he would "not think of any decision being made without our collaboration." That's sharing power.

CREATE AN ATMOSPHERE OF ACCEPTANCE FOR WOMEN. As leaders themselves, men can set the tone by "having women in positions of leadership," says one woman. She is aware that the environment of acceptance created by her male partner is a critical factor in her own acceptance by constituents. Women will struggle to break the glass ceiling until men help them by preparing the way. This means several things for men. First, they can help women be better understood in the patriarchy. Second, they can help organizations welcome change as women enter the denominational workplace. And third, they can as individuals continue to speak as men who personally believe in the value of women in leadership. For one man in this study it all adds up to "giving my partner access, for which I, in return, get someone to talk to."

ADVOCATE FOR WOMEN IN LEADERSHIP. Men know that they must play an active role in getting women elected or appointed to leadership positions. That's precisely why many of the men in this study advocate for and participate in mixed-gender teams. It's a way for them to advocate for women and personally benefit from the gifts that women contribute to the team. One man said, "Advocacy for women in ministry has been a theme for me for a long, long while. It has historically been our tradition to have women in ministry, but the congregations have been entirely too resistant." The men also know from experience that they often have to interpret the role of the female partner on the team and the value of having her on the team to constituents. Men need to be this aggressive about having women in leadership, even about having women on their teams.

AFFIRM WHAT WOMEN DO. "We'd like the men to share the praise and credit," said one churchwoman. Women have to work twice as hard to get half as far as their male peers. Many influences in the workplace tell women that they don't fit in or don't do things the accepted way. When women do excellent work, they need to be recognized. Too often their effort is taken for granted—but not by the men in this study. They know the value of a strong woman partner. They would agree with the man who said, "I know the women are good. I have made a decision to encourage them. It's a personal commitment."

HELP WOMEN ADVANCE. This requires helping women see and take advantage of opportunities in the system so that they can advance on their own merits. One man has encouraged his less experienced female partner to become involved in a number of different roles so she can become skilled and experienced in many. Another has encouraged his partner to use her skills in writing to become published. Yet another who is a team leader and head administrator has withheld jobs from men to keep positions open for qualified women and thereby maintain a gender balance in his team. Finally, one woman talked about how her male partner helped her build confidence by telling her she was capable of a senior pastorate. He kept telling her until she began to believe it. Today she is a senior pastor building another team. All of these examples represent the ways men can help women advance.

MENTOR WOMEN. "Whether you are a man or a woman, someone has got to show you the ropes," says one churchwoman. For women emerging as leaders, mentors should include men who know the system. One woman told of her intentional search for a male mentor. She picked a man who does not believe in the hero-leader model. He could therefore appreciate her style. At the same time, he could help her understand other men better. That's one thing male mentors do for women. Another way men can mentor women is by providing them with access to experiences such as those I discussed earlier. Third, men can do what Brian did for Martha when he "took her in" to leadership situations she might not otherwise have had access to. Martha not only gained access but also felt affirmed at the same time. "The whole way I was treated presented to others right up front that I was an equal partner," Martha recalled. "It was very affirming."

VALUE FAMILY CONCERNS. Family leave has been mandatory for some years, thanks to government legislation. In some settings, employers are also providing flextime, day care, lounges for nursing mothers who work, and other benefits. Too often these are seen as "women's benefits." The concerns they address—free time at home, quality child care, and infant nutrition—are also seen as women's concerns. This kind of thinking is based on the assumption that the welfare of the family is a woman's issue. The welfare of the family is, in fact, an issue for women and men—and for the church. Every benefit the workplace provides for the nurturing of children and others in the family, *regardless of who uses the benefit,* is a concern for men too. Wayne, for one, had to know this when he advocated for Erin even though her son's medical problems and her difficult second pregnancy kept her away from work. "If we had a different model it would not be considered 'disruptive' when women, who still carry the primary child-care role and have careers, need to have time for those responsibilities," Wayne said.

INCLUDE WOMEN IN DECISION MAKING. Just because women are present in leadership positions in the church does not mean that they are included when real decisions are made. Men in effective teams know this. It's one reason they are so committed to shared decision-making models in these teams. The other reason is, as they themselves frankly admit, they benefit from the wisdom that women bring to the decision-making process.

ARTICULATE THE GENDER TRAPS FOR MEN. All of the gender traps mentioned in Chapter Eighteen limit men's ability to team effectively with women, but the attitude traps are the most difficult to overcome because they are the most invisible to men. Men who carry around negative stereotypes of women, who accept patriarchal practices that limit women's advancement, or who continue to think of women first as sexual, are not equipped under any circumstances to team well with women. Yet they may not know why. Men who are free of these attitude traps can help their brothers by naming the trap and leading the way to more constructive attitudes about women. Remember the man who told me, "Women are my colleagues. I see them doing good jobs and doing them well. They have become my friends, not my sex objects." He is ready to help his male colleagues recognize the attitude traps.

INVITE OTHER MEN TO BEGIN THEIR CHANGE PROCESS. Men who deeply listen to women become sensitive to women's leadership concerns. They also become sensitive to the lack of awareness of their male colleagues. Many male team leaders in this study have told of the pressure they get to "show who's boss." They often get this pressure from men outside their team, even from superiors in the denominations. The firm resolve of these men not to be authoritarian allows women to participate in the team and forces other men outside the team to take stock. That's what is required. Men in this study also talked about their own change process and their disappointment with male colleagues who refuse to change. "As a younger man, I wanted to be more dominant. I've learned to change," one said. "Men who don't want women in leadership have a power issue," another commented, adding, "It gets played out as a gender issue." These men are both in a position to challenge and help their male colleagues to change. Talking to other men about this is important, one man said, "because we change not only by how we act but by how we talk about how we act."

Men in effective teams do not do these things "to help the women out," in the words of one. They do it for two reasons. First they "firmly believe that their women colleagues are gifted leaders." Second, they know that "we are part of the dominant structure and it is our job."

What Women Can Do

In Chapter Twenty I explained why the decision to be powerful is the most critical one for women. It is our preeminent task in becoming leaders alongside men. Once powerful, there is much more we can do as women to achieve parity with men and thus be effective partners with them. Women's tasks include the following (Becker, 1996):

GO PUBLIC. It starts with how we talk and ends up being how we think and know ourselves. "For us to obtain authority as women . . . we must risk making generalizations" (Schaper, 1990, p. 108). Our comfort is in applying what we know about leadership only to ourselves or the particular situation ("My style is to do *my* homework, listen to others, but at the same time, stick to *my* principles"). We become uncomfortable when we try to generalize ("Leaders should do *their* homework. Part of that is listening to others instead of making decisions in isolation"). We don't want to force this point of view on anyone else. Perhaps we don't even feel sure enough about our leadership to risk generalizing about it at all. Our tendency to particularize in this way weakens us. It limits the authority of our own style to us or to a particular situation.

We are keeping our own ideas about leadership a secret when we particularize. Instead, we can share our views and say not only that they are good for us but that they are instructive for all leaders. Men generalize like this all the time. We women are often offended when they do. But we cannot claim that men are doing wrong in generalizing what they know about leadership. Nor can we deny that men have gained by doing so. They claim community and *establish a common knowledge about what makes a leader* when they generalize. We, in contrast, choose isolation, the private understanding of leadership that never means anything to anyone but us. Thus we deny ourselves authority. We don't claim it for ourselves, and we don't get it from external sources. Our male partners in mixed-gender teams often wish we would claim this authority a bit more readily.

LEARN FROM MEN. If we have the courage to go public, we can then learn two skills from men who "can help us come to grips with what it means to have a powerful job and use that power effectively," said one laywoman. Men can teach us to be direct and to be unapologetically ambitious. "We need to be clear about what we want and what we need and who we are," said one team member. That's being direct. We can practice clarity most simply by speaking our minds in statements, not questions. Allow the uncomfortable silences that come when we are direct. Allow ourselves to be uncomfortable in those silences until we get the hang of being direct. "This business of trying to second-guess other people's feelings has not been productive for us as leaders," one woman declared. She advocates for being direct and accepting differences that are a normal part of the work environment. The men in this study would agree, some to the point that they work with their female colleagues to encourage this directness.

Ambition is another skill that women often address with ambivalence. We can also learn about it from men. "Work hard until you get it done." That's the formula one clergywoman offers. The attitude behind her energy: "I know that I can do things, and I can probably do many things better than anybody in the room, and if nobody else is going to volunteer, I'm going to do it, and I'm going to do it really well." We can do this without denying the value of relationships that are so important to us as women.

SPEAK UP. We women need to speak up. We are so used to being quiet, or what's little better, allowing ourselves to be silenced after we have already spoken. We get tired. Said one churchwoman of many years, "All women, no matter where we are in leadership, have a repeat experience of not being taken seriously. You go into a new setting with people who don't know you, and no matter how much experience you have, you feel that sometimes you have to start all over again. . . . I feel like I have to sell myself rather than just being accepted for who I am. It never stops for me." Women in leadership know what she means. Still, we have to speak up. Again, this is something our male teammates encourage because they know what a difference it can make outside the team.

One woman recalled a conversation she had with her teammate on this subject. Her partner said, "Darn it, you come in and raise the typical feminist issues that we're all tired of hearing about and we all just don't want to deal with . . . and darn it, you're right. We guys just get tired of it sometimes. But you are right. And I always have to go back and catch myself. . . . I have to deal with it."

A part of speaking up effectively is speaking in a language that men can understand. One woman commented about her team this way: "Early on we women realized that we were going to have to find some creative ways to continually communicate, to reiterate what our needs were . . . to help the men hear us." But we must also remember that "truly authoritative women would insist on talking their own language all the time, even among men" (Schaper, 1990, p. 108). This challenge reminds me of a woman in very senior circles in one denomination who often used the metaphor of cleaning house to explain to the men what needed to be done. They didn't like it, but they learned from it all the same. And they also learned a little bit about speaking *her* language.

NOTICE DIFFERENCES AMONG WOMEN. This requires listening. It seems we do so much listening. We listen to men. We listen to systems that debate around us about our suitability for leadership. I would urge that we focus our listening on each other as well. We need to get to know how women are different from each other. It's important because "there is a key generational difference among women in leadership now, with the younger trusting way too much in the women's movement to guarantee security and the older generation much too burned by the trouble we've already seen. There are so many interesting ways to be mistaken" (Schaper, 1990, p. 13). An older churchwoman observed something else that's different now for younger women: "They don't necessarily have to be the first. They don't have to break the barrier, but on the other hand . . . the more people get used to women, the more I think some of the problems that women have get ignored." There's so much more here beyond the generational differences, including differences for women of minority races who face triple jeopardy in negotiating the white male system, differences among laywomen and clergywomen, differences among women in conservative denominations, and more. It is essential that we begin to know and trust each other as women.

MENTOR OTHER WOMEN. When we know each other, we can mentor each other. We women, just like men, need mentors to succeed in becoming leaders and to help us define what leadership is for us (Gross and Peters, 1989). Surely we can learn from men, but to define ourselves and our style as different from men's (rather than deviant from men's) we need the mentoring of other women. There is great benefit for us in mentoring. We can tell each other our stories. We can speak our own language freely. "I think women learn differently than men. I would want to give them the assurance that they don't have to be anything else but themselves," said one laywoman. This is precisely why one lifelong volunteer in church leadership has been committed to helping other women become leaders too. "My leadership was not just to get things done but to develop others to be able to continue that leadership," she says. "We are always trying to reach out to all women."

BE OURSELVES BOLDLY. One woman asks, "How can we be in positions of leadership and still be dangerous leaders?" The answer, it seems to me, is that we must be true to our own way as leaders. Another team member puts it succinctly: "The secret of being a successful woman is to be a woman." Here I raise a caution about the things we learn from men. What we learn from them we must use as women. The balance is subtle. We must learn to survive in the patriarchy, to be sure. We can survive by not becoming overinvolved in the behind-the-scenes tasks of our organizations. Next, a delicate counterpoint to learning from men to be direct and ambitious is that we ought not to try to do everything ourselves. Third, we should share the relational tasks that need to be done with the men. Fourth, we can begin to expect more from men and less from other women. Above all, we must learn to focus on significant achievements. These skills require women to resist their internal radar and "reinforce behaviors that are more directly task-related" (Coger, 1985, p. 19).

At the same time, we can continue to be ourselves and thereby challenge the patriarchy. This is what is required of dangerous leaders. We do so by going public with our own style, holding it up as a useful model for men as well as women. We do so by allowing women a growing diversity of leadership styles. We do so over and over again when we speak our own leadership language. We do so when we make a commitment to be audacious. One young woman has concluded, "It's really important to be yourself, to be comfortable with yourself, not to try to fit a certain role."

ALLOW DISTANCE FOR OUR FEMALE LEADERS. "Women in leadership positions need to learn how to befriend each other. Women who are following women or who are relating to women in leadership positions need to learn to keep a distance," says one laywoman now in leadership herself. Too often we expect women leaders to be familiar friends, close to the rest of us who are the followers. We thus deny them the distance that authority requires in patriarchy. The result is that we hurt their chances to be effective leaders for men as well as women. This need we have for distance will not diminish until the current hierarchical systems have given way to much more integrated and flexible systems where *both men and women* can use a more familiar style.

Furthermore, women in leadership need to become comfortable with all kinds of power, including authoritative power. This particularly requires distance. "Awareness of this kind of power separates the leader from the group. It forces the leader to deal with differences; differences that are really inherent in the office. To pretend away such differences would be an act of denial" (Stortz, 1993, pp. 67–68). This in fact is one of the limitations of coactive power. It denies "differences in power between leader and group. It also denies responsibilities that rest—and rest only—with the leader" (p. 122).

BE THERE. We women have to be there, in the leadership of the church. This is demanding. In the patriarchy we suffer the stress of working in a male-dominated system, a stress that causes depression, weariness, and discouragement and ranges from "mildly irritating" to crippling of our leadership (Coger, 1985, p. 19). It is also demanding of our time and energy. Some of this stress is mitigated by working in teams with men who welcome our partnership. But in many ways it is still harder for us than for them. When we maintain our presence in spite of the stresses, things begin to change. Eventually, thanks to the presence of women and minorities in leadership, the patriarchy will give way to new systems.

LAUGH AS SARAH LAUGHED. When Sarah overheard God talking to Abraham about her impending pregnancy, she laughed. I do not believe she was being impudent or mocking God. She was laughing, as women must laugh, at the irony of her life. She was laughing at finally gaining what she had long ago given up. She was laughing that God told Abraham and not her. She was laughing because otherwise she would have to cry. It helps for women to have a sense of humor about the ridiculousness of bureaucracies that quibble over "what we can do." It helps for us to laugh with our male colleagues about the men who cannot yet accept our leadership, even though we are already leaders. The fact is, one man said, "the women have to be much more patient with us than we with them." Healthy, robust humor about our predicament falls to the women and to men and women together in effective teams. We should laugh and remember Sarah.

BE ANGRY AND BE MERCIFUL. We are most powerful as women when we "require the church and society to repent of their sins against us as women, while standing ready to forgive and receive the transformation that implies" (Schaper, 1990, p. 74). Think for a moment of the men or systems that have most abused us. Then imagine how we might forgive them at the same time that we refuse to let them abuse us again. If we can do this, we have found a measure of mercy in our own rage. We can be, as one man said, "strong but not alienating." If we can do this we can be challenging to our male colleagues and partners without being strident, a balance that men in mixed-gender teams appreciate and comment on. This is absolutely required. One woman described this as "being secure as a woman so that I know I don't have to be like a man and don't have to force feminism on anyone. At the same time I must confront what's wrong . . . and be able to step back myself when it's my issue." Without this level of discernment, we remain partners with those men and systems in our continuing abuse. With this discernment, we are ready for a new way of leadership that we can share with men without abuse.

The United States, with our "ideal if not actualized reality of equality for women" (Wessinger, 1996, p. 3), is an experimental arena for offering women leadership roles in congregations, agencies, and educational institutions of the denominations. If as men and women we can each do our part in modifying the patriarchal nature of our traditions, it is just possible that we might create fertile ground for many more mixed-gender teams.

How Teams Affect Systems

It's one thing for teams to model success for each other. But that's not enough. Systems have to change in order for teams to succeed in them. But I see little evidence that change comes from the systems themselves. It comes from the teams and the impact they have on the systems. To understand how this works, let's return to Blair and Mary. I thought Blair and Mary's move was supported by the denomination in some overt way. Apparently, it was not. Blair thought—and perhaps still thinks—that his and Mary's move had little impact on the denomination. I don't believe he is right, either. Understanding why Blair and I were both wrong will help us understand the relationship between teams and the systems in which they exist.

Creating Chaos?

Evidence is mounting that small changes can affect large systems in ways we had not heretofore predicted. According to chaos theory, "In a dynamic changing system, the *slightest* variation can have explosive results. . . . Even infinitesimal differences are far from inconsequential" (Wheatley, 1992, p. 126; italics in original). We have gained this new insight by applying what we have learned from quantum physics to our thinking. We now know that we do not live in a world ordered by Newtonian physics, where structures and systems are static and predictable. Instead, our world is made up of systems that are "never in the same place twice" but that over time "demonstrate an inherent orderliness" even though they are, in any given moment, chaotic. This may be true in our organizations as in our natural universe, Wheatley further suggests. "While we have lusted for order in our organizations, we have failed to understand its true nature" (p. 21). We have failed to see that disorder is a part of growth and self-renewal, and ultimately, order itself. "The things we fear most in organizations—fluctuations, disturbances, imbalances—need not be signs of an impending disorder that will destroy us. Instead, fluctuations are the primary source of creativity" (p. 20).

This perspective describes what I believe is the relationship between teams and the systems in which they exist. The evidence of the teams in this study is that they are an influence on organizational systems much more than systems are an influence on them. Furthermore, mixed-gender teams are creating some disorder as they affect systems that try to manage them rather than to observe and understand them. In some systems, mixed-gender teams are resisted, or at best, ignored.

I missed this point when I assumed that Blair and Mary's joint move to a new congregation was somehow promoted or supported by their presbytery. Mind you, their move was not resisted. Nor is there any evidence that their team is not supported within the presbytery. However, from the point of view of the church hierarchy, their move seems not to have been assisted so much as allowed to happen. Perhaps their move was a small incident that created a ripple only. This ripple has yet to have a long-term impact on the presbytery or the denomination in which Blair and Mary work.

What might that impact be? We do not know, but surely other people in the presbytery observed their move. Surely other people observe this team that has been effective for nearly a generation. Somewhere, somehow, it will have an effect on the system. And if scientific theory can be applied to our thinking about organizations, it could contribute in some way, at some time to explosive results. Scientists also now know that even very small differences at the beginning of a system's evolution can make prediction of the outcome impossible (Wheatley, 1992). If we apply this new science of unpredictability to our organizational thinking, we would suggest that the impact of Blair and Mary's partnership on the Presbyterian Church (U.S.A.) cannot be predicted this early in the game, not even with a shred of accuracy. Along with other influences in the denomination, it will have an impact in the future that we will be able to see in hindsight. And of course, Blair and Mary's story is only one of many stories of effective mixed-gender teams in this study. Taken together, the impact of

effective teams of men and women on church-related, not-for-profit organizational life will be another matter. Chaos theory would predict that
even though we cannot see the order in the change these teams are creating, it is there. Ultimately, it will make sense and it will become apparent,
because "if we look at a chaotic system long enough and with the perspective of time, it always demonstrates its inherent orderliness" (Wheatley, 1992, p. 21).

How Systems Respond to Teams

I've made two assertions about how mixed-gender teams and systems
interact. The first is that teams influence systems more than systems influence teams. The second is that mixed-gender teams are not, in the main,
viewed by the hierarchies in which they exist as important and positive
predictors of the future. To understand why I make these assertions, let
us look at the teams in this study.

From Brian and Martha to Blair and Mary and everywhere in between,
I heard stories about how systems do not effectively support mixed-gender
teams. Few and far between were the stories of ways in which systems
actively support them. Often it was simply the fact that the system broke
up the team in one way or another. With clergy teams, the splitting up was
sometimes overt, as with Brian and Martha, and sometimes covert, as in
the case of a team that was together only a few months before their
bishop began encouraging the female member to move. "It will be difficult for me to form another copastorate with a woman," predicted one
clergyman who has just lost his partner. "The bishop has told me that
there are no women qualified and the mood in the church is against the
copastorate model."

Sometimes the response of the hierarchy seemed benign, but the statistical evidence indicated underlying problems. One clergyman observed that
"overall the statistics in our denomination are discouraging for women.
There are more women in seminary but not an increase in those serving
parishes. The best opportunity for women in the parish right now is in a
copastorate with a male partner, where they have a chance to be secure as
they emerge as leaders. Congregations then have the privilege of recognizing what a great resource women are. But the truth is, there are not a lot
of mixed-gender teams who are not clergy couples. I know of only two in
our state." Many others agreed with this view. Collectively, this evidence
does not suggest any specific action on the part of the denomination
against mixed-gender teams. But it does indicate influences within systems
that are barriers to effective mixed-gender teams.

Many team members—both women and men—also spoke of men who are not willing or able to work effectively with women. This is a personal barrier first. It becomes a system barrier if the system accepts or even condones such behavior. Erin and Wayne's story illustrates the problems this barrier presents for women and for men who are their partners. Two clergy teams I interviewed in Iowa indicated that their denomination provides quarterly consulting for all teams, whether or not they are mixed gender. But this resource is not available throughout the denomination and is not widely available as I looked at other denominations.

Another system barrier I encountered was difficulty in getting approval for position descriptions for women entering teams. Erin, Pam, and Mary come to mind immediately as women who encountered this problem and ultimately had to accept titles that were less than the team hoped for. The problem in all cases was a church hierarchy unwilling for one reason or another to approve a title that would give the woman on the team status in the eyes of people outside the team. We have seen what problems teams encounter when the man is perceived to be higher in status than the woman. "We fashioned our roles apart from any consideration of what my title is," one woman indicated. "It has been a bit of an issue because I don't think everyone in the congregation is on board with our roles as equals. It's an extra stress." Teams attempting to avoid this problem by giving the woman team member an almost equal or equal title to the man seemed to run into problems with denominational approval quite often.

Clergy teams encounter all of the system responses I have summarized here. Other teams, including lay and clergy or even all laypeople working in educational institutions and other organizations of the church, encounter some of these responses more than others.

Peter, who reported no problems in the synagogue in bringing a woman aboard as associate, described three preexisting conditions in the congregation. First, he said, "Our women's organization died long before I came. It is expected here that any woman who participates in leadership would participate in the leadership of the whole congregation and not the leadership of a single-gender organization." Second, the men's organization was historically weak and folded into a mixed-gender group "that doesn't play the role that either a sisterhood or brotherhood plays in a classic congregation." Finally, "there was an effort on the part of the nominating committee over a number of years to make sure that women were included in the leadership of the congregation." These criteria, in addition to the clergyman's own advocacy, made bringing in a woman associate "the expected thing to do." This list is instructive of the kinds of things that systems need to do to promote strong mixed-gender teams. Unfortunately, it is the exception rather than the norm to get them done. They were done in one congregation, but they are not widely done in Reform Judaism nor, for that matter, in other denominations.

The spiritual formation team also told of strong support in their educational institution for their mixed-gender team. "The administration supports us being a team. That is important," said Cecilia. "In almost all the other seminaries, one person is the spiritual director and if that person can get anybody else to help, they consider themselves lucky. The fact that we can be a team, and it is respected and supported by the administration, is significant. It sort of evolved here as they hired each one of us but it is recognized as a value to the point that, as I leave the seminary, the team is looking for someone to replace me. It's not just 'You've got enough people on the team. You don't need a woman, or another member.' It is presumed that I will be replaced." As in the previous example, the support comes from the organization in which the team exists (the seminary) and not from the wider denomination (the Roman Catholic Church).

Apart from these explicit examples of ways that mixed-gender teams are not supported by the systems in which they exist, it seemed to me that they are largely ignored. This is another way of saying that their real importance goes unnoticed. They are not considered to be predictors of the future that we should all aspire to in the workplace. If they were, they would be getting a lot more attention. Bishops and other church officials would want to know more about what makes a successful mixed-gender team so they could replicate it in other places. Partner organizations would want to learn from the successful example set by teams like the Lutheran relief team. Techniques used in successful teams would be sought and examined. Men and women who are not succeeding would want assistance from those who are. More schools would seek out the mentoring of effective mixed-gender teams such as Blair and Mary, who did mentoring at Yale Divinity School in New Haven until they moved. I could go on and on.

But few of these things are happening in larger systems that now have effective mixed-gender teams. If systems have any influence on teams it seems to be mildly negative, designed more to neutralize the teams than anything else. But the best teams resist negative system influence and try to remain as little affected by system polity as possible.

The fact of the matter is that our denominational systems are not yet equipped to support effective mixed-gender teams very well. They are designed to support other models, and they have not yet figured out why or how to change. That's why they do not have much positive impact on these successful teams. It's the other way around. These teams are positively influencing systems. And in the end, it is the teams who will show our systems how to change.

How Teams Affect Systems

In order to help systems change, effective mixed-gender teams model for systems as well as for other teams. This is their broader modeling role. It's a bit harder to discern this modeling role at first because we do not yet know the final impact these effective teams will have on systems. We can, however, look at how these teams work in systems as *predictors* of the future. These teams model six trends that I believe are important. Mixed-gender teams show us all of the following things.

• *Mission is achieved best by the integration of action and reflection.* We are so busy. We want to get things done. In our nonprofit organizations and our denominations, we want to bring faith to the faithless, feed the hungry, heal the sick, bless the dying, comfort the children, counsel the troubled, and help the poor reach self-sufficiency. We are very busy doing these things. That is laudable. But what we are able to achieve in line with our chosen mission is not done through activity alone. It is done by counterpointing action with reflection.

Observing effective mixed-gender teams, one can hardly miss seeing how well they integrate reflection and action. At some point, they achieve a new way of working together that is not like any other way they have worked in the past. Activity takes its proper place and ceases to create a treadmill for them. These teams are busy, to be sure. But their activity is purposeful and reaps multiple rewards because it is subject to reflection and learning that comes from reflection. For these teams, the value added often comes from having a cup of coffee together rather than adding more tasks to the list of things to do.

• *There is measurable value in entering into relationship with each other.* The value added we can achieve in having a cup of coffee and reflecting with each other comes from our relationships. Men and women in effective mixed-gender teams are not afraid to form relationships with each other that go far beyond the superficial. Their relationships allow them to talk honestly with each other about what they are doing and what (else) needs to be done. In knowing each other, they are able to decide how to go about their work most effectively. I believe we shall see a growing trend toward deeper relationships among those who are the very best at achieving a mission together. Real relationships allow people to be and do their very best together. That is what achieving our mission requires of us today, and in the future.

• *Systems must be increasingly adaptable and flexible.* Effective mixed-gender teams show us how to organize and manage a self-generating, adaptable system. They demonstrate that such systems are not only a good idea but a real possibility. They dispel the notion that such systems take too much time and aren't really productive. They provide examples of the many different ways in which an adaptable system can be organized to work. Effective mixed-gender teams are important models of adaptable systems. Each team is in its own way a system. Each has designed ways to function that work for the team. Each is, in its own way, flexible to the people in it and adaptable to the environment both inside and outside the team.

We're hearing more and more about the value of adaptable systems. We learn it from scientific observation (Wheatley, 1992). We see the need for organizations and their leaders to "imitate nature's ability to adapt structures to changing environments, to let power balances shift, and to surrender control for trust in dynamic interconnectedness" (Ashe, 1997, p. 148). In much of the literature on leadership and the debates about leadership style, we see this trend. Leaders need to be adaptable to systems that are themselves adaptable (Heifetz, 1994; Helgesen, 1995; Lipman-Blumen, 1996; Drucker, 1998). The church too is changing. In an environment where change has historically been slow, some observers (Glaser, 1983; Russell, 1993; Ashe, 1997) predict cataclysmic change just ahead as the church gives up its impermeable systems in favor of others that are more adaptable. Effective mixed-gender teams demonstrate adaptable systems for us and thereby show us the way to the future.

• *Flexible systems (teams) can exist in inflexible environments.* Although each mixed-gender team is a system in its own right, each has also figured out ways to thrive as a system in a larger context that is often hostile and at best neutral. Men, especially those who are team leaders or who hold a senior position, have a great deal of responsibility for keeping the team healthy and flexible when external structures are inflexible. In such situations, as we have seen in the preceding two chapters, people outside the team do not understand what the team is really about. They pressure the team to be less flexible, less adaptable, and less effective when they ask, "Who's the boss?" That's just one example of a challenge flexible teams face in inflexible systems.

We might hope for a time when our organizations will be more flexible themselves. But in the meantime, these teams demonstrate that it is possible for flexible systems (the teams) to exist in larger environments (organizations or denominations) that are hierarchical and inflexible. We can even go so far as to predict, as I have in this chapter, that flexible systems will influence their environment so as to break down its inflexibility.

• *Conflict can be constructive.* Earlier I addressed the myth of the harmonious team. It's important here again as a predictor of a trend. We can observe in the teams in this study that none exists without conflict. Team members have also told us that conflict is an important part of the give-and-take as they strive to achieve a mission together. Conflict is not a problem to be avoided at all costs. Much to the contrary, it is a necessary part of getting the work done. Out of conflict, these teams forge new ways of working together that help them accomplish their mission, sometimes in ways they themselves did not expect. Constructive conflict is a part of the relationships that I mentioned earlier in this section.

At the same time, conflict has to be of the right kind to help rather than hinder the team. Remember what Ben said about his work with Fredrica and Karen in introducing new leadership paradigms to the organization: "Personal issues need to be dealt with personally and organizational problems need to be dealt with organizationally." And remember what Diane said about the theological institute team: "Working together means being honest, working things through. Sometimes you work to clarity and sometimes you don't achieve it. But you can't just vent whenever you want. You pay a price. It can be hazardous to the long-term relationship if you are foolish. You have to ask, 'Is it going to help or hinder?' Just because it's going to make you feel better, it's not necessarily going to improve trust."

Ultimately, effective mixed-gender teams demonstrate the value of the right kind of conflict in our systems. They show us the possibility and the limitation of conflict. Their experience should indicate to us that systems need new ways of understanding and integrating the right kind of conflict into our ways of working together.

• *Diversity is critical to our success in mission.* The most effective mixed-gender teams demonstrate a very sophisticated understanding of diversity. They see it as "the door to opportunities rather than the lid to Pandora's box" (Lipman-Blumen, 1996, p. 239). For them, diversity is critical to their success; it connects directly to their work. They have moved far beyond valuing diversity because it gives access to people who have been denied access in the past. This approach to diversity is an admirable place to start, but as effective teams know, it does not give us anywhere to go with a diverse workforce. Nor do the best mixed-gender teams settle for the access and legitimacy paradigm, which values a diverse workforce because of the insight that new ethnic workers can give us to new constituencies. Instead, these teams consider diversity essential to accomplishing their mission as a whole. They know that diverse teams are more effective in practice because the mix of ideas is richer. They also know that communication and role shifting is more challenging in a diverse team. But for them the results are worth the challenges. They have come to understand that they must have women and men and people of different ethnic backgrounds on the team to do their best work. Remember what the spiritual formation team told Binh: "It's not just that we let you join us. We need you to join us."

In the future, this new and deeper understanding of diversity will be increasingly important for all our systems. All of our organizations will need the wisdom that "women, Hispanics, Asian Americans, African Americans, Native Americans—these groups and others outside the mainstream . . . don't bring with them just their 'insider information.' They bring different, important, and . . . relevant knowledge and perspectives about how to actually *do work*" (Thomas and Ely, 1996, p. 80). With this new knowledge, our organizations will be able to achieve their missions more creatively and more effectively for increasingly diverse constituencies.

Showing the Way to the Future

Mixed-gender teams need not be the only influences on our work life showing us these trends. In fact, they probably will not be. A trend is set by a number of different influences converging. But the evidence is that change in our workplace is upon us. Change in the nature of the church is upon us. Observers of the church predict that the church is entering a new epoch, one that will not be European and male but will instead be "the church of both sexes" (Glaser, 1983, p. 44). Glaser makes a case for gender equity in the Roman Catholic Church particularly. His is but one voice predicting a very different kind of church in the future. A generation ago Robert Ellwood was already predicting that the influence of women on religious traditions had begun to shape a "possible American

DISCUSSION QUESTIONS FOR TEAMS

Part One: Reflecting and Taking Action

FOR PERSONAL REFLECTION

1. Does my team have an effective and mutually satisfying ministry together? Why or why not?
2. Does my lifestyle provide time and space for reflecting?
3. How do I reflect?
4. Do I see my personal reflection as part of my spiritual repentance?

FOR TEAM DISCUSSION

1. How does our team reflect? Can we list specific ways in which we reflect together?
2. How does reflecting benefit our team?
3. How can we reflect more? Do we need more reflective time? Do we need more structure for reflection? What rituals would help?
4. Discuss the nine criteria for mixed-gender teams to discern your common understanding of them.
5. Do the nine criteria "speak to" our team?
6. How important is each criterion to the overall growth and effectiveness of our team?

Part Two: Learning

FOR PERSONAL REFLECTION

1. What are my leadership traits?
2. What contributions do I make to the team?
3. What role or roles do I play in the team?
4. What "holds me back" in my team interaction?
5. What inspires me to use all my talents in the team?

FOR TEAM DISCUSSION

1. How are we each different or similar as leaders? As followers?

2. What traits do we believe will be required of leaders in the future of this organization (or this congregation)?

3. What are the specific leadership contributions of the women in our team? Of the men?

4. What have we learned about each other as leaders in reading this section, in talking together, and in working together?

5. How do we define ourselves as a team?

6. Where are we in the four stages of team development: forming, storming, norming, or performing?

7. How does diversity influence our team?

8. Is our team effective? How do we know? How do our constituents know?

Part Three: Believing

FOR PERSONAL REFLECTION

1. What do I believe about the participation of women in leadership?

2. Does our team welcome women and men equally?

3. Are my values congruent with the mission of our team?

FOR TEAM DISCUSSION

1. How have we each come to be leaders and members of this team?

2. Do we have a theology of gender equity? If so, what is it? Should we write it?

3. Do we feel that men or women can be more effective in influencing our organization (or denomination) to be more welcoming of women as leaders?

Part Four: Naming and Including

FOR PERSONAL REFLECTION

1. What do I know about myself as a leader, follower, and partner?

2. What are my personal prejudices about mixed-gender leadership,

and how do they limit my thinking or acting for the mission of this organization (or congregation)?

FOR TEAM DISCUSSION

1. How do we know each other as leaders, followers, and partners?

2. How has working together changed us as individuals?

3. How has working together improved our work?

4. How does racism or sexism in our workplace, our denomination, or our community limit our effectiveness as a team?

5. How well are we using the four ways of naming and including each other that are typical of effective mixed-gender teams (believing in the strength of each of us, trusting each other, achieving and maintaining parity, and knowing the benefits of being part of the team)?

Part Five: Communicating and Working Together

FOR PERSONAL REFLECTION

1. How do I communicate in the team? Do I speak and listen? Am I assertive with my opinion? Do I participate as much, more, or less than others?

2. How comfortable am I with confrontation?

3. What gender traps frustrate or anger me?

FOR TEAM DISCUSSION

1. How do the women and men in our team use language and conversation differently or in the same ways?

2. How often do we as individual team members (and as a whole team) talk to each other?

3. What do we talk about in our team? Can we list instances of work talk, team talk, and personal talk?

4. How do we talk about God?

5. What is our idea-action-feedback cycle?

6. How do we handle misunderstandings in the team?

7. How do we recognize one another's gifts and accomplishments?

8. How do we handle each of the elements of working together discussed in Chapter Seventeen (making decisions, maintaining

accountability, honoring boundaries, giving permission, developing a spiritual dimension, and having fun)?

9. If we consider a recent team project that went well and another that didn't go well, what was the difference?

10. How is our team growing spiritually?

11. How do we have fun together?

12. What gender traps do we each find most frustrating, difficult, or insurmountable?

Part Six: Influencing

FOR PERSONAL REFLECTION

1. What are the sources of my own power?

2. What are my own attitudes and biases about the use of power?

3. Am I able and willing to use power constructively?

4. What tempts me to abuse power?

FOR TEAM DISCUSSION

1. How do we define power in our team?

2. How do we use power as individuals? As a team?

3. Do we follow the power rules for effective teams listed in Chapter Twenty-One (share power, appreciate the team leader's role, embrace power, use different kinds of power, talk honestly about power, define our own power, consider power an ally, view power as abundant, be humble about having power, use power with enthusiasm)?

4. How do people outside our team view the power of our team? Is it consistent with how we use power in our team?

5. How do we share power with each other? How do we share power with others in the organization (or congregation)?

6. Does our team leader get pressure from constituents to "take over" the team? If so, how does he or she resist?

Part Seven: Modeling

FOR PERSONAL REFLECTION

1. What are the most important actions I can take to be an effective team member?

FOR TEAM DISCUSSION

1. How does our team use the nine criteria to create an effective team?

2. What are the most important actions men in our team can take to be effective team members? To make the team more effective?

3. What are the most important actions women in our team can take to be effective team members? To make the team more effective?

4. In what ways does our organization or our denomination support our mixed-gender team?

5. How well does our team use the six ways suggested in Chapter Twenty-Three to influence our organization or denomination (using action and reflection to achieve mission, being adaptable, promoting relationships, being flexible even in inflexible environments, using conflict constructively, and promoting true diversity)?

REFERENCES

Alpert, Rebecca, and Milgram, Goldie. "Women in the Reconstructionist Rabbinate." In Catherine Wessinger (ed.), *Religious Institutions and Women's Leadership: New Roles Inside the Mainstream.* Columbia: University of South Carolina Press, 1996.

American Management Association. "Senior Manager Teams: Profiles and Performance." *Management Review,* Sept. 1998, pp. 37–44.

Anand, Anita. "Of Virtue and Power." *Christian Social Action,* Oct. 1990, pp. 18–25.

Ashe, Kay. *The Feminization of the Church?* Kansas City, Mo.: Sheed & Ward, 1997.

Becker, Carol E. "In Any Age: Can We Hear God?" In Duncan Ferguson (ed.), *New Age Spirituality: An Assessment.* Louisville, Ky.: Westminster/John Knox Press, 1989.

Becker, Carol E. *Leading Women: How Women Can Avoid Leadership Traps and Negotiate the Gender Maze.* Nashville, Tenn.: Abingdon Press, 1996.

Bednarowski, Mary Farrell. "Outside the Mainstream: Women's Religion and Women Religious Leaders in the Nineteenth Century." *Journal of the American Academy of Religion,* 1980, 48, 207–231.

Bednarowski, Mary Farrell. "Widening the Banks of the Mainstream: Women Constructing Theologies." In Catherine Wessinger (ed.), *Women's Leadership in Marginal Religions: Explorations Outside the Mainstream.* Urbana: University of Illinois Press, 1993.

Belenky, Mary Field, Clinchy, Blythe McVicker, Goldberger, Nancy Roule, and Tarule, Jill Matteck. *Women's Ways of Knowing.* New York: Basic Books, 1986.

Bendroth, Margaret. *Fundamentalism and Gender: 1875 to the Present.* New Haven, Conn.: Yale University Press, 1993.

Billington, Jim. "The Three Essentials of an Effective Team." *Harvard Management Update,* Jan. 1997, pp. 3–5.

Buchanan, Constance H. *Choosing to Lead.* Boston: Beacon Press, 1996.

Campbell, Joan Brown. "Toward a Renewed Community of Women and Men." In Melanie A. May (ed.), *Women and Church: The Challenge of Ecumenical Solidarity in an Age of Alienation.* New York: Friendship Press, 1991.

Carroll, Jackson, Hargrove, Barbara, and Lummis, Adair T. *Women of the Cloth*. New York: HarperCollins, 1983.

Chinnici, Rosemary. *Can Women Re-Image the Church?* Mahwah, N.J.: Paulist Press, 1992.

Chittister, Joan D. *Job's Daughters: Women and Power*. Mahwah, N.J.: Paulist Press, 1990.

Coger, Marian. *Women in Parish Ministry: Stress and Support*. Washington, D.C.: Alban Institute, 1985.

Coutu, Diane L. "Briefings from the Editors: Trust in Virtual Teams." *Harvard Business Review*, May-June 1998, pp. 20–21.

de Castillejo, Irene Claremont. *Knowing Woman: A Feminine Psychology*. New York: HarperCollins, 1973.

Drucker, Peter F. "There's More Than One Kind of Team." *Wall Street Journal*, Feb. 11, 1992, p. 16.

Drucker, Peter F. "Management's New Paradigms." *Forbes*, Oct. 5, 1998, pp. 152–176.

Ellwood, Robert S., Jr. "The Study of New Religious Movements in America." *Council on the Study of Religion Bulletin*, June 1979, pp. 71–72.

Faludi, Susan. *Backlash: The Undeclared War Against American Women*. New York: Crown, 1991.

Finn, Virginia Sullivan. "Ministerial Attitudes and Aspirations of Catholic Laywomen in the United States." In Catherine Wessinger (ed.), *Religious Institutions and Women's Leadership: New Roles Inside the Mainstream*. Columbia: University of South Carolina Press, 1996.

Foucault, Michel. "Two Lectures." In Colin Gordon (ed.), *Power/Knowledge: Selected Interviews and Other Writings, 1972–1977*. New York: Pantheon Books, 1980.

Fox, Matthew. *Original Blessing*. Santa Fe, N.M.: Bear, 1983.

Fox, Matthew. *The Reinvention of Work: A New Vision of Livelihood for our Time*. San Francisco: Harper San Francisco, 1994.

Glaser, John W. "Epoch III: The Church Feminized." *Commonweal*, Jan. 28, 1983, pp. 44–45.

Gray, Helen T. "Women's Leadership Roles Challenge Tradition." *Progressions*, Feb. 1992, pp. 14–16.

Gross, Lora, and Peters, Ted. "Role Models for Women Seminarians." *Dialog*, 1989, 28(2), 92–102.

Gutek, Barbara A. "Sexuality in the Workplace: Key Issues in Social Research and Organizational Practice." In Jeff Hearn, Deborah L. Sheppard, Peta Tancred-Sheriff, and Gibson Burrell (eds.), *The Sexuality of Organization*. Thousand Oaks, Calif.: Sage, 1989.

Guzzo, Richard. "The Intersection of Team Effectiveness and Decision Making." In Richard Guzzo, Eduardo Salas, and Associates, *Team Effectiveness and Decision Making in Organizations*. San Francisco: Jossey-Bass, 1995.

Hamilton, Michael. "Women, Public Ministry, and American Fundamentalism, 1920–1950." *Religion and American Culture*, Summer 1993, pp. 171–196.

Hearn, Jeff, and Burrell, Gibson. "The Sexuality of Organization." In Jeff Hearn, Deborah L. Sheppard, Peta Tancred-Sheriff, and Gibson Burrell (eds.), *The Sexuality of Organization*. London: Sage, 1989.

Heifetz, Ronald A. *Leadership Without Easy Answers*. Cambridge, Mass.: Harvard University Press, 1994.

Heilbrun, Carolyn G. *Writing a Woman's Life*. New York: Ballantine, 1988.

Helgesen, Sally. *The Feminine Advantage: Women's Ways of Leadership*. New York: Doubleday, 1990.

Helgesen, Sally. *The Web of Inclusion*. New York: Doubleday, 1995.

Heuser, Roger, and Shawchuck, Norman. "Different Teams, Different Leadership Styles." In Roger Heuser (ed.), *Leadership and Team Building: Transforming Congregational Ministry Through Teams*. Mathers, N.C.: Christian Ministry Resources, 1999.

Hill, Linda A. *Managing Your Team*. Boston: Harvard Business School, 1994.

Howe, Margaret E. *Women and Church Leadership*. Grand Rapids, Mich.: Zondervan, 1982.

Hunt, Mary E. "Power: A Feminist Theological View." *Waterwheel*, 1998, *11*(4), 1–2.

Hurty, Kathleen. "Ecumenical Leadership: Power and Women's Voices." In Melanie A. May (ed.), *Women and Church: The Challenge of Ecumenical Solidarity in an Age of Alienation*. New York: Friendship Press, 1991.

Hurty, Kathleen. "Women Principals: Leading with Power." In Diane Dunlap and Patricia Schmuck (eds.), *Women Leading in Education*. Albany: State University of New York, 1995.

Inskeep, Kenneth, and Mroczek, Jacqueline. *Sexual Harassment Study Report*. Chicago: Evangelical Lutheran Church in America, 1993.

Jackman, Michele, and Waggoner, Susan. *Star Teams, Key Players: Successful Career Strategies for Women in the '90s*. New York: Henry Holt, 1991.

Jackson, Susan E., May, Karen E., and Whitney, Kristina. "Understanding the Dynamics of Diversity in Decision-Making Teams." In Richard Guzzo, Eduardo Salas, and Associates, *Team Effectiveness and Decision Making in Organizations*. San Francisco: Jossey-Bass, 1995.

Jacobi, Jolande. *The Way of Individuation*. New York: Meridian Books, 1965.

Jewett, Paul. *The Ordination of Women*. Grand Rapids, Mich.: Eerdmans, 1980.

Jobes, Gertrude. *Dictionary of Mythology Folklore Symbols.* Metuchen, N.J.: Scarecrow Press, 1962.

Jung, Carl. "On Psychic Energy." In *The Structure and Dynamics of the Psyche, Collected Works,* Vol. 8. (2nd ed.) Princeton, N.J.: Princeton University Press, 1966.

Kanter, Rosabeth Moss. *Men and Women of the Corporation.* New York: Basic Books, 1977.

Katzenbach, Jon R. "The Myth of the Top Management Team." *Harvard Business Review,* Nov.-Dec. 1997, pp. 83–91.

Katzenbach, Jon R., and Smith, Douglas K. "The Discipline of Teams." *Harvard Business Review,* Mar.-Apr. 1993a, pp. 111–120.

Katzenbach, Jon R., and Smith, Douglas K. *The Wisdom of Teams.* Boston: Harvard Business School, 1993b.

King, Martin Luther, Jr. *Where Do We Go from Here?* New York: Harper-Collins, 1967.

Lapp, Cynthia. "God-Talk, Girl-Style." *Waterwheel,* Fall 1998, p. 6.

Lawless, Elaine J. "Not So Different a Story After All: Pentecostal Women in the Pulpit." In Catherine Wessinger (ed.), *Women's Leadership in Marginal Religions: Explorations Outside the Mainstream.* Urbana: University of Illinois Press, 1993.

Lehmann, Edward C., Jr. *Gender and Work: The Case of the Clergy.* Albany: State University of New York, 1993.

Lerner, Michael. *Surplus Powerlessness.* Oakland, Calif.: Institute for Labor and Mental Health, 1986.

Lindley, Susan Hill. *You Have Stepped Out of Your Place: A History of Women and Religion in America.* Louisville, Ky.: Westminster/John Knox Press, 1996.

Lipman-Blumen, Jean. *The Connective Edge: Leading in an Interdependent World.* San Francisco: Jossey-Bass, 1996.

McCarter, Neely Dixon. *The President as Educator.* Atlanta, Ga.: Scholar's Press, 1996.

Miller, Jean Baker. *Toward a New Psychology of Women.* Boston: Beacon Press, 1986.

Mills, Albert J. "Gender, Sexuality, and Organizational Theory." In Jeff Hearn, Deborah L. Sheppard, Peta Tancred-Sheriff, and Gibson Burrell (eds.), *The Sexuality of Organization.* London: Sage, 1989.

Montgomery, Helen Barrett. *Western Women in Eastern Lands: An Outline Study of Fifty Years of Woman's Work in Foreign Missions.* New York: Garland, 1987. (Originally published 1910.)

Morrison, Ann. *The New Leaders: Guidelines on Leadership Diversity in America.* San Francisco: Jossey-Bass, 1992.

Motte, M. "A Vision of Ecumenical Mission: Challenge During the Decade." In Melanie A. May (ed.), *Women and Church: The Challenge of Ecumenical Solidarity in an Age of Alienation.* New York: Friendship Press, 1991.

Nuechterlein, Anne Marie, and Hahn, Celia A. *The Male-Female Church Staff.* Washington, D.C.: Alban Institute, 1990.

O'Toole, James. *Leading Change: The Argument for Values-Based Leadership.* New York: Ballantine, 1996.

Overton-Adkins, Betty J. "Beyond Managing and Celebrating Diversity: Implications for Women's Leadership." *Leadership Journal,* 1997, *1*(2), 19–25.

Pagels, Elaine. *Adam, Eve, and the Serpent.* New York: Random House, 1988.

Paul, Diana Y. *Women in Buddhism: Images of the Feminine in the Mahayana Tradition.* (2nd ed.) Berkeley: University of California Press, 1985.

Prusak, Bernard. "Woman: Seductive Siren and Source of Sin?" In Rosemary Radford Ruether (ed.), *Religion and Sexism.* New York: Simon & Schuster, 1974.

Rhodes, Lynn. *Co-Creating: A Feminist Vision of Ministry.* Louisville, Ky.: Westminster/John Knox Press, 1987.

Rieff, David. "The Death of a Good Idea." *Newsweek,* May 10, 1999, p. 65.

Rosener, Judy. "Ways Women Lead." *Harvard Business Review,* Nov.-Dec. 1990, pp. 119–125.

Ruether, Rosemary Radford. *New Woman, New Earth: Sexist Ideologies and Human Liberation.* New York: Crossroad, 1975.

Ruether, Rosemary Radford. "Women in Utopian Movements." In Rosemary Radford Ruether and Rosemary Skinner Keller (eds.), *Women in Religion in America: The Nineteenth Century.* New York: HarperCollins, 1981.

Ruether, Rosemary Radford, and McLaughlin, Eleanor (eds.). *Women of Spirit: Female Leadership in the Jewish and Christian Traditions.* New York: Simon & Schuster, 1979.

Russell, Letty. *Church in the Round.* Louisville, Ky.: Westminster/John Knox Press, 1993.

Schaef, Ann Wilson. *Women's Reality: An Emerging Female System in a White Male Society.* (2nd ed.) San Francisco: Harper San Francisco, 1985.

Schaper, Donna. *Common Sense About Men and Women in the Ministry.* Washington, D.C.: Alban Institute, 1990.

Scholtes, Peter R. *The Team Handbook.* Madison, Wis.: Joiner Associates, 1988.

Shawchuck, Norman, and Heuser, Roger. *Leading the Congregation.* Nashville, Tenn.: Abingdon Press, 1993.

Sheppard, Deborah L. "The Image and Self-Image of Women Managers." In Jeff Hearn, Deborah L. Sheppard, Peta Tancred-Sheriff, and Gibson Burrell (eds.), *The Sexuality of Organization.* Thousand Oaks, Calif.: Sage, 1989.

Stortz, Martha E. *Pastor Power.* Nashville, Tenn.: Abingdon Press, 1993.

Stortz, Martha E. "Naming and Reclaiming Power." In Musimbi R. A. Kanyoro (ed.), *In Search of a Roundtable: Gender Theology and Church Leadership.* Geneva, Switzerland: WCC Publications, 1997.

Tannen, Deborah. *You Just Don't Understand.* New York: Ballantine, 1990.

Tannen, Deborah. *The Argument Culture: Moving from Debate to Dialogue.* New York: Random House, 1998.

Tavard, George H. *Woman in Christian Tradition.* London: University of Notre Dame Press, 1973.

Terry, Robert W. *Authentic Leadership: Courage in Action.* San Francisco: Jossey-Bass, 1993.

Thomas, David A., and Ely, Robin J. "Making Differences Matter: A New Paradigm for Managing Diversity." *Harvard Business Review,* Sept.-Oct. 1996, pp. 79–90.

Wessinger, Catherine. "Woman Guru, Woman Roshi: The Legitimation of Female Religious Leadership in Hindu and Buddhist Groups in America." In Catherine Wessinger (ed.), *Women's Leadership in Marginal Religions: Explorations Outside the Mainstream.* Urbana: University of Illinois Press, 1993.

Wessinger, Catherine. "Women's Religious Leadership in the United States." In Catherine Wessinger (ed.), *Religious Institutions and Women's Leadership: New Roles Inside the Mainstream.* Columbia: University of South Carolina Press, 1996.

West, Cornell. *Race Matters.* Boston: Beacon Press, 1993.

Wheatley, Margaret J. *Leadership and the New Science: Learning About Organization from an Orderly Universe.* San Francisco: Berrett-Koehler, 1992.

Yocum, Rena M. "Presents and Presence." In Melanie A. May (ed.), *Women and Church: The Challenge of Ecumenical Solidarity in an Age of Alienation.* New York: Friendship Press, 1991.

INDEX

A

Abandonment, women's fear of, 260

Abraham and Sarah, 304

Abuse of power, 15; anger and mercy for, 304–305; confusion of power and, 259, 260–261, 267, 268; exclusion as, 255; exploitation as, 254–255; manipulation as, 255; in Ned's story, 25–26; temptation of, 261, 279–280; by types of power, 255–256; women's experience of, 259, 304–305

Academic institutions, power and influence in, 244–245

Acceptance for women, atmosphere of, 297

Access and legitimacy paradigm, 313

Accountability: in cooperative method, 43, 44; failures of, 213–214; maintaining, 19, 213–214; men's fear of loss and, 237; in teams, 63, 69

Achievement pressures: "What does it feel like?" trap and, 223; "Work twice as hard" trap and, 226–227, 297

Acknowledging each other. *See* Naming

Action: as men's gift, 239; reflection as inner, 31–32; relationship of reflection to, 11, 28–30, 31–32, 310

Action traps for men, 238–239

Active criteria and tasks: of communicating (criterion six), 14, 173–178, 179–198; discussion questions for, 317–319; of influencing (criterion eight), 15–16, 243–280; listed, 10; of modeling (criterion nine), 16–17, 283–314; overview of, 14–17; of working (criterion seven), 15, 199–240. *See also* Communicating (criterion six); Influencing (criterion eight); Modeling (criterion nine); Working (criterion seven)

Activists, 54

Adam and Eve, 92

Adaptable systems, 311

Advancement, supporting women's, 297–298

Affirmation, 19, 197–198, 297

African Americans, negative prejudices of, 159

African Methodist Episcopal, 97

Alpert, R., 96

Ambition, 301

American Baptist church, 77

American Management Association, 70

American social history: individualism, cooperation, and authoritarianism in, 49–51, 52; melting pot metaphor in, 157; recent trends in, 52–54; women as speakers in, 182; women's leadership in, 58–59

Anand, A., 263

Androgyne, God as, 187

Anger, 304–305

Antiracism training, 34, 44, 45, 162–164

Antiracism work, in "Ben, Fredrica, and Karen" example, 43, 44–46

53–54; current demands on, 52–53; definitions of, 49; gender differences in, 55–59; hero model of, 49–51, 52, 54, 57; learning about, 11–12, 48–59; as learning challenge, 48; new models for, 51–54; parity in, achieving, 103–104, 164; power and, 258; power gaming and, 262–263; team talk about, 192; in teams, 66, 68–69, 274–278. *See also* Connective leaders; Hero-leader model; Influencing; Power; Women in leadership

Leadership, women in. *See* Women in leadership

Leadership in teams, 66, 68–69, 274–278

Leadership styles, 27; cultural determination of, 58–59; prevailing white male worldview and, 88–89; respect for different, 168; respect for different, among women, 303; respect for different, in "Ben, Fredrica, and Karen" example, 46–47, 48; women's, 51, 52, 55–59, 88–89, 303

Leadership teams, 66

Learning (criterion two), 41–73; about leadership, 11–12, 48–59; about team building, 12, 60–73; in "Ben, Fredrica, and Karen" example, 41–47; discussion questions for, 315–316; mentoring and, 220–221; overview of, 11–12; team modeling of, 291, 292, 293; verification of, 21–22

Learning organization, Lutheran relief team as, 105, 119–120

Lehmann, E. C., Jr., 58

Lerner, M., 260

Letting go of attitudes, 33

Life scripts: naming oneself in, 149–150; quest plot in, 146–148;

sharing of, 144–146; of spiritual formation team members, 144–145; of women versus men, 146–148; writing, 143–148

Lilly Endowment grant, 199

Lindley, S. H., 58, 86, 93, 95, 97, 98

Lipman-Blumen, J., 49–50, 52, 53–54, 55–56, 58, 147, 257, 258, 311, 313

Listening: to differences among women, 302; in "Eleanor and Peter" example, 179; men's challenges for, 29, 184, 296; men's versus women's expectations for, 28–29; reflecting and, 28–30; women's challenges for, 29–30, 302

Loss, fear of, 235–238

Loyalty tests, sexist jokes as, 194–195

Luke Skywalker, 253

Lummis, A. T., 98

Lutheran relief team, 63, 105–109, 110, 162; accountability in, 213; capacity building them of, 108, 109; change policy of, 119; cross-cutting issues of, 105; gender equity model of, 105–109; gender equity statement of, 106, 113, 115–121, 293–294; learning stance of, 105, 119–120; mentoring of, 221; policy of, toward cultural differences, 119; Rethinking project of, 105, 107, 192, 291; sense of urgency and mission of, 111–112; social policy of, 117; theological position of, 117

M

"Make me comfortable" trap, 225–226

Male supremacy belief, 90–91

Manipulative power, 255; men's suspicion of, 237, 255

Mara, 93–94